Education and Imagination

Education and Imagination explores the application of Jungian perspectives in educational settings, establishing the creative imagination as a critical and necessary feature of learning throughout the lifespan. The book identifies various facets of applying contemporary Jungian thought to the issue at hand, in chapters that range from scholarly critiques to practical project reports.

This straightforward and accessible resource addresses issues at the interface of education and imagination and the possible contribution of insights from Jungian psychology, in a practical, theoretical and imaginative way. Topics include:

- a synthesis of Jung and Vygotsky
- learning difficulties
- storytelling, socialization and individuation.

Contributed to by authors professionally involved in education and training on the one side, and actively engaged with Jungian studies on the other, *Education and Imagination* will make essential reading for those involved in educational and training contexts, as well as the wider public of teachers, trainers and students.

Raya A. Jones lectures at the School of Social Sciences, Cardiff University, UK.

Austin Clarkson is a musicologist and professor emeritus of music, York University, Canada.

Sue Congram is an organizational consultant whose practice centres on leadership. She teaches in the UK and abroad.

Nick Stratton has been a consultant in vocational education since 1996, and was previously research manager at City and Guilds Institute.

Education and Imagination

Post-Jungian Perspectives

Edited by Raya A. Jones,
Austin Clarkson, Sue Congram
and Nick Stratton

Routledge
Taylor & Francis Group

LONDON AND NEW YORK

MT

First published 2008
by Routledge
27 Church Road, Hove, East Sussex BN3 2FA

Simultaneously published in the USA and Canada
by Routledge
270 Madison Ave, New York, NY 10016

*Routledge is an imprint of the Taylor & Francis Group, an Informa
business*

© 2008 Raya A. Jones, Austin Clarkson, Sue Congram and
Nick Stratton

Typeset in Times by
RefineCatch Limited, Bungay, Suffolk
Printed and bound in Great Britain by
TJ International Ltd, Padstow, Cornwall
Paperback cover design by Gerald Myers

This publication has been produced with paper manufactured to
strict environmental standards and with pulp derived from
sustainable forests.

British Library Cataloguing in Publication Data
A catalogue record for this book is available from the British Library

Library of Congress Cataloging-in-Publication Data
Education and imagination : post-Jungian perspectives / edited by Raya
A. Jones . . . [et al.].
    p. cm.
Includes index.
ISBN 978-0-415-43257-3 (hardback) – ISBN 978-0-415-43258-0
(pbk.) 1. Education–Philosophy. 2. Educational psychology.
3. Jung, C. G. (Carl Gustav), 1875–1961–Influence. I. Jones,
Raya A.
LB14.7.E37 2008
370.15–dc22

2007042489

ISBN: 978-0-415-43257-3 (hbk)
ISBN: 978-0-415-43258-0 (pbk)

9/9/09

Contents

Contributors

Austin Clarkson, MA (Eastman School of Music), PhD (Columbia University), musicologist and educator, is an emeritus professor of music, York University, Toronto. He also held positions at Columbia and Yale universities. He designed a university course on the creative imagination based on Jungian principles and practices and is preparing a book on that curriculum in collaboration with twelve participants. He directs a group of artist-teachers that provides programmes on the creative process for children and adults (see www.exploringcreativity.ca). Active as an author on contemporary concert music, he is general editor of the music and writings of the composer Stefan Wolpe. Together with the Jungian analyst Beverly Bond Clarkson, he has led workshops on the creative process for Jungian groups in Canada and the United States.

Sue Congram, C.Psychol., is an independent organization consultant whose broad and varied portfolio centres today on the praxis of leadership as an organizational process. Her background is in Gestalt-centred learning, which informs her professional work through a holistic and creative form of inquiry. She teaches Gestalt in organizational practice in the UK and abroad. She became interested in the work of Jung a few years ago when seeking greater depth of meaning in her work and life. This has led to incorporating Jungian ideas in management and leadership learning, and a Jungian perspective to her research into corporate leadership. Under her previous name of Sue Clayton, she is the author of *Sharpen your Team's Skills in Supervision* (McGraw-Hill 1999), *Sharpen your Team's Skills in Developing Strategy* (McGraw-Hill 1996), *Simply People* (The Space Between 2001) and co-author, with Trevor Bentley, of *Profiting from Diversity* (Gower 1998).

Terence Dawson, PhD, is an Associate Professor of English Literature at Nanyang Technological University (NTU), Singapore. His main fields of interest are the application of Jungian psychology to literature, the relation between literature and the other arts, the psychological implications of the long eighteenth century and the legacy of Jean-Jacques

Rousseau. He is the author of *The Effective Protagonist in the Nineteenth-Century British Novel: Scott, Brontë, Eliot, Wilde* (Aldershot and Burlington 2004) and co-editor, with Polly Young-Eisendrath, of *The Cambridge Companion to Jung* (Cambridge University Press 1997; 2nd edn 2008).

Darrell Dobson, MEd, PhD., has been a secondary school English and Drama teacher since 1992. His research focuses on the professional knowledge and reflective practices of teachers who use the arts and Jungian psychology to promote transformation. He is the editor of *Jung: The e-Journal of the Jungian Society for Scholarly Studies* (www.thejungiansociety.org) and is vice-president of the organization. Dobson is the author of *Transformative Teaching: Promoting Transformation through Literature, the Arts and Jungian Psychology* (Sense, forthcoming).

Phil Goss is a Jungian Analyst and Senior Lecturer in Psychotherapy and Counselling at the University of Central Lancashire. He is a member of Association of Jungian Analysts (London) and IAAP with a private practice in the Lancaster area. Goss has been a teacher and manager in special educational, and has a particular interest in Jungian perspectives on learning difficulties and the development of meaningful learning experiences for pupils in this context.

Allan Guggenbühl, Prof. Dr. Psychologist FSP/analytical psychotherapist SGAP, is a professor at the University of Education of the State of Zurich, Director of the Institute of Conflict Management and Mythodrama, Zurich, and the Department for Group Psychotherapy for Children and Adolescents at the Educational Counselling Centre in the State of Bern. His extensive publications have been translated into English, French, Swedish, Dutch, Italian, Russian, Czech, Japanese and Chinese. He is the author of several books, including *Das Mythodrama* (IKM 1999) and in English translation: *Men, Power, and Myths: The Quest for Male Identity* (Continuum 1997) and *The Incredible Fascination of Violence: Dealing with Aggression and Brutality among Children* (Continuum 1996).

Raya A. Jones, PhD, is Lecturer in Psychology in Cardiff School of Social Sciences (formerly the School of Education). Her main research interests are the philosophy and history of psychology, with a focus on Jungian, narrative and social constructionist approaches. Earlier research concerned emotional and behavioural difficulties in school. She currently serves on the executive committee of the International Association for Jungian Studies. She has published extensively in peer-refereed journals in both Jungian and non-Jungian contexts, and is the author of *The Child–School Interface: Environment and Behaviour* (Cassell 1995) and *Jung, Psychology, Postmodernity* (Routledge 2007).

Charlotte Hua Liu, MEd, is an experienced language teacher and university tutor, and currently a PhD candidate at the University of Adelaide, Australia. Her research areas are Vygotsky's educational psychology-philosophy and semiotics, discourse studies, micro educational sociology and language education. In her field research she has worked with a large number of students and teachers in China and Australia.

Carolyn Mamchur is a professor at Simon Fraser University, Canada, and author of psychology texts, articles, poetry and children's books, including *Insights* (Ontario Institute 1984), *A Teacher's Guide to Cognitive Type Theory and Learning Style* (Association for Supervision and Curriculum Development 1996), *The Popcorn Tree* (Fitzhenry and Whiteside 1998) and *In the Garden* (Pemmican 1993). She has written ten feature film scripts and a half-hour drama for CBC. For her PhD at the University of Florida she studied with the founders of the Centre for Application of Psychological Type, and did postdoctorate work at the Jung Institute in Switzerland, furthering her studies in the application of psychological type theory. As a writer and educator, she is presently focusing her interest in psychology and creative writing, particularly screen writing and the use of the archetype in creating authentic characters.

Robert S. Matthews, PhD, Grad Dip Ed, is a lecturer at the School of Education, University of Adelaide, Australia. He is also the Vice-President of the C. G. Jung Society of South Australia. His research interests are in analytical psychology as applied to classroom interactions and to learning theory, Vygotskian pedagogy and holistic approaches to education.

Madeline Sonik, MA, MFA, PhD, is a writer and anthologist whose fiction, poetry and creative non-fiction have appeared in literary journals internationally. Her books include her first novel, *Arms* (Nightwood 2002), a collection of short fiction, *Drying the Bones* (Nightwood 2000), a children's novel, *Belinda and the Dustbunnys* (Hodgepog 2004) and anthologies, including *When I Was a Child* (Oberon 2003) and *Entering the Landscape* (Oberon 2001) and *Fresh Blood: New Canadian Gothic Fiction* (Turnstone 1998). She holds a PhD in Education, an MFA in Creative Writing and an MA in Journalism. She has taught as a sessional instructor in the Department of Theatre, Film and Creative Writing at the University of British Columbia and has designed and implemented part-time and continuing education Creative Writing courses using Jungian approaches at Camosun College, Victoria, BC.

Nick Stratton, MA, has been a consultant in vocational education since 1996, and previously a research manager at City and Guilds Institute. He holds an MA in Jungian and Post-Jungian Studies and is currently a PhD candidate at the University of Essex. Stratton has been a member of the management committee of the Further Education Research Association since 1980. He is the creator of the Professional Agent website at www.p-agent.com.

Chapter 1

Introduction

A debt to Jung

Raya A. Jones, Austin Clarkson, Sue Congram and Nick Stratton

> The debt we owe to the play of imagination is incalculable.
>
> (Jung 1973 [1921]: para. 93)

At the time of writing, an internet search on the phrase in the epigraph yielded nearly 100 instances of its appearance. The quote is available in collections of quotes. It is often placed motto-like in contexts that bear no relation to Jungian psychology and with no bibliographical accreditation other than its attribution to Carl Jung. A de-contextualized catchy phrase, free-floating in cyberspace and plucked so as to lend a ring of profundity to various projects, its fate attests to a dire fragmentation of knowledge in the Age of Information. Much of formal education nowadays is modularized into bite-sized packages. Pedagogy is fenced in by benchmarks, formal learning objectives, evaluations and appraisals. The scope for holistic learning and teaching is limited. The toll on bringing imagination into education is incalculable.

In referring to 'education' in the book's title we have in mind the social institution that is centred on pedagogy and which comprises formal and semi-formal settings ranging from the school to lifelong learning such as training in the workplace or courses taken for leisure. Those diverse contexts share at least four characteristics distinguishing them from other contexts of human activity. First, there is an interpersonal transaction within which someone is empowered to impart knowledge or a skill to those who lack it, and who are required or wish to acquire it. Power asymmetry is a core characteristic of any pedagogic transaction. Second, with the position of power comes a duty of care or mentoring. Positioned as a teacher, one has a duty to nurture the learner's development. This confers upon teachers a right and duty to judge the desirability, not only of particular material, but also of the method of its transmission. Pedagogic methodologies are polarized along a continuum from the didactic to Socratic 'midwifery'; that is, from putting things in the learner's mind to bringing out something from within the learner. The third characteristic, then, is having a teaching rationale (with an emphasis on 'rational'). Pedagogy requires skills that practitioners must acquire and continue to develop in their workaday practice. As teachers, we often learn from our students in that their responsiveness to what we do teaches us about the effectiveness of our material and method. Thus, fourth, a teacher is also a learner.

The term 'imagination' invokes the romantic connotations of creativity, originality and spontaneous fantasy. It might well seem like the anathema of education *qua* the social institution described above. The Oxford English Dictionary provides several definitions of imagination, out of which the closest to the use of the term in this book is:

> **4.** The power which the mind has of forming concepts beyond those derived from external objects (the 'productive imagination'). **a.** The operation of fantastic thought; fancy. **b.** The creative faculty of the mind in its highest aspect; the power of framing new and striking intellectual conceptions; poetic genius.
> (OED Online: www.oed.com, accessed 4 March 2007)

This 'power which the mind has' seems to violate the power asymmetry inherent in the roles of teacher and learner. We may teach the skills of painting, but not kindle the student's creativity or ignite the spark of genius that makes a truly great artist. We may provide opportunities for expressing one's imagination, but cannot dictate the creative outcome; and so forth.

This book's contributors grapple with tensions at the interface between imagination and education, and negotiate its ambivalence with particular attention to Jungian ideas. Jung himself had little to say about education as such. In a lecture to teachers, Jung (1946) informs his audience what analytical psychology is about, rather than advising them about pedagogy or examining the learning process. He held a somewhat negative, distrustful view of education, claiming that centuries of education forced human reason to 'develop from the subjective, individual sphere to the objective, social sphere', producing 'a readjustment of the human mind' to its modern intellectual capacities which alienate us from our true nature (Jung 1952: para. 17). He made the statement quoted in the epigraph in his preamble to introducing the theory of the psychological types. In that context, Jung contested the psychoanalytical theories of Adler and Freud. Both theories 'reject the principle of the imagination since they reduce fantasy to something else'; that is, treat patients' imaginings as symptomatic of repressed wishes or unconscious conflicts (Jung 1973 [1921]: para. 93). Jung goes on to aver:

> For everyone whose guiding principle is adaptation to external reality, imagination is . . . something reprehensible and useless. And yet we know that every good idea and all creative work are the offspring of the imagination, and have their source in . . . infantile fantasy. . . . The

dynamic principle of fantasy is *play*, a characteristic also of the child, and as such it appears inconsistent with the principle of serious work. But without this playing with fantasy no creative work has ever yet come to birth. The debt we owe to the play of imagination is incalculable.

(Jung 1973 [1921]: para. 93)

Jung implicitly contrasts rational, reality-directed thinking with fantasy or imagination – a distinction elaborated in a monograph that was first published in 1912 and later revised (Jung 1952) without altering his position regarding the two kinds of thinking. The 'fantasy versus rationality' dichotomy was hardly unique to Jung. His exposition of it perpetuated assumptions that were taken for granted in his milieu in the wake of eighteenth- and nineteenth-century Romanticism. The Romantics advocated a notion of knowledge which emphasized creativity, basing the idea partially on German Idealism which posited the existence of a special mental faculty superior to discursive reason (Baumer 1974). To them, the imagination was 'the vessel through which the Infinite or Eternal expressed and became conscious of itself'; and some claimed that we touch reality more deeply in dreams and ecstasy than we do in wakefulness, because those states are removed from sense perceptions (ibid.: 203). Romantic Man was sharply contrasted with the Rational Man of the Enlightenment or the 'classical' tradition: Romantic Man was seen as 'more many-sided and more complicated. In him "reason" was not preeminent . . . but took orders from the deepest feelings or intuitions' (ibid.: 203).

The Romantic positing of the imagination as diametrically opposed to rational thought reverberates, not only in Jung, but also in the prevailing perception that imagination is maligned in education. Few would dispute that, in much of school and university teaching, the guiding principles are indeed to do with adaptation to external reality. Analytic reasoning or logical thinking, as well as factual knowledge of the world, are nurtured; 'imagination' seems relegated to indulgence in the creative arts. Perception of the education/imagination interface as a domain of tensions and ambivalence has generated various theses – such as Greene's (2000) reflections in *Releasing the Imagination* – and initiatives, notably the Imaginative Education Research Group at Simon Fraser University, Canada (www.ierg.net) led by Kieran Egan (e.g., Egan and Madoc-Jones 2005). Those do not refer to Jung or Jungian ideas. How can 'Jung' help us?

The Jungian imagination

Jung's analytical psychology has branched into several schools of thoughts (Samuels, 1985), associated with psychotherapy (rather than education). Nevertheless, certain concepts and techniques can be adapted for pedagogical purposes, as we seek to demonstrate.

The book's contributors draw upon Jungian and post-Jungian theories, albeit selectively. It is not necessary to have a prior knowledge of Jungian thought in order to make sense of how the contributors to this book apply particular ideas. If you are unfamiliar with Jung's psychology and wish to learn more, highly accessible accounts of 'basic' Jungian thought can be found in numerous introductory textbooks, such as Murray Stein's (1998) *Jung's Map of the Soul*. Clifford Mayes (2005) also provides a good easy-to-read review of the basics in the first half of *Jung and Education*. However, such 'primers' seldom acknowledge debates and controversies, and thus do not capture the pluralism of the post-Jungian intellectual world, a pluralism or multivoicedness which underpins the present collection too. Some of the contributors differ in their interpretation of some concepts. For that reason, our editorial decision has been to leave the definitions (which are inseparable from an interpretation) of specific terms to the authors using them in their chapter. Suffice it here to give an indication of the most recurrent terms and their importance vis-à-vis the general theme of the present book.

Three terms recur in several of the chapters: individuation, active imagination and archetypes. All three are at the heart of Jungian psychology, although Jung used them in different ways at different times. This has left their precise meaning open to continuous debate, reinterpretation and ongoing reformulation influenced by ways of thinking other than Jung's own. *The Handbook of Jungian Psychology* edited by Papadopoulos (2006) provides state of the art reviews of those (and other) key Jungian ideas, the issues they have raised, and debates surrounding them.

Briefly, *individuation* is usually defined in the Jungian context as either the process or state of achieving an inner integration of disparate elements of the Self, both conscious and unconscious elements. Fine-grained meanings of the term vary along a continuum from those that imply a process of becoming to those indicating a state of being. The same could be said regarding uses of the term *active imagination*. In clinical practice, it generally refers to a technique for eliciting and working with unconscious material. By evoking unconscious contents, activating the creative imagination brings to conscious awareness images and feelings that serve the individuation process. Viewed as a state of being, the essence of active imagination is the ability to bear the tension between the conscious and the unconscious (Chodorow 1997). Understood as a process of becoming, active imagination may be facilitated in activities using the visual arts, dance, writing, poetry, storytelling and theatre work.

A distinction should be drawn between active imagination, on the one hand, and imaginative exercises and other classroom activities that have conscious goals and predictable results, on the other. Active imagination is concerned with the creative (productive) rather than the re-creative (reproductive) imagination. The Jungian community is divided regarding the practical application of active imagination. Some believe that it belongs only in the therapeutic consulting room under the supervision of an analyst. Others have found that properly framed exercises facilitate the evoking of spontaneous images and feelings in ways that can be highly beneficial in non-clinical settings (Clarkson 2005; Clarkson and Worts 2005).

Archetype is Jung's both most famous and misunderstood hypothesis outside the Jungian community. Within the Jungian community, it seems to have generated more controversy and interpretative diversity than any other concept. Whereas the differentiation into a focus on 'being' versus 'becoming' could be viewed as unproblematic in the case of either individuation or active imagination – like looking at different sides of a coin – some definitions of archetypes are incommensurable with each other. One way to capture the scope of the term is to imagine it as a spectrum of interpretations and reformulations. On one end of the definitional spectrum, 'archetype' implies a concrete product of the imagination: a definite motif, such as the hero, mother, wise old man, rebirth and more. At this end (which is furthest away from Jung's position), the term has been used by literary critics, such as Northrop Frye (1957), so as to denote narrative images that are commonly found in literary works, making no assumptions about the psychological process of their production. At the opposite end, the term captures Jung's idea of a dynamic psychological process, whereby certain images (such as hero, etc.) arise within subjective experience at certain stages of the individuation process. The hypothesis of the *collective unconscious* is crucial to understanding his idea. Jung posited the existence of a biologically given, common-to-all ('collective') configuration of the psyche. The theory of archetypes is premised on the proposition that some products of the creative imagination – especially motifs that recur universally – are due to that basic configuration (i.e., the collective unconscious) rather than merely material derived from actual experiences (the personal unconscious).

Jung's own thinking about archetypes changed over time, but he remained consistent in locating them in the inner dynamics of the embodied psyche. He emphasized that archetypes are a dynamic lived experience charged with emotion. They are emotionally loaded images. An image alone 'is simply a word picture of little consequence. But by being charged with an emotion, the image . . . becomes dynamic, and consequences of some kind must flow from it' (Jung 1964: 96). To Jung, archetypes both predispose how human beings experience the world and express actual experiences. In a late formulation, Jung used the metaphor of a spectrum: 'the dynamism of instinct is lodged as it were in the infra-red part of the spectrum, whereas the instinctual image lies in the ultra-violet part' (Jung 1969 [1954]: para. 414). Linking image to spirit, he comments in a footnote that 'blue, the colour of air and sky, is most readily used in depicting spiritual contents, whereas red, the "warm" colour, is used for feelings and emotions' (ibid.: n. 122). Yet, to Jung, violet is more appropriate, for as the 'mystic' colour it reflects 'the indubitably "mystic" or paradoxical quality of the archetype in a most satisfactory way. Violet is a compound of blue and red, although in the spectrum it is a colour in its own right' (ibid.: para. 414). The abstract idea towards which Jung labours is that an archetype is simultaneously an image in its own right and a '*dynamism* which makes itself felt in the numinosity and fascinating power of the archetypal image' (ibid.: para. 414, italics in the original).

It is worth noting how Jung's use of the spectrum metaphor quickly shifts from a convenient heuristic to a lucubration about colour symbolism – symbolism that itself attests to the 'violet' vibrancy of certain images. Throughout his work, Jung communicates his ideas in a dizzying array of metaphors while, in the same breath, theorizing about why symbolic images so powerfully captivate us, and why they appear and reappear, as if of their own accord, in dreams, myths, art, religions and even science.

Active imagination is described directly by Austin Clarkson (Chapter 8), Sue Congram (Chapter 10), Phil Goss (Chapter 3), Robert Samuel Matthews and Charlotte Hua Liu (Chapter 2) and Madeline Sonik (Chapter 7), and is implicit in the description of mythodrama by Allan Guggenbühl (Chapter 5). The concept of individuation is central to the contributions by Terence Dawson (Chapter 4), Raya A. Jones (Chapter 6), as well as Sonik (Chapter 7), although it implicitly enters most, if not all, the other chapters. Similarly, references and allusions to archetypes are implicit in all chapters though most directly enter the projects described by Darrell Dobson (Chapter 9) and Nick Stratton (Chapter 11). In Chapter 12, Carolyn Mamchur reviews Jung's identification of the psychological types, a theory applied in education by her (Mamchur 1996) and others (e.g., Lin et al. 2005).

Applying 'Jung' in education

Speaking to teachers in 1924, Jung described analytical psychology as 'an eminently practical science' which does not 'investigate for investigation's sake, but for the immediate purpose of giving help' (Jung 1946: para. 172). While his practical concerns as a psychotherapist were different from those of a teacher – and, addressing teachers, he was mostly concerned with imparting insights from psychotherapy – his 'practical science' standpoint may strike a chord with educators too. To Jung, analytical psychology is 'concerned with the actual, day-to-day, happenings of human life . . . it is the hopes and fears, the pains and joys, the mistakes and achievements of real life that provide us with our material' (ibid.: para. 171). Likewise, in extrapolating an outlook from the clinic to the classroom, the concern is ultimately with the implications for actual happenings and real people. Our premise is that a Jungian slant could enhance teaching and learning across the lifespan, not only by placing the whole person at the centre of learning and teaching processes (as any holistic approach does), but also by providing a unique framework for considering and promoting personal wholeness. It gives us a language with which (a) to make rationally visible the role that creative imagination plays in the process of achieving such wholeness (i.e., individuation), and (b) to create techniques that may facilitate the process, such as active imagination techniques.

In presenting this book, we are hardly the first to apply 'Jung' to education. At least two other works deserve a mention for their excellence. One is by Clifford Mayes (2005), who presents an original approach to curriculum and instruction. Mayes attributes to Jung a view of education as 'inherently archetypal' and as ideally addressing the whole child, not just aiming to develop technical skills in the service of 'consumer society and its military-industrial machinery' (Mayes 2005: 97). That standpoint can certainly be found in Jung, though Mayes' paraphrase recontextualizes it in present-day society (especially North American). Reflecting on his own teaching experiences, Mayes describes various aspects of the teacher–student reciprocal roles in archetypal imagery: e.g., student as Hero, teacher as Spirit, i.e., sage, guide or mentor (ibid.: 126 ff.). He also considers personal and archetypal transference in the classroom. The other noteworthy contribution is Bernard Neville's (2005) handbook. It is aimed at teachers interested in holistic approaches, and is fundamentally grounded in James Hillman's archetypal psychology – a post-Jungian 'school' utilizing esoteric jargon of Greek gods and goddesses (absent in Jung's own work). Discussing the difference between religion and archetypal psychology, Hillman asserts that in the latter,

> gods are *imagined*. They are approached through psychological methods of personifying, pathologizing, and psychologizing. They are formulated ambiguously, as metaphors for modes of experience. . . . All psychic reality is governed by one or another archetypal fantasy, given sanction by a God.
>
> (Hillman 1975: 169–170)

In this vein, Neville (2005) discusses the teacher-natures of fourteen deities, from Zeus and Hera to Hestia and Hermes, which represent complexes manifest in both males and females. Throughout his book, Neville confidently describes tried-and-tested practices such as active imagination, psychodrama, personality type and meditation; and critically though sympathetically reviews the theoretical contributions of Jung, Freud, Milton Erickson, Assagioli and several others.

Hillman's archetypal psychology, which rests on a 'language game' in which characters from Greek mythology are spoken of as if they exist, is a postmodernist departure from Jung's own discourse. While some of the contributors to the present book may go along with Hillman, others are sceptical of his framework and distance their own reading of Jung from his (though that particular dispute does not arise in this book). More broadly, to some of Jung's followers, postulations such as the collective unconscious and archetypes provide quasi-scientific explanations for phenomena of the imagination. To others, the same hypotheses serve as convenient labels, metaphors, even poetic images in their own right, which help us to talk about creativity and imagination. Rather than impose a singular Jungian doctrine, our aim in this volume has been to sample the multivoiced nature of the post-Jungian world.

The debt to Jung is greater than merely importing certain ideas so as to construct imaginative methods of instruction or to rationalize the promotion of creativity in our students. His legacy also provides a lens through which to reflect on our own individuation within our professional role – a theme explored in this volume by Darrel Dobson (Chapter 9). Jung's own concern was primarily with intra-personal dynamics. Those may enter our inter-actions with our students as personal projections about them. In this vein, Guggenbühl-Craig (1971) pointed to the 'split archetype', for example the bipolar motif of the wounded healer. Pointing to the dangers of health pro-fessionals regarding sickness as belonging solely to the patient, he implored healers to maintain awareness of their own wounded pole. A similar split archetype is inherent in the encounter between teachers and students, which parallels an 'inner tension between the states of being a knowledgeable adult and an unknowing child', as Guggenbühl-Craig notes; the

> archetype by which the good teacher is fascinated is that of the knowing adult–unknowing child. A good teacher must stimulate the knowing adult in each child. . . . But this can only happen if the teacher does not lose touch with his own childishness.
>
> (Guggenbühl-Craig 1971: 104–105)

It could be argued that the insight into the play of split archetypes in dyadic teacher–learner interactions retains an emphasis on the 'bounded' individual, an emphasis that characterizes Jung's own work (Jones 2007). It deflects attention from the socio-political ecology of the pedagogic relationship; that is, the fact that any interactions (including reciprocal perceptions) between persons who are positioned in relation to each other as teacher and student necessarily take place within a social-normative order of prescribed rights and duties.

For those of us working in educational contexts, our development as teachers could benefit, not only from having some techniques and rationale for nurturing our students' creative imagination, but also from an awareness of how various archetypal projections enter the very system which prescribes our encounters with students. A Jungian perspective sometimes helps. For example, drawing upon Jung's idea of the shadow (the inner 'other' which forms in opposition to the ego), Uhrmacher (1997) describes the 'dark' side of curricula. In this volume, Phil Goss (Chapter 3) explores collective projec-tions which manifest in certain attitudes within British special education, while Allan Guggenbühl (Chapter 5) considers how the myth of the innocent child, among other archetypal themes, may account for educators' ambivalence about letting students engage their own imagination.

An overview of the book

The idea for the book grew out of the editors' involvement in the International Association for Jungian Studies (IAJS: www.jungianstudies.org). We distributed a call for chapters to members of the IAJS, and subsequently made the selection for this volume from a large body of submissions. Wishing to give a platform to what may come up from the 'field', we did not exercise any prescriptions as to which viewpoints are to be represented. In the same spirit, we did not impose expectations regarding the extent to which contributions should embody a critical engagement with theory or describe pedagogic practices. Our strategy has resulted in a collection spanning the full spectrum from practical project reports to scholarly critiques. Compared with similar books that have a single author, and therefore present a singular standpoint, *Education and Imagination* has the advantage of presenting a variety of perspectives and levels.

The chapters are organized roughly from the theory-focused to the practice-centred. We deliberately refrained from dividing the book into discrete theory and practice parts, partly in view of the considerable overlap of the two domains in some chapters, and partly as an expression of resistance to the modularization of knowledge. It may be more helpful to draw upon Jung's description of the four functions of consciousness. Jung plots *thinking* and *feeling* as opposite poles of the rational axis; *sensing* and *intuition* as opposite poles of the irrational axis (e.g., Jung 1973 [1921]). Here, the criterion would be, which function do particular chapters most readily call out in the reader? Some chapters require us (readers) to think, to ponder ideas, whereas other chapters evoke feeling-based judgements about the projects they describe.

Starting at the 'thinking' extreme of the rational axis, Robert Matthews and Charlotte Hua Liu present a *tour de force* and a conceptual synthesis of works by two influential thinkers. The theme of Chapter 2, 'Education and imagination: a synthesis of Jung and Vygotsky' is premised on an understanding of creative imagination as a developmental faculty that is common to all (as opposed to being unique to the artistically gifted), is relevant in all domains of learning, and therefore should be actively promoted through educational policy and practice. Towards that goal, Matthews and Liu compare the concept of the creative imagination in Vygotsky's 'phylogenetic' psychology with Jung's 'archaic' psychology (to do with the collective unconscious). Vygotsky located imagination in the interplay between realistic and fantasy (autistic) thought within a functional unity. He regarded its maturation as a high point of conscious development, which holds the key to greater integrity of consciousness and the possibility of transcending one's socialization. Jung similarly emphasized the crucial role of the imagination in assisting the process of individuation, and developed the method of active imagination for consciously working with fantasy material.

Whereas Chapter 2 is theory-focused, and its writers implicitly seek to advise policy and practice through thinking about the role of the imagination, Chapter 3, 'Learning difficulties: *shadow* of our education system?' may advise policy and practice by inviting us to think about our own attitudes. Based on his work with young people with profound and multiple learning difficulties, Phil Goss scrutinizes the ideal of inclusion in British special education. While the ideal holds that all students should have an equal access to school education, those with severe learning difficulties challenge the conventional expectations that education is about achievement and passage to adulthood. Goss skilfully guides us through an active imagination process, enabled by Jungian imagery (such as the shadow puer/puella, anima) whereby we – as teachers, parents, carers, or other stakeholders – may explore what such students represent to us, engaging with our own projections and attitudes which are revealed in our reactions to severe learning difficulties. Goss calls for a deeper reflexive debate on 'special' students, a debate grounded in imaginative and affective responses to 'them', which is arguably necessary before genuine educational inclusion could happen.

In Chapter 4, 'Rousseau, childhood and the ego: a (post-)Jungian reading of *Emile*', we return to a comparison of theories, as in Chapter 2. As in Chapter 3, we may tacitly continue to engage active imagination so as to reflect on our expectations; in this case, about the possibility of instruction for authentic imagination. Terence Dawson critiques Rousseau's provocative thesis vis-à-vis Jung's description of individuation. In order to allow for the development of a truly autonomous individual, ready to take his place in society, Rousseau would have the educator shield the growing child from any social influences, ideology and tradition. Dawson explores that argument in the light of Jung's definitions of the ego and the persona and their respective functions, showing how Jung's view serves to uncover an unsuspected dimension to *Emile* and how Rousseau's argument suggests a need to tighten Jung's definitions of the persona and the ego.

If Dawson's critique provokes us through our reaction to Rousseau's extreme recommendations, the theme of Chapter 5, 'Education and imagination: a contradiction in terms? Experiences from mythodramatic crisis intervention in schools' provokes us through Allan Guggenbühl's reflections on his experiences leading an international project that used mythodrama towards conflict management in schools. Viewing the imagination as a powerful tool for developing new perspectives – a tool unrestricted by morals, political correctness or social codes – Guggenbühl submits that it is a valuable resource for dealing with conflict. Structured activities using fairytales and myths create a safe place for students to acknowledge their fantasies, however aggressive their themes might be, and in this way may help to discover new solutions to crisis. Yet, some schools regard such activities as inimical to the inculcation of students into the normative order. Guggenbühl identifies prevailing negative attitudes towards giving free rein to students' imagination, attitudes that are indeed the antithesis of Rousseau's *Emile*.

Continuing the thread of using fairytales and myths in schools, Chapter 6, 'Storytelling, socialization and individuation', examines some of the debates for and against engaging young children with fairytales, including empirical research into children's emotional attachment to stories. Raya A. Jones identifies tensions between Jungian and non-Jungian views on traditional storytelling in terms of their implicit assumptions about personal development, social process and education. Non-Jungian educators and psychologists who recommend using fairytales, myths and legends in the education of young children often point out their utility as pedagogic tools, such as promoting literacy and communication skills, and multicultural awareness. The socializing significance of fairytales has been both endorsed favourably and contested by various psychoanalysts, scholars and social commentators. In contrast, the classical Jungian viewpoint construes fairytales as expressions of the collective unconscious, which are distilled in the course of their repetitive retelling over generations, and thus represent snapshots of the individuation process.

While the previous chapters present 'arguments' (at both the thinking and feeling poles of the rational axis), Chapter 7, 'Literary individuation: a Jungian approach to creative writing education', moves into a description of techniques. Madeline Sonik proposes a method of teaching creative writing which assists students in producing literary art of substance. It encourages students to transcend the concerns of the ego (including an attempt to make oneself 'sound creative') and, instead, to relocate the source of creativity in the 'unknown'. By observing movements of the unconscious, the ego may acquire greater awareness and maturity, which ultimately serves one's artistic development. Sonik explores the potential of specific Jungian concepts (e.g., the shadow, archetypal image, synchronicity and the technique of amplification) towards assisting students to achieve a creative relationship between consciousness and the unconscious.

Chapter 8, 'The dialectical mind: on educating the creative imagination in elementary school', both returns to theory and takes us further into concrete practice. Austin Clarkson describes a programme in which a curriculum for creative imagination, originally designed for adults, was adapted for elementary school children. The structured programme involves alternating reflective and productive exercises, and enables participants to express authentic images and feelings in original pictures, poems and stories. It evokes meaningful and often transformative experiences, as Clarkson shows through his analyses of drawings produced by children participating in the programme. Clarkson also considers the philosophical foundations for the creative imagination, contending that although images and symbols retain a heuristic value in contemporary society, children at increasingly younger age are subject to mandated, standardized tests for literacy and numeracy that focus on instrumental rationality, to the detriment of the child's holistic development.

Austin Clarkson features in a research study reported in Chapter 9, 'The symbol as teacher: reflective practices and methodology in transformative education'. In this chapter, Darrell Dobson critically examines transformative learning and links it to 'archetypal reflexivity' practices, notably archetypal narratives. In keeping with the epistemology and methodology of narrative inquiry, 'narrative' is understood here as both the phenomena being studied and the means of representing the research. Dobson discusses the findings of his inquiry into the professional knowledge of three experienced teachers (Clarkson among them). All three understand analytical psychology and the arts as a means of transformative learning, and regard education as primarily a process of unfolding, or drawing out, of the personality or psyche. This process requires learning to work with symbols that guide one's personal and professional development.

Chapter 10, 'Arts-informed learning in manager-leader development', continues the focus on adult professional development in the context of the corporate world. Sue Congram describes a training programme designed for women who are in leadership positions or aspire to such positions. Conventional management and leadership learning has paid little attention to the self in the leader role. Instead, greater emphasis is given to developing role incumbents' capabilities to meet practical imperatives. Congram's programme adapts a particular form of active imagination, and aims towards deepening awareness and fostering a change of perspective. The programme involves non-prescriptive artwork such as drawing, painting, collage, textural art and mask work. Congram integrates insights from Gestalt as well as Jungian psychology in her rationale for arts-informed learning in the workplace.

Similarly with adult learners in mind and describing a specific programme, as in Chapter 10, and with a theme that overlaps the idea of the symbol as teacher in Chapter 9, the next chapter, 'Learning assistants for adults', describes the development of innovative software for sustaining learner motivation and encouraging self-development. In Chapter 11, Nick Stratton recounts his personal journey from conception to completion of the material. His model pivots on the representation of the learner's past, present, future and 'effecting change' in four support roles (the guard, mirror, guide and joker respectively), which have their counterparts in the classical Jungian catalogue of archetypes. Learners are invited to personify and amplify those role-players and to maximize their 'engagement' qualities. The software is structured to mimic individuation along developmental pathways.

We end the volume at the 'feeling' extreme with Chapter 12, 'Chasing the shadow'. In her highly evocative narrative, Carolyn Mamchur describes the journey to individuation that was undertaken by graduate students who took a course designed to improve classroom interactions. The students chose three possible applications of Jung's theory of psychological types, and examined type theory with a focus on personal development culminating in facing the 'shadow'. The final class was held at Mamchur's cabin in the mountains, and was described by students as the most meaningful learning experiences in their educational careers. Three case studies provide an insight into that experience. In writing this chapter, Mamchur deliberately avoided providing a concluding section that would artificially cap the account with some contrived statement. Instead, her narrative takes us from the feeling to sensing function. The final words deposit us in that cabin in the mountains through the words of one student, who wrote, 'The light outside has changed through the enormous windows and the cedars have gained their evening sober elegance. Their tops wave, dark and lovely, their live green scent mingles with the smoky breath of just-lit evening fires.'

It is a powerful reminder indeed that creative imagination involves a sense of wonder, freshness of vision and open-endedness.

References

Baumer, F. L. (1974) Romanticism. In P. P. Wiener (ed.) *The Dictionary of the History of Ideas* (Vol. 4). New York: Charles Scribner's Sons.

Chodorow, J. (1997) *Jung on Active Imagination*. London: Routledge.

Clarkson, A. (2005) Educating the creative imagination: A course design and its consequences. *Jung: The e-Journal of the Jungian Society for Scholarly Studies* 1: 1–17.

Clarkson, A. and Worts, D. (2005) The animated muse: An interpretive program for creative viewing. *Curator: The Museum Journal* 48: 257–280.

Egan, K. and Madoc-Jones, G. (eds) (2005) Special Issue: Education and Imagination. *Teaching Education* 16: 1–88.

Frye, N. (1957) *Anatomy of Criticism*. Princeton, NJ: Princeton University Press.

Greene, M. (2000) *Releasing the Imagination*. San Francisco, CA: Jossey-Bass.

Guggenbühl-Craig, A. (1971) *Power in the Helping Professions*. Dallas, TX: Spring.

Hillman, J. (1975) *Re-Visioning Psychology*. New York: Harper Perennial.

Jones, R. A. (2007) *Jung, Psychology, Postmodernity*. London: Routledge.

Jung, C. G. (1946) Analytical psychology and education. *The Collected Works of C. G. Jung* (Vol. 17). London: Routledge & Kegan Paul.

—— (1952) Symbols of transformation. *The Collected Works of C. G. Jung* (Vol. 5). London: Routledge & Kegan Paul.

—— (1964) Approaching the unconscious. In C. G. Jung, M.-L. von Franz, J. H. Henderson, J. Jacobi and A. Jaffé, *Man and his Symbols*. London: Aldus.

—— (1969) On the nature of the psyche. *The Collected Works of C. G. Jung* (Vol. 8). London: Routledge & Kegan Paul. (Original work published in 1954.)

—— (1973) Psychological types. *The Collected Works of C. G. Jung* (Vol. 6). London: Routledge & Kegan Paul. (Original work published in 1921.)

Lin, L., Cranton, P. and Bridglall, B. (2005) Psychological types and asynchronous written dialogues in adult learning. *Teacher College Record* 107: 1788–1813.

Mamchur, C. (1996) *A Teacher's Guide to Cognitive Type Theory and Learning Style.* Alexandria, VA: Association for Supervision & Curriculum Development.

Mayes, C. (2005) *Jung and Education: Elements of an Archetypal Pedagogy.* Lanham, MD: Rowman & Littlefield Education.

Neville, B. (2005) *Educating Psyche* (2nd edition). Greensborough, Victoria: Flat Chat Press.

Papadopoulos, R. K. (ed.) (2006) *The Handbook of Jungian Psychology.* London: Routledge.

Samuels, A. (1985) *Jung and the Post-Jungians.* London: Routledge & Kegan Paul.

Stein, M. (1998) *Jung's Map of the Soul.* Chicago, IL: Open Court.

Uhrmacher, P. B. (1997) The curriculum shadow. *Curriculum Inquiry* 27: 317–329.

Chapter 2

Education and imagination

A synthesis of Jung and Vygotsky

Robert S. Matthews and Charlotte Hua Liu

Pao zhuan yin yu
(Chinese idiom: 'To throw out a rock, in the hope of eliciting jade')

This chapter is a theoretical exploration of the writings on imagination by Jung and Vygotsky and the beginnings of a synthesis of their views relevant to the educational arena. We believe the two are compatible along their holistic serving epistemological lines and the developments of each find their complement in the other. The intention in bringing them together is that the spiritual depth of Jung will be combined with the spiritual height of Vygotsky.

We agree with other advocates exploring Jung and education, that the accent on the whole child is the essential point. The implications of this for analytical psychology we believe would be to view the developing child within the frame of their entire psyche, inclusive of the collective unconscious and situated in a cultural, historical and social world. What does holistic development require of the school process? We are in a paradox between inner and outer requirements. The archaic aspect of our inner world may wish for a life different to that of our cultural system. Does the social collective provide a good enough life consistent with our deeper nature? We believe this to be the tension we move through when looking to apply Jung to school education. The developing ego, as Edinger (1992 [1972]) attests, must loosen (but not sever) its ties with the Self. There is a pedagogic role to assist ego in becoming self-responsive enough to stand in the world and take up life's tasks, as the collective has deemed appropriate (job, family, etc.). In analytical psychology this tension is articulated in the pedagogic situation through a delineation of directed and non-directed thought.

Vygotsky maintained the conscious psyche emerges from a monadic interaction of mind, unconscious and behaviour. He sought to develop a dialectical psychology which viewed the mental and physical as two qualities within this monadic system. To understand imagination, one needs to view the unconscious and conscious coming together, a unifying of realistic and fantasy thinking.

The complementarity of Jung and Vygotsky, we argue, arises from their respectively profound understanding of the whole person. For the purposes of this chapter we will discuss how these understandings bridge to education, specifically, through their accounts of imagination. Views of fantasy and imagination are sought to be mapped out from Jung and Vygotsky's perspectives. Both made similar distinctions between the imagination that serves reality adapted thought and the imagination that serves the inner life. Although Jung followed the track of the latter through the depths of the unconscious, Vygotsky pursued the former to the heights of conscious awareness of the external world. What is left unsaid in Jung, Vygotsky provides wonderfully with regards to the school education of children and adolescents. What is left unsaid in Vygotsky, Jung offers as a fulfilment of life's journey for the mature adult.

The following accounts of Jung and Vygotsky are around the theme of the imagination, made separately and in that order. A final section then follows on their synthesis and pedagogic implications.

JUNG, EDUCATION AND THE IMAGINATION

Developmental view of Jung

It is not an easy matter for those interested in applying analytical psychology to the education of children and adolescents, as Jung's psychological focus was on the second half of life. This is not to say that the early years of psychological development were not of great importance for Jung, but his exploration of the mythic dimension of the psyche drew him deeply to explore how the adult ego encounters and integrates the deeper stratum of the unconscious. Consequently Jung's developmental ideas are not concisely articulated in his writings but rather lay embedded across his work. The most immediate writings of pedagogic importance are the series of lectures on educating children, which were compiled in his *Collected Works Volume 17*. These lectures deal with a sharing of therapeutic insights to aid a teacher's awareness of their students' psychological qualities of relevance to the classroom situation, qualities such as transference and giftedness. Unlike Vygotsky, however, he did not attempt any rigorous theory or model of learning. The following is a very brief developmental picture.

The collective layer of the unconscious plays a pivotal role throughout the development of one's conscious self, one's ego. 'The [archetype of the] Self, like the unconscious, is an a priori existence out of which the ego evolves. It is, so to speak, an unconscious prefiguration of the ego' (Jung 1958a [1954]: para. 391). Edinger (1992 [1972]: 7), taking up Jung's position, comments that '[i]n earliest infancy, no ego or consciousness exists. All is in the unconscious. The latent ego is in complete identification with the Self. The

Self is born, but the ego is made.' Archetypal elements are not a developmental property, but are understood to be a priori existences of the psyche. The centre of consciousness, the ego, arises 'out of the clash between a child's bodily limitations and environmental reality. Frustration promotes islets of consciousness which coalesce into the ego proper' (Samuels et al. 1986: 51).

During the first few years of life, the developing ego is in considerable identification with archetypal energies, particularly the Self, and this is exhibited as an inflation to the exigencies of the outside world. Relationships with parents are of course crucial, especially the child's relationship with the mother (or primary carer). The infant is awash with the images which arise out of the interaction of archetype and experience (Samuels et al. 1986: 80). The parental identifications are the source of later projections experienced by teachers in the transferential exchange.

In typical development, the ego attains adequate differentiation into an emerging identity after the time of puberty, as 'normally the psyche attains relative independence only after puberty' (Jung 1954: para. 107). As the child develops a successful identity, their new found assurance arises from an increased stability in the face of demands from both their inner and outer worlds. The transition to adulthood is ideally framed by a growing sense of independence, so crucial for the demands of adult life. The process of ego development is accompanied by at least a partial severance to the objective unconscious (Jung 1954: para. 211). There appears to be a cyclic movement, beginning in childhood and continuing throughout life, of the ego moving away and toward the Self, leaving and returning to the archetypal connection (Edinger 1992 [1972]: 5). If too strong a separation occurs then the child's psychic life risks a breakdown. For substantial loss of contact with the archaic being within can disrupt the regulatory process of psyche. This is brought to mind through the Jungian catchcry urging teachers to be mindful of the heart of their students rather than merely the knowledge content of their lessons.

Directed and non-directed thought

In 'Symbols of transformation' (Jung 1956 [1952]) Jung begins with a delineation of two kinds of thinking, directed (or realistic) and non-directed (or fantasy) thinking. This delineation, not uncommon at the time, was profoundly extended by Jung to introduce his view that the unconscious operated ultimately as an archaic reservoir of human history. In this view much of our imaginal life is beyond the direction of ego, it arises from the tension of conscious life with the objective stratum of our unconscious. This delineation is worth discussing in detail as it is used by Jung to frame his historical understanding of the role of imagination and lays the ground work for using imagination as an approach to integrate unconscious contents and so assist individuation.

Directed thought is *reality orientated*, both with regards to the adaptation of its content and in its communicative purpose.

> Any very intensive train of thought works itself out more or less in verbal form – if, that is to say, one wants to express it, or teach it, or convince someone of it. It is evidently directed outwards, to the outside world. To that extent, directed or logical thinking is reality-thinking, a thinking that is adapted to reality, by means of which we imitate the successiveness of objectively real things, so that the images inside our mind follow one another in the same strictly causal sequence as the events taking place outside it.
>
> (Jung 1956 [1952]: para. 11)

Such thought is under the direction of ego, but is prone to tire. It takes significant conscious effort to maintain, as ego has only a limited portion of the psyche's libido at its disposal.

On the other hand, non-directed or fantasy thinking is 'supra-linguistic' for Jung, it 'moves in inexpressible images and feelings' (ibid.: para. 11). The flow of fantasy does not tire the ego, 'working as it were spontaneously, with the contents ready to hand, and guided by unconscious motives'. Such thought 'turns away from reality, sets free subjective tendencies, and, as regarding adaptation, is unproductive' (ibid.: para. 20).

Jung argues that western culture has undergone a great shift in emphasis between these two modes of thought. That since antiquity we have seen a decline in the mythological imaginings of non-directed thought and a corresponding increase in directed thought as libido culturally passed from the former to the latter. Thus the 'secret of cultural development is the *mobility and disposability of psychic energy*. Directed thinking, as we know it today, is a more or less modern acquisition which earlier ages lacked' (ibid.: para. 17, italics added). During these earlier ages, the focus was strongly in favour of the fantasy products of the psyche, which resulted in a rich mythic life, but now we lean heavily towards adaptation with a scientific world. Directed thought is a tool of culture that dominates today's classroom, indeed one could define the classroom as a cultural means of the promotion and conditioning of directed thought.

> Directed thinking or, as we might also call it, thinking in words, is manifestly an instrument of culture, and we shall not be wrong in saying the tremendous work of education which past centuries have devoted to directed thinking, thereby forcing it to develop from the subjective, individual sphere to the objective, social sphere, has produced a readjustment of the human mind to which we owe our modern empiricism and technics.
>
> (Ibid.: para. 17)

Jung is not seeking to undermine this development, but does realize its tendency to foster a one-sided psychic life that may later require adjustment for successful individuation. A counterbalancing respect for the imagination is vital for the healthy psychic system as through it, 'directed thinking is brought into contact with the oldest layers of the human mind, long buried beneath the threshold of consciousness' (ibid.: para. 39). To redeem the natural regulating process of the psyche, Jung will later formalize his approach into the technique of active imagination.

Jung's view that the flow of images constituting non-directed thought involves an objective layer of the unconscious was a departure from Freudian theory and in part heralds the direction of his future work.

> The unconscious bases of dreams and fantasies are only apparently infantile reminiscences. In reality we are concerned with primitive or archaic thought-forms, based on instinct, which naturally emerge more clearly in childhood than they do later. But they are not in themselves infantile, much less pathological. . . . The instinctive, archaic basis of the mind is a matter of plain objective fact.
>
> (Ibid.: para. 38)

Non-directed thought may be a relatively conscious occurrence as in daydreams or reverie, or the more unconscious dreams of our night-time slumber or '[f]inally, in split-off complexes there are completely unconscious fantasy-systems that have a marked tendency to constitute themselves as separate personalities' (ibid.: para. 39).

Thus the modern propensity for directed thought encourages a suppression of our archaic side that may go too far and require restitution in years to come. Yet with Vygotsky we will see a role for the archaic being within directed thought itself. The collective has won, at considerable effort, a great store of objective knowledge, i.e. agreed upon knowledge that is to be socially inculcated through the classroom experience. This knowledge was originally produced with the archaic being's assistance, and its reconstitution within the learner's conceptual system similarly requires instinctual assistance. It is not that we lose contact with the archaic being this way, only our instinctual self is utilized for collective conscious production of scientific not mythological understanding; useful for realistic adaptation, but not for inner adaptation as there is a loss of contact with the mythic landscape of the inner world. This is the paradox of the modern classroom: how do we assist our students' adaptation to reality but at the same time give the inner world and its regulatory capacity the liberation it needs?

Active imagination

Through Jung's therapeutic encounters and the intense inner work that he voluntarily undertook with his own fantasy life (see Jung 1995 [1963]: 194–225), there arose understandings that working with the imaginal world is a way to integrate the psyche. The image holds the key that can allow consciousness to integrate what lies missing in the unconscious. For the 'image is a condensed expression of the psychic situation as a whole, and not merely, or even predominantly, of unconscious contents pure and simple' (Jung 1971 [1921]: para. 745). If it can be approached in earnest by consciousness then a new attitude may arise, one that consciousness would not have found itself.

> In whatever form the opposites appear in the individual, at bottom it is always a matter of consciousness lost and obstinately stuck in one-sidedness, confronted with the image of instinctive wholeness and freedom. This presents a picture of the anthropoid and archaic man with, on the one hand, his supposedly uninhibited world of instinct and, on the other, his often misunderstood world of spiritual ideas, who, compensating and correcting our one-sidedness, emerges from the darkness and shows us how and where we have deviated from the basic pattern and crippled ourselves psychically.
>
> (Jung 1958b: para. 190)

The functional process of this synthesis between image and ego, Jung termed transcendent, the technique he evolved for its practice, he termed active imagination. This process provides the means to recover from the cultural one-sided emphasis on directed functioning (ibid.: para. 139). The transcendent function works to mediate and integrate conscious and unconscious factors. In the union of these factors a new way of being emerges. It is transcendent 'because it makes the transition from one [conscious] attitude to another organically possible, without loss of the unconscious. The constructive or synthetic presupposes insights which are at least potentially present in the patient and can therefore be made conscious' (ibid.: para. 145).

The activation of the transcendent function is not a straightforward matter. In the therapeutic process, it is the analyst who takes on the conscious role and guides the client in the encounter with their unconscious material.

> In actual practice, therefore, the suitably trained analyst mediates the transcendent function for the patient, i.e., helps him to bring conscious and unconscious together and so arrive at a new attitude.
>
> (Ibid.: para. 146)

Certain reservations withstanding (stated in his Prefatory Note, ibid.), Jung believed that a client may undertake this process themselves. When the therapy had matured to a certain point, and the client's ego strength was established, it was fruitful for them to practise engaging their ego with the active flow of their own imaginal contents, their active imagination.

To practise active imagination one must first elicit suitable unconscious material. Spontaneous fantasy material is preferred over dreams for their more 'composed and coherent character' leading to a greater chance of sensible encounter with consciousness (although dream fragments may be used as initial points of spontaneous fantasy) (ibid.: para. 155). Spontaneous fantasy material will be visual and/or auditory. Some prefer to concretize the fantasy process, or are required to do so through frustration with any spontaneous outpouring. This may be done in many ways, by writing, drawing, modelling or even dancing their fantasies. Of the external product Jung says it is 'influenced by both conscious and unconscious, embodying the striving of the unconscious for light and the striving of the conscious for substance' (ibid.: para. 168).

In the wakened state the conscious mind can fully engage with the unconscious material and the possibility for transcendence to a new attitude arises. The attitude of the conscious engagement is crucial for success. The ego must involve itself in ethical judgement with the imaginal outpourings. If one falls into a wholly passive aesthetic stance, then the images pass through consciousness unchecked, no conscious voice answers the unconscious position (ibid.: para. 176) and there will be no integration. Alternatively if the ego maintains it is the producer of such images, that they are cognitively governed, then one falls into the power principle (von Franz 1998: 112). Alternatively, as commented on by Von Franz:

> [If] one enters genuinely into the inner happenings with a sober spirit of ethical commitment and serious search for greater consciousness, then the flow of inner images commences to contribute to the growth of personal wholeness, that is, to individuation and to the creation of an inner security which is strong enough to withstand the assaults of both outer and inner problems.
>
> (Von Franz 1998: 113)

Successful active imagination leads to a deeper sense of authenticity:

> For what is now happening is the decisive rapprochement with the unconscious. This is where [the alchemical self] insight, the *unio mentalis*, begins to become real. . . . What you are now creating is the beginning of individuation, whose immediate goal is the experience and production of the symbol of totality.
>
> (Jung 1955: para. 753)

The functional point to active imagination depends on the ego state maintaining its view of the imagination as an object of unconscious expression, only then can a true alchemical dialogue follow with its transformative effects.

Jung makes a crucial point concerning the quality of the imagination, it must be active, i.e. purposive. He distinguished the flow of images encountered as an 'active, purposeful imagination' and not fantasy as 'mere nonsense' (Jung 1977 [1935]: para. 396).

> A fantasy is more or less your own invention, and remains on the surface of personal things and conscious expectations. But active imagination, as the term denotes, means that the images have a life of their own and that the symbolic events develop according to their own logic – that is, of course, if your conscious reason does not interfere.
>
> (Ibid.: para. 397)

Active imagination shows both the necessity and the limitation of the directed functioning of consciousness. Its capacity for relation to the objective, its propensity for discrimination, differentiation and meaning, and most importantly according to Jung, its moral capacity are all essential elements that need be brought to bear on the material of the imagination brought forth by the unconscious if the transcendent function is to evoke a new attitude. Its limitation is also evident here. The ego alone cannot generate the new attitude, it arises only with the assistance of the irrational, and will need to find acceptance from both.

THE UNCONSCIOUS AND ACTIVE IMAGINATION FROM VYGOTSKY'S PERSPECTIVE

In our readings of Vygotsky, the majority of references to psychoanalytic literature were to Freud (indeed Vygotsky wrote the introduction to the Russian translation of 'Beyond the Pleasure Principle'). Several references to Jung can be found, but they are only passing citations and show little engagement with his work (note that Vygotsky died in 1934, prior to the publication of many of Jung's most significant works). Despite an apparent lack of direct intellectual encounter, we believe that Vygotsky's vision of the irreducible functioning of the phylogenetic analogue in the developing mind is compatible with Jung's notion of the collective unconscious. In the following space, we devote our discussions first to comprehending aspects of Vygotsky's educational philosophical premises. Specifically, we describe Vygotsky's historical philosophy of learner potentials, covering the archaic, phylogenetic analogue in the geological structure of the individual psyche, and the role of the unconscious in active learning. This is followed by discussions of the role of imagination in active learning. Lastly, we engage in pedagogical connections in the light of the established theses thus rounding out a position from which we may formulate an initial synthesis between the two great writers.

A historical philosophy of learner potentials

A correct view of human developmental potential must be one that embraces our historical past. A Vygotskyan theoretical edifice establishes for its foundation a profound reverence for 'the greatest depths of our being' (Vygotsky 1971: 207), to rest on our historical, objective unconscious being for a development-oriented educational psychology. For understanding the genesis of higher mental functions, it is recognized by Vygotsky that our history, akin to Jung's thousand-year-old man, lives in all contemporary individual beings. Reviewing Blonskii's 'Psychological Essays', Vygotsky (1981) comments:

> This unified genetic scheme embraces both everyday human behavior and the history of its development, which spans many thousands of years. It would be more accurate to say that it considers everyday human behavior from the point of view of this long history. In this regard, it provides a splendid picture of it since the historical point of view can be applied to general psychology, to the analysis of the behavior of modern humans.
>
> (Vygotsky 1981: 156–157)

Phylogeny and ontogeny

The question is: how did the archaic being of our phylogeny come into its deep existence, exerting its influence as the 'centre of gravity' in even perceptual fields of young children? Vygotsky (1978: 35) attributes the 'centre of gravity' phrase to Kurt Koffka. As David Jaravsky ([1987], quoted in Robbins 2001: 43) commented, Vygotsky 'dreamed of a psychological analogue to the "biogenetic" law that ontogeny recapitulates phylogeny'.

> In the development of the child, two types of mental development are represented (not repeated) which we find in an isolated form in phylogenesis: biological and historical, or natural and cultural development of behavior. In ontogenesis both processes have their analogs (not parallels). This is a basic and central fact, a point of departure for our research: differentiating two lines of mental development of the child corresponding to the two lines of phylogenetic development of behavior. This idea, as far as we know, has never been expressed; nevertheless it seems to us to be completely obvious in the light of contemporary data from genetic psychology, and the circumstance that it has thus far stubbornly escaped the attention of researchers seems completely incomprehensible.

> By this, we do not mean to say that ontogenesis in any form or degree repeats or produces phylogenesis or is its parallel. We have in mind something completely different which only by lazy thinking could be taken to be a return to the reasoning of biogenetic law.
>
> (Vygotsky 1997: 19)

Unlike the process of human developmental history, where the development of human beings as a collective group moves from one stage to another, and where the new system does not begin until the old unfolds to its end, in ontogeny (the developmental process of an individual) the old and the new, the ancient and the contemporary coexist and develop simultaneously. Ontogenetic development consists of cultural and natural lines of development in intertwinement and mutual penetration. This last point we will revisit later. For now, our goal is to highlight that for Vygotsky, first, the collective, historical phylogenetic development, in the form of an objective entity, lives and plays an integral part in all contemporary beings' psychological (unconscious) systems; and second, without a full understanding of the existence and functioning of this 'ancient brain' (Vygotsky 1981: 156) we will not be able to appreciate completely the ontogenetic potential in our present beings. The collective unconscious is recognized as an infinite source of our unified and unique path of growth.

Geological structure of the human psyche

Further, the everyday human individual psyche is conceptualized as one of a historical, multilayered, hierarchical nature. Quoting Ernst Kretschmer's law of stratification in the history of brain development, Vygotsky (1981) aligns his position with the view, not of the disappearance of lower mental functions in the genetic process, but of their subordination to the new functional centres formed in higher mental functions (lower and higher functions differ in their degrees of integration of the conscious and the unconscious):

> In my opinion, one of the most fruitful theoretical ideas genetic psychology has adopted is that the structure of behavioral development to some degree resembles the geological structure of the earth's core. Research has established the presence of genetically differentiated layers in human behavior. In this sense the geology of human behavior is undoubtedly a reflection of 'geological' descent and brain development.
>
> (Vygotsky 1981: 155)

The historical unconscious and the contemporary consciousness interact and subject each other to their influences. Being integrated with the conscious, the historical unconscious finds new forms of expression; and merged with the phylogenetic, consciousness is allowed sustained, coherent growth. Between the historical unconscious and the contemporary conscious there is now a newly formed centre in the whole of the mental functioning structure.

The unconscious in active learning

Doubts have been raised concerning learning theories, including those of Vygotsky, which propose the role of environments in the development of the mind. It has been said that these have failed to address how the external world is bridged across to the internal mind. Paramount in the challenges has been what is called the 'Fodor paradox'. Stated simply, it is paradoxical that to learn one has to know what one does not yet know. Specifically, two aspects underlying Vygotsky's learning theories have been identified. On the one hand, it is believed that higher, more complex mental functions grow from lower, more elementary mental functions. For example:

> [T]he results of our analysis of rudimentary functions [are] . . . that this process consists in the transition from one form of behavior – the lower – to another, which we arbitrarily call the higher, as being more complex in genetic and functional respects. The line dividing the two forms is the relation of stimulus-response. For one form, an essential characteristic is a full – in principle – determinacy of behavior by the stimulus. For the other, the same essential characteristic is autostimulation, the creation and use of artificial stimuli-devices and determining one's own behavior with their help.
>
> (Vygotsky 1997: 53)

On the other hand, social cultural environment is considered to have decisive impacts on development. A paradox is observed between the internally specified, biological process and the external, cultural process of development, to which Vygotsky's notion of internalization is seen as an unsatisfactory answer.

We believe that, in order to resolve the so-called 'learning paradox', the historical collective unconscious, as amplified by Jung, with which Vygotsky has interwoven aspects of his theoretical edifice, will be an indispensable key.

This is an extension of an old idea. 'It has been hypothesized by Russian psychologists that children possess miniature systems of knowledge, which are primary image models' (Robbins 2001: 52). Also, quintessential in Chinese traditional philosophies, including Taoism and Confucianism, is the conceptualization of a unified world of humans, nature, and ether (otherwise sometimes translated as sky or god), as expressed in the phrase *Tian Ren He Yi* (ether and human unified). The unification of ether and human gives rise to a deepest inner source of inexhaustible life energy, commonly shared by all members of the universe. Inhabitants of the universe manifest varied and unique representations of the common life origin; such is depicted in the phrase *Yue Ying Bai Chuan* (the moon with one hundred reflected images in rivers of the same number). Varied and unique as they are, all reflections share a common archetypal existence.

Vygotsky is of the belief that the recognition of 'a basic primordial and universal principle common to all living matter' (Vygotsky and Luria 1994: 12), which might or might not be Freud's notion of the death instinct, is an important precondition for explaining the 'spiral' process of human development (ibid.: 17). In any case, and consistent with Jung, the pleasure and survival principles alone, characterizing the individual ontological life, are viewed as in no way adequate for understanding the whole of human behaviour and learning.

When individuals, as well as human and world are so decisively interconnected by the common, primordial layer of the psyche, humans are not considered born as *tabula rasa*, but as history-bearing lives. Even in the infant, evidence has been found of active shaping of the environment for intellectual participation. In investigating the ontological history of the indicatory gesture in the baby, Vygotsky identifies the birth of self-awareness through meanings socially introduced into one's own actions:

> [A]t first the indicatory gesture is simply an unsuccessful grasping movement directed at an object and designating a forthcoming action. . . . Here we have a child's movements that do nothing more than objectively indicate an object.
>
> When the mother comes to the aid of the child and comprehends his/ her movement as an indicator, the situation changes in an essential way. The indicatory gesture becomes a gesture for others. In response to the child's unsuccessful grasping movement, a response emerges not on the part of the object, but on the part of another human. Thus, other people introduce the primary sense into this unsuccessful grasping movement. And only afterward, *owing to the fact they have already connected the unsuccessful grasping movement with the whole objective situation, do children themselves begin to use the movement as an indication. The functions of the movement itself have undergone a change here: from a movement directed toward an object it has become a movement directed toward another human being.* The grasping is converted into an indication. Thanks to this, the movement is reduced and abbreviated, and the form of the indicatory gesture is elaborated. *We can now say that it is a gesture for oneself.*
>
> (Vygotsky 1981: 160–161, italics added)

Concluding the study, Vygotsky observes that '[w]e could therefore say that it is through others that we develop into ourselves and that this is true not only with regard to the individual but with regard to the history of every function' (ibid.: 162). In fact, the whole essence of the cultural line of individual development consists of the fact that '*the individual develops into what he/she is through what he/she produces for others'* (ibid.: 162, italics in the original).

Highlighted in the above analysis is the full and complete integration of the individual and the social. To reconcile the fact that higher mental functions (functions directed to self-regulate) grow out of lower ones (those directly and fully initiated by external stimuli) with the social nature of inner development, the core is the perception of individuals', including infants', active initiation and recreation of social situations for intellectual internalization. The Fodor paradox presumes, on the other hand, an essential separatism between humans and their environment.

> It may be said that the basic characteristic of human behavior in general is that humans personally influence their relations with the environment and through that environment personally change their behavior, subjugating it to their control.
>
> (Vygotsky 1978: 51)

But Vygotsky's is a monist view of human–universe interconnections, whose components, though connected, should never be reduced to identity with one another. Individuals, as varied, unique, sometimes opposite and conflictual representations of Jung's archetypal psyche, interact and influence one another in a functionally, rather than substantially, coherent manner.

Also, in answer to the paradox, 'to know what is not yet known', the psychological activity of self-regulation in learning is not a consciously aware construct by necessity or by nature. The infant's internal development of the indicatory gesture proceeds 'by first being an indication, i.e., functioning objectively as an indication and gesture for others, being comprehended and understood by surrounding people as an indicator. Thus, the child is the last to become conscious of his/her gesture' (Vygotsky 1981: 162).

The life and expression of the innate, archetypal origin are best continued in the context of social, ontogenetic activities. And unless we work hard and long in the pursuit of learning, leading to increasing subject–object integration and conscious–unconscious dialogue, the profound unity in the depth of the values and meanings of life will be beyond us. Among other implications, the dialectical monist psychology of learning underlines what is depicted in the Chinese phrase *Sheng Er You Zhi, Er Zhi Ye Wu Ya* (life is natured by knowing, knowing by infinity).

The unconscious, active imagination and school learning

In proposing a historical monist perspective of learning and education, Vygotsky provides a bridge between subjectivism and objectivism in their radical forms. In a monist view, realistic and autistic (using Bleuler's definition), or directed and undirected thinking are not separately identified as conscious and unconscious; on the contrary, they present opposites forming a dialectic whole. In dreams, for example, we manifest a generalized thinking different from thinking in the awakened state not in terms of nature, but in terms of functional structure. Understanding conceptual generalizations in dreams holds the promise of revealing the original functional nature of our ancient, complexive thinking.

> An extremely interesting phenomenon can also be observed in adult thinking. Although adult thinking has achieved the formation of concepts and generally operates on that foundation, not all the adult's thinking is based on these operations. In dreams, for example, one can observe the ancient primitive mechanism of complexive thinking, the concrete fusion, condensation, and shifting of images. As Kretschmer has correctly noted, the study of the generalizations that are observed in dreaming is the key to the correct understanding of primitive thinking. It does away with the prejudice that generalization in thinking emerges only with the most developed form of thinking, only with thinking in concepts.
>
> (Vygotsky 1987: 155)

The conceptualization of imagination in human development for Vygotsky is another example of the dialectic-monist standpoint. Rather than a homogeneous, recurrent form of mental activity, imagination is considered an integral part of the whole of the physio-psychological functional system. In the development of scientific conceptual learning, 'imagination and thinking are opposites whose unity is inherent in the very first generalization, in the very first concept that people form' (Vygotsky 1987: 78). From the very start, learning and understanding is featured with the irreducible organic structure of generalization, and any generalization or abstraction is 'at one and the same time a flight from life and a more profound and accurate reflection of life' (ibid.). Imagination and scientific conceptual learning are ever intertwined processes – thus Vygotsky breaks free from the myth of the clandestine, independent nature of imagination and that of the purely rational and objective origin of scientific concepts.

The creative imaginative act in the mind is described to consist of four processes (Vygotsky 2004). First, in the process of disassociation, the complex whole is broken up into individual parts, with some isolated and retained, and others left out. Next, in the change or distortion process, the parts retained are reworked. External features are transformed, exaggerated or minimized so that impressions should correspond to our internal state. Then the association process involves the unification of transformed parts and impressions in constructing a generalized conceptual system, which may take various forms, 'from the purely subjective association of images to objective, scientific association corresponding, for example, to geographical concepts' (Vygotsky 2004: 28). Eventually, the complete creative act is seen in externalized crystallized images.

Throughout such an extremely complicated process, it is commented, the human need to adapt to the environment is acting as the social guiding force, creating challenges and feelings of discontentment in the individual. However, questions stated in the Fodor paradox remind us that this is not the complete story of the origin of creative imagination. For example, in the process of a simple finger movement by the infant developed into first a social gesture and later internalized symbolic act for oneself, the work of the mind involved is highly sophisticated. At first, elements have to be disassociated from the situation containing the originally innocent finger movement on the infant's part and the whole series of reactions on the mother's part – e.g., seeing, approaching, questioning and seeking an answer concerning the intention of the finger movement, trying out and fetching a number of different things in view, etc. The singled out elements will then need to be cast in exaggerated reflections in the mind, serving as the raw materials for a hypothetical connection. Later, the hypothetical system will be crystallized and tested in similar, repeated actions. The infant's desire for food or amusement certainly triggers and lays the ground for the unfolding of the whole process. However, what is inside the 'unlearned' toddler that sustains the internal learning process?

A line from Goethe, a poet oft-quoted by Vygotsky, is appropriate here: 'Did our eye not contain the sun's power, how could it perceive the sun at all?' (quoted in Guggenbühl-Craig 1971: 90). Young as it may be in ontogenetic and biological age, the infant celebrates a phylogenetic inheritance, where the collectively shared archetypes exist as objective entities. Thus, witnessing the livelihood and growth of the ancient existence in all, in learning we fantasize, in fantasies we understand:

> Tables, chairs, and the *idea* of the table and the chair; the world and the idea of the world (god); the thing and 'numen,' the unknowable 'thing in itself'; the connection of earth and sun, of nature in general and law, (Logos), god. The bifurcation of man's knowledge and the *potential* for idealism (= religion) is already *given* in **the first, elementary** abstraction.
>
> (Lenin, quoted in Vygotsky 1987: 78, emphases in the original)

The spiral, revolutionary growth of the human psyche as a whole originates from the integration of both the conscious and the unconscious, and from incessant interaction with scientific knowledge, which itself embodies unity of human and world. In this belief, never is it self-evident that such is a natural evolutionary process. Until strenuous and persistently reflective commitment is engaged the object–subject unity will not be realized.

In school learning, the ancient archetypal thinking presents to us a profound inner drive, the drive to make connections. Briefly, within disciplines we are aided in our reflections on the internal logic systems which pertain to specific subject domains. But there is also a formal aspect to all disciplinary learning, representing the transcendent forces of the collective, objective unconscious.

> There is significant commonality in the mental foundations underlying instruction in the various school subjects that is alone sufficient to insure the potential for the influence of one subject on the other (i.e., there is a formal aspect to each school subject). . . . In attaining conscious awareness of cases, the child masters a structure that is transferred to other domains that are not directly linked with cases or grammar; . . . the mental functions are interdependent and interconnected. . . . Because of the foundation which is common to all the higher mental functions, the development of voluntary attention and logical memory, of abstract thinking and scientific imagination, occurs as a complex unified process.
>
> (Vygotsky 1987: 208)

Imagination and classroom teaching

Three points stand out when considering Vygotsky's writings of features of the proximal developmental environment: teaching through engagement, the ideal form, and collective subjectivity.

Teaching through engagement

Pavlov's dogs performed the way they did because of the experimental environment that was set up for them (Vygotsky 1997). The educator's role is none other but to create and make use of the powerful forces in the totality of the social learning activity and individual experience. The environment, natural or social, is conceived not as a separate, external existence benignly indifferent. The environment is always composed of social relationships – between humans, humans and world, humans and history. In the classroom process, the student is exposed to relations to the teacher, the activity, the text and co-learners. The nature of the labour arranged for different classroom participants, for instance, may or may not situate the student in a relationship with the learning activity in an intellectual manner. The good educator coordinates environmental factors in such a way that the learner is, with all his/her historically inherited experiences, engaged with intra-psychological struggles and challenges for forming new (re)active connections and systems.

No doubt, to Vygotsky, the thesis that in education, nothing is passive and everything is active underlines all of a professional educator's endeavour. 'Thus is the educational process an active one on three levels: the student is active, the teacher is active, and the environment created between them is an active one' (Vygotsky 1997: 54). For active engagement of learning, it is particularly important that such is achieved without direct, intentional interference with learners' perception, apperceptions and internal representations (Robbins 2003: 131–133). While perception may denote more immediate sensational experiences of the environment, apperception consists always of active (but not necessarily conscious) constructions of meanings and connections. Vygotsky defines apperception and its importance for learning in the following way:

> The subjectivity of understanding, the meaning introduced by us ... is the sign of any understanding. As Humboldt quite rightly put it, any understanding is a non-understanding; that is to say, the thoughts instilled in us by someone's speech never coincide entirely with the thought in the mind of the speaker. Anyone listening to a speech and understanding it apperceives the words and their meaning in his own way, and the meaning of the speech will be a subjective one every time, no more and no less than the meaning of a work of art.
>
> (Vygotsky 1971: 42)

Considering the complex world of the individual psyche, to introduce from the external prescribed, encoded apperception is an impossible task. Teacher–student interactions in the social environment need, then, to provide 'affordances' (van Lier 1996) but not transmissions for the development of internal connections. This requires the relationship of inner resonance between subjectivities in the collective group. To this we will come back shortly.

For our present purpose, every form of human labour has a dual nature – where both the mental and the physical participate in the environment in different ways (Vygotsky 1997). The teacher participates in the classroom social environment in two ways: as the director of the social environment and on the other hand, as a part of this same environment. The work of an active, imaginative educator is not to take the place of the educational mechanism such as a book, a map, a dictionary or a learning partner. In fulfilling these roles, the educator's physical labour outweighs the psychological operation. A true educator teaches not by teaching, but rather by engaging learning and self-teaching.

The ideal form

In our earlier discussions of the analogy between phylogeny and ontogeny, the recapitulation, within the individual, of the former in the latter was contended. Now, the same issue exists for the educational environment. In phylogeny, it was said that stages of development unfold in sequence; the next stage does not begin until the previous one comes to its end. In ontogeny, however, *both the beginning and the end of development need be present in analogous forms to the history of human evolution*. The ideal or final form is defined as such:

ideal in the sense that it acts as a model for that which should be achieved at the end of the developmental period; and final in the sense that it represents what the child is supposed to attain at the end of his development.

(Vygotsky 1994: 348)

In phylogeny it would be impossible to imagine that a final form of evolution existed from day one of the history, guiding and inspiring the direction of development. In the education of the individual, however, the influence of the ideal form is the rule regulating the development of higher mental functions. All higher mental functions were once social and later internalized.

This principle [of the environmental influence] consists of the fact that the child's higher psychological functions, his higher attributes which are specific to humans, originally manifest themselves as forms of the child's collective behavior, as a form of co-operation with other people, and it is only afterwards that they become the internal individual functions of the child himself.

(Vygotsky 1994: 353)

In the individual ontological development, unlike the process of historical human evolution, the ideal form needs to be present, alongside the primary, rudimentary form from the very beginning of development. The ideal form is involved in the development, interacting reciprocally with the elementary. The integration later becomes the individual's 'internal asset, his property and a function of his personality' (Vygotsky 1994: 353). The principle of the ideal form in the environment is hence also the principle of the environment functioning as the *source* of development, and not just the *context* of it.

The only useful education is the education that leads, and not lags behind development, it is stated. One very important mission of teaching is to reveal for learners the internal logic and intrinsic connections in matters (Vygotsky 1987). Only when the ideal form, the intrinsic, integrated system is presented, is the potential flight away from the concrete and situational possible and so the ability to see beyond reality is fostered in the learner.

Collective subjectivity

As discussed earlier, to reconcile the apparent tension in the two underpinning aspects of pedagogic endeavours, it is important that the educator act not as the owner and transmitter of knowledge in its final form – knowledge in its final form, i.e. the scientific concept, has to be in the form of the learner's intrapsychological, apperceptive integration of the subjective and the objective – but only as the mediator of the ideal form of learning. Such is also prescribed by the creative nature of the teacher's labour.

To interact as a mediator for learning is not to say that the teacher's labour and his/her knowledge are to become peripheral in the classroom collective. On the contrary, they are to be infused with the learning mind in such a profound way that teaching and learning does not occur within the confinement of consciousness alone. The environment and the social situation, woven with discursive and ultra-discursive interactions into coherent wholes, are the best allies of the teacher.

In all interactions and engagement with knowledge, the teacher is to participate with all his/her passions, curiosity and personality, but not will. In this sense, 'a teacher who is sober-minded teaches no one' (Vygotsky 1997: 349). Among learners, a sense of communal care and respect needs be fostered. To a significant extent, the seemingly intellectual incapacity developed in individuals to see and think beyond isolated mindsets and to take in social nutrients for internal expansion has its origin in the lack of emotional and intellectual affinity in proximate life contexts.

But Vygotsky's emphasis on the influences of a cohesive collective has often been read superficially. Self-defence is offered for potential misunderstanding:

> The goal of the school is not at all a matter of reducing everyone to the same level, on the contrary, one of the goals of the social environment that is created in the school is to achieve as complex, as diversified, and as flexible an organization of the various elements in this environment as possible. It is only necessary that these elements not be in any way irreconcilable, and that they be linked up together into a single system.
>
> (Vygotsky 1997: 79)

Where a Vygotskyan sense of collective cohesiveness is formed, the collective binding conceived is generated on the highest level. Individuals need not be similar or identical in opinions or will; indeed, disagreements, differences, and even oppositions are only necessary conditions for individual learning. Social relationships, composing proximal learning environments is defined in terms of a profound, psychological encounter and infusion. The expansion of the self takes as precondition entering and immersing into previously foreign paradigms of thinking so that fortification, enrichment, or change could happen as a result of integration.

Conclusions

Before synthesis is attempted of Jung and Vygotsky, we would like to briefly summarize our discussions of the latter so far. Vygotsky identifies his psychology as 'height psychology', as differentiated from 'depth psychology'. However, height and depth psychologies are not separate and independent from one another. It has been our point of view in this chapter that depth psychology gives birth to and then is extended by height psychology. In general, the developmental approach to educational psychology is always to view 'oneself and others within the highest possible explanatory principle possible' (Robbins 2001: 97–98). This is possible only on the basis of scientific constellation of the deep structures of the human psyche. Nature is within the human development itself; and to fully understand nature, we need a thorough account of development.

In a Vygotskyan developmental psychology, the conscious and the unconscious form two ends of one continuum in the individual's psychological whole. It is true in the perspective that not only various stratas of the psyche cannot be isolated from one another, but more importantly, enabled by integration, development will bring higher, qualitatively different forms of existence, transcending boundaries of rationality and affects.

In this context, imagination is moved from the peripheral to the centre. Instead of being a mysterious, fixed entity, imagination is considered an intrinsic feature of a particular structure of mental processes, resulting from a particular integration of the conscious and the unconscious, an integration of scientific learning and primary fantasies.

SYNTHESIS

Recent educational psychology literature shows a marked interest to understand the pedagogic role of imagination, creativity and play in the classroom. The predominant approach is that of identifying key characteristics of the 'creative genius' in order to provide attributes that educators may steer the budding creative learner towards. As has been argued elsewhere (Craft et al. 2001; Matthews and Liu, submitted), this approach is of limited value to classroom educators. Descriptions of mature traits are accounts of the fossilised remains of a living developmental process. A child forges their imaginative faculty through years of practice. It is here that the teacher needs to mediate; it is here that we need to understand in order to assist the teacher. We need a methodology that is open and flexible to the living system, inclusive of the whole child. We believe the synthesis of Jung and Vygotsky is most suited to this end.

Ultimately combining Jung and Vygotsky along the lines of imagination provides us with a reframing of the role of the archaic being in the modern classroom. The pedagogic evolution of our culture has harnessed our imagination in order to explain the scientific over the mythic, the reality adapted over the inner adapted. Historically we witness a rise in the outer adapted use of the archaic being to re-create the collective artefacts of our inheritance and a diminution of our inner gaze inhibiting the archaic being's purposive expression in our lives.

We wonder if this parallel realization cannot find synthesis. That the split between inner and outer cannot be reconciled in some manner. By pointing towards the essential role of the image producing aspects of psyche in the most abstract of problems, and the most materialistic of problems, we wonder if a greater respect for our imagination as a great cultural phenomenon, equally as worthy as pure rational thought, is not possible. It may then be reasonable to accept that the inner world of the student *is* always present, no matter what the learning task, and then the next questions dawn, how do we nurture such a wonderful quality, what respect must we pay her, what are the characteristics of the learning process that pervert the flow of our inner world and how do we balance such things? To be a culture conscious of the ego–Self connection, right throughout life's learning process.

Jung explored imagination to offer us a path to the wholeness of our psyche during the second part of life. By bringing the two poles of directed and non-directed thought together, our ethical ego engages with the outpourings of our deep, active imagination, the most removed from directed functioning, and produces a technique to assist the expansion of psychic life. This is the healing of our modern cultural rift. The emphasis on directed thought, so promoted within our educational system, can be addressed later in life. The movement towards individuation is the gift we are all given no matter our place in history. Its means adapts to the context in which one lives. But one must ask the question, can our educational system become a more balanced, more holistic endeavour?

We are not unaware, nor unsupportive, of the strong interest in assisting children to explore the imaginal in the classroom. However, we are cautious to first understand the developmental process before we would wish to predicate actions of teachers in the classroom. We believe that Vygotsky may well offer an approach to achieve such a purpose. His functionally unified understanding of the imagination, holds within it a developmental view that may soothe the cultural division of conscious and unconscious within pedagogic practice itself.

For Vygotsky, his unified view of realistic and autistic thought, emerging in objective imagination, is an invaluable extension to include the creative in every cognitive act. With this view, the archaic being is not lost in directed thought, but assists in our formulations of concepts necessary for outer adaptation. It would appear that culturally, this role of the archaic being is unconscious. Ego is too much enamoured with thinking itself the centre of the psyche. In directed thought, the ego inflatedly believes it is in complete control. Vygotsky tells us otherwise. That this inflation is prevalent throughout our educational system, engenders a stultification of learning and not a flourishing. If we do not give our inner nature its due in the learning of directed thought, then we do indeed teach for a one-sided view in the classroom.

Jung offers a union of conscious and unconscious in later life, Vygotsky may offer a cultural reframing, to connect the artificial polarity of directed and non-directed thought. If we can culturally withdraw our inflation of ego in our belief that ego alone is responsible for rational advance, and respect the role of the archaic man in directed thought, then perhaps the way will become possible to give the inner life its due as well. The spirit is ever present, whether the ends are for realistic or inner adaptation. A theoretical framework that sustains such a position, such as arises through this synthesis of Jung and Vygotsky, is a worthy pursuit for pedagogical inquiry.

References

Craft, A., Jeffrey, B. and Leibling, M. (2001) *Creativity in Education: Current Perspectives on Policy and Practice*. London: Cassell.

Edinger, E. F. (1992) *Ego and Archetype*. Boston, MA: Shambhala. (Original work published in 1972.)

Guggenbühl-Craig, A. (1971) *Power in the Helping Professions*. Dallas, TX: Spring.

Jung, C. G. (1954) The development of personality. *The Collected Works of C. G. Jung* (Vol. 17). London: Routledge and Kegan Paul.

—— (1955) Mysterium coniunctionis. *The Collected Works of C. G. Jung* (Vol. 14). Princeton, NJ: Princeton University Press.

—— (1956) Symbols of transformation. *The Collected Works of C. G. Jung* (Vol. 5). London: Routledge and Kegan Paul. (Original work published in 1952.)

—— (1958a) Transformation symbolism in the Mass. *The Collected Works of C. G. Jung* (Vol. 11). London: Routledge and Kegan Paul. (Original work published in 1954.)

—— (1958b) The transcendent function. *The Collected Works of C. G. Jung* (Vol. 8). Princeton, NJ: Princeton University Press. (Original work published in 1916.)

—— (1971) Psychological types. *The Collected Works of C. G. Jung* (Vol. 6). London: Routledge and Kegan Paul. (Original work published in 1921.)

—— (1977) The Tavistock Lectures: On the theory and practice of analytical psychology. *The Collected Works of C. G. Jung* (Vol. 18). Princeton, NJ: Princeton University Press. (Original work published in 1935.)

—— (1995) *Memories, Dreams, Reflections*. London: Fontana. (Original work published in 1963.)

Matthews, R. S. and Liu, C. H. (submitted) Creative imagination and science education. *International Journal of Education*.

Robbins, D. (2001) *Vygotsky's Psychology-Philosophy: A Metaphor for Language Theory and Learning*. New York: Kluwer Academic and Plenum.

—— (2003) *Vygotsky's and A. A. Leontiev's Semiotics and Psycholinguistics: Applications for Education, Second Language Acquisition, and Theories of Language*. Westport, CT: Praeger.

Samuels, A., Shorter, B. and Plaut, F (1986) *A Critical Dictionary of Jungian Analysis*. London: Routledge and Kegan Paul.

van Lier, L. (1996) *Interaction in the Language Curriculum: Awareness, Autonomy and Authenticity*. London: Longman.

von Franz, M.-L. (1998) *C. G. Jung: His Myth in our Time*. Toronto: Inner City Books. (Original work published in 1972.)

Vygotsky, L. S. (1971) *The Psychology of Art*. Cambridge, MA: MIT. Press.

—— (1978) *Mind in Society: The Development of Higher Psychological Processes*. Cambridge, MA: Harvard University Press.

—— (1981) The instrumental method in psychology. In J. V. Wertsch (ed.) *The Concept of Activity in Soviet Psychology*. Armonk, NY: M. E. Sharpe.

—— (1987) *Collected Works of L. S. Vygotsky* (Vol. 1), edited by R. W. Rieber and A. S. Carton. New York: Plenum.

—— (1994) *The Vygotsky Reader*, edited by R. van der Veer and J. Valsiner. Oxford: Blackwell.

—— (1997) *Collected Works of L. S. Vygotsky* (Vol. 4), edited by R. W. Rieber. New York: Plenum.

—— (2004) Imagination and creativity in childhood. *Journal of Russian and East European Psychology* 42(1): 7–97.

Vygotsky, L. S. and Luria, A. (1994) Introduction to the Russian translation of Freud's *Beyond the Pleasure Principle*. In R. van der Veer and J. Valsiner (eds) *The Vygotsky Reader*. Oxford: Blackwell.

Chapter 3

Learning difficulties

Shadow of our education system?

Phil Goss

This chapter explores the archetypal dynamics that may lie behind the long-standing debates about the ideal and reality of inclusion in the education system of England and Wales. 'Inclusion' broadly refers to the principle that all pupils, irrespective of special educational need (SEN), should be included in the mainstream of education provision. The focus for this exploration is the needs of pupils with severe learning difficulties (SLD) and profound and multiple learning difficulties (PMLD). By playing imaginatively with what these pupils may represent in relation to some of Jung's archetypal figures of the psyche I aim to stimulate reflection on how these pupils might genuinely find their place within the education system. To complement this discussion, disguised examples will be given of how these archetypal representations may show themselves, based on pupils I have worked with.

Pupils with SLD and PMLD, due to their neurological and other impairments, have been conventionally categorized as functioning with IQ of less than 70, and sometimes as low as 30 or below. These children and young people require intensive support to learn the most basic literacy, numeracy and self-help skills, which will mainly reflect attainment at Level 1 and below of the National Curriculum (Teachernet 2007). Some will use signs and symbols, though some can manage simple conversations. For those experiencing PMLD, communication is non-verbal, for example indicating a simple preference through head movement or pressing a switch. For the latter range of pupils, high levels of dependency on teachers, teaching assistants and nursing staff for their complex medical needs are the norm.

In my experience of working with pupils across the range highlighted, families and carers of these pupils often present significant emotional needs arising from the high levels of attention and care required by their child, the level of psychological adjustment required by the very nature of having a child with SLDs or PMLDs, and the variable level of services and general social acceptance offered towards them and their child. To use Jungian parlance, a *black sheep* complex is at work here, where society is a parent who feels uncomfortable with the presence of an unexpected child and the real child's family becomes as identified with this archetype as the child is.

Isolation, misunderstanding and a kind of ambivalence about whether to shower this child with resources and protection, or put her or him out of view where they can no longer disturb our sense of who we are, are all hallmarks of the historical relationship of the child with learning difficulties with wider society. Working with such pupils can lead to teachers identifying with this isolation and 'specialness' themselves, for example by feeling as if they are specialists on the fringe of the teaching profession (Youell 2006: 97).

These themes inform the longstanding struggle to identify the right 'place' for these pupils in our schooling system. Special schools have been the established means for providing for specialized input for pupils with SLD or PMLD since the 1970 Education Act (O'Hanlon 1995) but there has since been a growing clamour to provide more inclusive learning environments for them – to facilitate their social development, and dissolve prejudices against them.

The introduction of the National Curriculum aimed to incorporate learning requirements for all pupils into one framework (DfEE 1988). Although practitioners have lobbied to get more realistic approaches to teaching the least able pupils included in this framework (e.g. Byers 1999, on the National Literacy Strategy) the principle of having a 'curriculum for all' has now been broadly accepted. Continued debate, however, has heightened the sense of this being something the educational establishment – and wider society – continues to search its soul about. In recent years, there has been a growing questioning of these principles, as a debate in the House of Commons testified (Hansard 2005).

Baroness Warnock (1997) herself has regretted the implied advocacy of wholesale classroom integration in her committee's original report (DES 1978). The 1978 report had argued for recognizing all pupils' entitlement to integrated experiences of education. The Warnock committee's vision incorporated the argument that special needs should not perpetuate categories such as 'learning difficulties' but provide a continuum which focuses on needs as they arise. This paved the way for legislation, the 1981 Education Act, which moved schooling in the UK closer to an acceptance, if not a proper implementation, of the principle of inclusion. Central government's guidance, which complements recent SEN legislation, makes it clear that schools 'should actively seek to remove barriers to learning that can hinder or exclude pupils with special educational needs' (DfES 2001: para. 7). What remains a psychological reality, however, is ambivalence about inclusion.

Do we really want pupils with unfamiliar learning and social needs in our mainstream classrooms – some so potentially needy or disruptive that the learning of more able and settled pupils may be subsumed or even overlooked? Or can we, as a 'civilized' society, justify deciding we cannot cope with – or do not want – the most needy pupils in the midst of others learning algebra at Key Stage 2 or preparing for their GCSE Modern Foreign Languages viva? While government pushes legislation through, a case can be made for a complementary process of reflection on what pupils with learning difficulties represent for us and our projections about learning they catch. By using a Jungian framework, this chapter makes a small stab at galvanizing this process.

Inclusion for individuated schools?

The influential currency of the concept of inclusion arises from two main sources. One is the momentum of equal opportunities legislation and advocacy of disability rights since the 1950s (Campbell and Oliver 1996: 62–80). The other stems from the belief pupils who would otherwise be taught separately in special schools will benefit from being taught with their peers – expectations will be higher, effective learning and behaviour modelled, and this will facilitate social integration (Peacey 2005: 162–163).

There is evidence of innovative inclusive practice (e.g. Thomas et al. 1998: Ch. 3) based on an emphasis on the rights of individual learners, the quality of the learning environment and on the capacity of mainstream teachers to develop skills in managing specialized needs. Inclusion aims to replace the concept of 'integration' (Allen 1999) which hallmarked perspectives in the 1980s with its binary emphasis on recognizing differences within shared educational experiences with: 'a philosophy of acceptance . . . providing a framework within which all children . . . can be valued equally, treated with respect and provided with equal opportunities at school' (Thomas et al. 1998: 15).

We see a kind of polarization in the debate about inclusion – it is either an ideal to be achieved for everyone's benefit, or an illusion because it is mistaken to think pupils with complex needs can be catered for in contexts which are not specialized. While there is a continuum of views held across government, media and wider society, at either ends we see the kind of polarities which Jung referred to as part and parcel of human experience. He wrote of the need for some kind of synthesis of two opposites to take place, via confrontation and dialogue. He called the psychological element which can bring this about the 'transcendent function' (Jung 1958: para. 131) which finds a way forward to transcend the impasse. To facilitate this fully in the inclusion debate, there is a need to get to grips with the archetypal influences at work behind the aspirations and projections held about pupils with SEN and the ideal of inclusion.

The notion of inclusion corresponds to the psychological ideal of the integration of disparate parts into a unitary whole. Although this ideal is usually associated with individual development, it can also have something to say about our collective aspirations. Jung described the purposive process of life to be *individuation* – or 'A person's becoming himself' (Samuels et al. 1986: 76) – and this could be applied to initiatives relating to the school system 'becoming fully itself', rather than splitting off elements which are a struggle to incorporate. This struggle has difficult educational and social implications which are often not highlighted in the more upbeat narratives on inclusion promoted by policymakers. Allen (1999: 23–24) usefully provides an analysis of the dynamics of power lying below the surface by applying Foucault's (1977: 208) 'box of tools' notion to the child identified as having SEN. Allen (1999) describes how such pupils are constantly exposed to 'hierarchical' observation, to comparison against 'normal' standards (which could be linked to attitudes of 'intellectual subordination' towards pupils with SEN; see Benjamin 2002: 142), to classification and documentation of identity, and to an association with the 'special' or 'inclusive' learning environment they are taught in. This places the pupil in the central gaze of others, and surely means she or he will catch a powerful range of projections from those around her or him. So, what archetypal forms might these take?

The pupil with learning difficulties – *shadow, puer/puella or trickster?*

A crucial factor in the *individuation* process is, according to Jung, our capacity to notice, and begin to integrate, our *shadow*. Jung meant by this those aspects of ourselves we are uncomfortable and ashamed about or, 'that which we have no wish to be' (Jung 1966 [1946]: para. 470). In the context described, it is possible to make related assertions about these pupils, who until the late 1960s were not deemed as educable, and were instead generally institutional-ized for a lifetime of dependent care. In this sense, they have only recently been 'seen' properly – like an individual who has slowly come to notice their *shadow*. It is no wonder, then, that we have encountered psychological tension about what we 'do' with, and for, these pupils now we have recognized their right to be part of 'us'.

Another important aspect of the notion of *shadow* is its implication of *failure* – those faulty and unappealing aspects of ourselves we would prefer to keep out of the light. In this respect, pupils with SLD and PMLD represent the *shadow* of our achievement driven schooling culture with their (comparatively) very limited levels of achievement.

When we meet or work with such a pupil, we are unconsciously confronted with our own areas of weakness – our own learning difficulties. This can promote our own unwillingness to face the presence of limited intelligence, physical disability and at times unpleasant behaviours and medical needs. One pupil I worked with – a boy of 12 who experienced very significant communication difficulties and needed to be supported to walk – personified many of these *shadow* aspects. At times he demonstrated formative learning and social skills. However, his behaviours – seeming to relate to a deep-seated rage at not being understood, and to the loss of communicative and motor functions in an accident – included violent responses to staff who tried to engage with him. His physical appearance, dangerous behaviours and highly dependent care and medical needs could generate fear, and a kind of repulsion, at times. So, not only was he someone who struggled to learn, but also he conveyed a powerful image of all those aspects of being human we would rather not be – unattractive, very dependent and antisocial. To give learners like this young person the attention, care and teaching they deserve requires a capacity to be aware in ourselves of what they may represent of *us*. However much we trumpet the notion that pupils with learning difficulties need to be enabled to achieve as much as possible, it is important to recognize what we may be unconsciously defending ourselves against by taking a one-sided, overly positive approach to the potential of children and young people with significant learning difficulties, and by imagining this is enough to bring about meaningful inclusion.

So, the suggestion here is that a little soul searching of what educational failure represents for us would inform our approach to pupils experiencing learning difficulties, and help us recognize why it seems so important to *include* these pupils in the main body of our education system. It is also important to notice another archetypal representation that a pupil with SLD or PMLD may carry for us – that is of the eternal child, or *puer/puella* as Jung designated this figure. The boy or girl who does not grow up: this archetype transmits its presence in the clinical setting through a lack of groundedness and unwillingness to engage in reality. This figure can also have a somewhat hypnotic appeal – and I would argue that such pupils carry this. Pupils with disabilities can be treated with a protective care and a kind of perverse adulation for what they represent. From my own experience of teaching and managing these pupils in special schools, fundraising for them can be like pushing at an open door, as (to try not to resort to caricature) these are poor, defenceless children *who will never grow up*, and therefore unreservedly deserve our care and charity. In this perspective, the knowledge that the vast majority will never have a job, a partner or children (and many, sadly, will not live long) renders them as the repositories of our projections about not growing up – both our secret wish that we don't have to, and our fears that we may not have really attained true adulthood, as society expects.

So, although special educationalists have quite rightly emphasized the need to provide age-appropriate curricula and attitudes towards young people with SLD or PMLD., it may be that this representation of *puer-puella aeturnus* in the education system serves a purpose for the rest of us. This may contribute a hidden barrier to full *inclusion*, as there might well be a part of us (the *collective shadow* of the enlightened, caring, *inclusive* learning community) which wishes to keep the eternal child as a talisman against falling into that state ourselves. A glaring example of this in public policy is the way that a fully funded education package is supplied to individuals with significant learning difficulties up to the age of 19 before services become more variable as the student enters adulthood, as if government and society find it hard to face up to the reality that these young people are no longer children and they may still need the level of care the 'eternal children' we have set them up to be demands.

One of many examples of how young people with significant learning difficulties are seen as 'eternal children', from my own experience, is of a 19-year-old woman who was due to leave the school to go into adult provision. Unfortunately the options available in the local area were very limited, since her care needs were so significant that the special needs provision at the local college lacked the resources to cater for her. Instead, she would spend most of her (short) adult life being cared for at home with some limited social services support for her parents. What was striking was how easily we all accepted this as 'natural' after sixteen years of supposedly 'preparing her for adult life'! She was unable to speak but that was no excuse for us not being able to offer this adult any sort of meaningful choice in the matter at all. This situation can be replicated as a matter of course because, I suggest, we unconsciously buy into this *puer/puella* complex.

One of Jung's most established psychological principles is that of *compensation* – the way in which our unconscious alerts us to when our psyche is out of balance (Samuels et al. 1986). It can be speculated, using this principle, that we turn to this presence of *puer/puella* to convince ourselves that our schools are not just about achievement, not only about proving they are 'successful' in the stern eye of the Office for Standards in Education (Youell 2006: 151) but also that this is a system which has *soul*. A system which, due to how closely its 'success' or 'failure' is tied up with government agendas, might have lost its sense of *soul* and so may be unconsciously projecting what is left of it onto pupils with SEN, especially those with significant learning difficulties.

I will return to this theme, but it highlights the sense that there may be some powerful collective projections at work. This may include polarities of projection which oscillate between *shadow* (the failed aspects of our learning and development) and *puer/puella* (the eternal child who needs our care and protection). The ethos of special schooling has conventionally suggested the presence of this polarity – keeping pupils who seem so 'different' at arm's length as well as idealizing those who work with them. My own anecdotal experience is of repeated responses of 'oh you must be so patient' when I told people that I taught pupils with learning difficulties. This supposed saintliness and self-sacrifice of working with 'eternal children' remains in the air around special schooling.

One more archetypal figure is worth mentioning in regard to the pupil with learning difficulties – the *trickster* (Jung 1968 [1954]). This figure is the equivalent to the *fool* in the Tarot pack – at first sight a character who doesn't know what she or he is doing and becomes the figure of fun or disparagement for the wider community; a scapegoat for our projections about immaturity and lack of good sense. However, there is another dimension to *trickster* which is more relevant: the capacity for subverting conventions. The current debates about *inclusion* tend to be rooted in rational reflection on systems, physical access, curriculum and assessment. What the living presence of pupils with significant learning difficulties does is to challenge long-held pedagogic, standards-based approaches to successful schooling (e.g. Marzano 2003). In this respect, this kind of learner is acting as *trickster* to all our well-established ideas about how learning should happen. They challenge the convention that achievement is about high level benchmarks which all pupils should aspire to. They undermine the idea that subject-based curricula are going to meet the needs of all pupils. They require the teacher to be more than an effective transmitter of learning and discipline.

Instead, the teacher in the *inclusive* classroom has to greatly broaden and deepen their capacity to differentiate learning experiences, oversee social integration and attend to complex behaviours and medical needs. There is a sense that the presence of *trickster* in the system – in the shape of these pupils with SLD or PMLD (as well as those presenting a whole range of other SEN, e.g. those on the autism continuum, or experiencing visual/hearing impairments) – is acting as the driver for change. The 12-year-old boy mentioned above acted as *trickster* in the sense that he starkly exposed the limitations of the skills and resources of the school, as well as the underdeveloped awareness of some professionals. He did this, apparently, by adopting what Sinason (1992: 111–135) calls a 'secondary handicap'; that is, exaggerating the *shadow* characteristics that he noticed other people presumed him to have – the 'unacceptable' behaviours, physical appearance and disabilities (he clearly sometimes consciously exaggerated his physical ailments and challenging behaviours). This strategy in turn drove the school to update policies and practices.

If, as in the above example, we can recognize this *trickster* quality for what it is – confronting us with our own tendencies towards rigidity and the reification of outdated notions of achievement – then we can begin to see how our projections onto these pupils may contribute to where inclusion gets stuck.

Anima and the 'special child' as carrier of education's soul

Notions of inclusion hold resonance because they offer us an organizational, pedagogical and political way of trying to leapfrog over rigid archetypal influences and turn them into something which we have 'overcome'. However, the fact that in the UK we refer to people for whom the terms 'mentally handicapped' or 'mentally retarded' have not entirely fallen out of circulation (at least outside the *de rigeur* jargon of policymakers and service providers) reminds us that the historical perception of, and feeling for, their inherent separateness remains deeply rooted. There would be many people living now who may remember how the place of people with learning difficulties in our society was once assumed to be in lifetime institutional care – an assumption made irrespective of social position or financial influence, and which reflected deep-seated beliefs about the enfeebled and dependent nature of mental handicap (Sinason 1992). We now live in the shade of the world of our fore-bears where the 'solution' to difference was *exclusion*, and the current debates bear testimony to this. This point is important, I believe, as the way things have changed so radically in no more than half a century means, not only that we are playing 'catch-up' with inclusive thinking, but also that the ghost of the 'uneducable' child is still in our midst.

Bearing this in mind, the capacity we have had as an educational establishment to embrace the principle of inclusion – if not yet the ramifications of the practice of it – suggests that something significant has got hold of that previously embedded assumption about excluding the learning disabled (in order to protect 'us' from 'them' and vice versa?) and turned it inside out.

Behind social and political shifts in western societies which have facilitated the pursuit of equal opportunities and valuing of achievement, the huge systems which strive to effectively implement such principles need to provide a sense of ongoing rationale for what they do. In the case of the education system, this requires a rationale for why achievement is so important, while holding up the core significance of equal opportunities. Here, the achievements of the least able become crucial, as they supposedly demonstrate these two principles can work together. In this respect what the system does for those who find learning most difficult provides not just a rationale, but arguably the *soul* of its work, offering inspiration to all other learners and giving a deep sense of meaning to the role of education which driving thousands of able A level students to higher grades does not provide. This is not to belittle the value of high achievement, but rather to suggest the principle of educational inclusion provides a sense of psychological and even spiritual purpose to what nurseries, schools and colleges across the UK do.

Inclusion becomes one of the 'higher' values which both replaces or even unconsciously apes the Victorian Christian principles on which so much in our educational establishment was based. More than this, the presence in the system of groups of learners who were previously outside it, throws a reflection back onto that system which implies that it is capable of *losing its soul* without every member of society having access to it. In this sense, the pupil with significant learning difficulties is the carrier of *soul* onto whom we can all project our aspirations for being properly *included* ourselves, as well as to have a truly *inclusive* society. Our muddled thoughts and feelings about success and failure – how we define these terms and why failure is 'bad' – can all be safely contained by this figure, whose need for our help and skilled teaching allows us to concentrate on the redeeming *soul* quality of what we are doing, instead of confronting our own anxieties about how well or not we may do as learners.

This notion of *soul* has, in the post-Jungian canon, been most notably developed by James Hillman. He ascribed Jung's concept of *anima* as the archetypal carrier of soul. While *anima* is most commonly associated with the presence of the feminine in men as part of the *anima–animus* dyad, it also carries great affective power. As Hillman (1985: ix–x) writes: 'The call of soul convinces; it is a seduction into psychological faith, a faith in images and the thought of the heart. . . . Anima attaches and involves. . . . We cannot remain the detached observer' (reprinted in Moore 1990: 87). When we are in this *anima* consciousness, the unconscious archetypal influences become as important as, and conjoined with, the workings of ego consciousness. This state enables us to have the 'psychological faith' mentioned here by Hillman, and the faith we have in *inclusion* is a dimension to this *anima* presence of *soul* embodied by the pupil with significant learning difficulties.

The young *puella* woman described above, throughout her school career, carried this *soul*. Her needs were so acute that days when she smiled and gurgled at songs sung in her class group were treasured and clearly 'fed' the nurturing needs of those around her. This is not to decry these dynamics or the meaning she brought into the lives of those who worked with her, but rather to acknowledge that there was a transaction taking place here in which she *brought soul into the learning environment*. When these episodes of warm responding happened during inclusive activities at a local mainstream school this effect was felt powerfully by the pupils and staff there too. One could describe these moments as conveying a quality of veneration of the meaning carried by the presence of abnormality (Littlewood 1993), which in turn suggests numinosity as well as offering a reference point for 'social morality' (Lewis 2003: 134).

If this reading of the current embodiment of education's *soul* as residing in the presence of the previously banished pupil with SLD or PMLD has value, then it may be worthwhile considering what unbalanced or uncomfortable aspects of the education system as a whole are being 'ministered to' by the presence of these learners.

Actively imagining the real place of learning difficulties

The conclusion to this chapter will suggest ways in which the use of 'active imagination' (Jung 1976 [1935]) could possibly facilitate an approach to inclusion which more genuinely gets to the underlying archetypal 'blocks' to embracing it. The suggestion here is this might get us to a more grounded position in relation to what can really be achieved; a position genuinely in the best interests of pupils with significant learning difficulties, as well as the learning communities they become part of through being *included*.

To lay the ground for this proposal, here are three propositions based on the discussion provided this far. The education system in England and Wales has adhered to a commitment to promoting achievement in schools which has struggled with another key principle – equality of opportunity. This pertained most graphically to the right of people with learning difficulties to have access to the education system. Since acknowledging this problem, the system is now *compensating* by championing the principle of inclusion without having properly engaged in a process of reflection and psychological confrontation to enable this to happen in a realistic and meaningful way. This includes taking into account what holds meaning for the pupil with learning difficulties within the learning experiences they are offered (Goss 2006). The reality is therefore more complicated than just promoting a principle – and in this respect pupils with SLD or PMLD (or with other SEN) act as *trickster* to challenge our assumptions, as well as our own motives for pursuing inclusion.

Secondly, and more specifically, educationalists across the age phases have not properly faced up to our own projections onto pupils with learning difficulties, in terms of what they represent as learners. My suggestion is they can represent both *shadow* and *puer/puella* projections, reflecting what De Groef (1999: 43) characterizes as our 'binary representation of disability'. The *shadow* fears we have about our own learning weaknesses, and our less physically and socially appealing features, get projected via our wish to 'help' them. *Puer/puella* is constellated through this wish too, but via the sense of reassurance we get that however much we teach and support them they will remain the equivalent of the *eternal child* of the schooling system. This can give them their aura of 'specialness' – their dependence and trust in the greater knowledge of those around them in some ways paralleling the dynamic of mother–infant interactions (Hobson 2002: 29–60). This parallel is provided in an attempt to suggest the unconscious ways we may struggle with an urge to infantilize these pupils, despite all our conscious claims for our determination for them to be as independent as possible. While acknowledging the speculative tinge to these assertions about archetypal influences, there is a case for taking 'time out' to look at our own unconscious needs and projections in this area.

Finally, the idea of seeing *anima* (or in this case 'soul') as embodied in the presence of the pupil with significant learning difficulties throws into relief the possibility that there has been an insidious 'loss of soul' in the current schooling system. It is beyond the scope of this chapter to scrutinize this possibility in detail, other than to hazard the view it is in our preoccupation with measurable outcomes and demonstrable benefits to society as a whole, that we may have chosen to avoid the deeper questions of how education can contribute to individual and social growth, mutuality and meaning. Attending to human frailty, which these pupils represent, does indeed offer some *anima consciousness* feeling of *soul*. There is a need, arising from this location of education's *soul* in the ideal of inclusion, to scrutinize where the wider goals of education are missing *soul* before we can fully 'know' what feeds our collective will for this laudable goal.

What arises from these propositions is a suggestion that a process of reflection and re-envisaging what *inclusion* might really mean within the UK schooling system would be of real benefit to the planning of provision, training and individualized learning careers of pupils (and adults) with learning difficulties. Jung's model of *active imagination* is proposed here as the starting point for successful facilitation of this process.

By *active imagination* Jung meant a process that is available to each of us and which enables us to confront aspects of our unconscious which are trying to catch our attention and tell us something we might need to be aware of in order to move our conscious awareness forward (Chodorow 1997: 10). The process involves allowing images or figures from the unconscious to come into mind by allowing, rather than forcing, them to do so. For those of us who may work with pupils with learning difficulties, the suggestion here is that noticing, negotiating with and confronting whatever images emerge (and the associated thoughts and feelings) in relation to people with SLD or PMLD may help us to get closer to what they represent for us. We may notice what we project onto them from our own past and present, as well as in relation to our own aspirations for the future – for ourselves and for schools and wider society.

As the *active imagination* process is supposed to be without predetermined 'agenda', I propose that applying these principles via expressive therapy structures might be the most effective way to channel this initiative which all stakeholders in the inclusion process could partake in. One obvious way is through applying effective art therapy techniques (Gilroy 2006: 120–150). The first step would be to relax and reflect quietly with the theme of learning difficulties held loosely in mind, and notice any images arising.

The next step would be to draw or paint the image which has come through most strongly – it could be an animal, plant, building, mode of transport, or maybe a version of someone with learning difficulties as they are. This would be done bearing in mind the principle that the picture is not to be viewed for its artistic or stylistic merit, but for what it represents (Case and Dalley 1992). This in itself throws up a relevant question: if I am anxious about other people (or myself) judging the 'quality' of the picture, what does this say about my unconscious fears and conscious attitudes towards learning difficulties?

What should emerge from this process is a developing internal and hopefully interpersonal dialogue about what we mean and feel by 'learning difficulties' and a deepening engagement with questions such as 'why *inclusion?*' and 'what is *inclusion?*' The art therapy approach is not the only possible strategy available; discursive, dramatic, writing and other creative strategies could also be used (Oaklander 1988). What I am proposing here is a process that would be valuable for *all* teachers, school leaders, support staff, governors, local education authority (LEA) advisers and policymakers at the Department for Children, Schools and Families (DCSF) to get at least one experience of in order for the deeper levels of the inclusion agenda to be properly teased out. I am aware this seems rather a grand proposal, but it is about offering the tools of *imagination* to the real world of education as it currently struggles with that issue. It is a case which I believe is worth making in order to shift the psychological 'logjam' around it. If such an enterprise were to be undertaken, built into teacher training, schools' in-service training (INSET) days and DCSF/LEA policymaker 'blue-skies' consultations, then some of this deeply set, historical baggage around 'learning difficulties' could at least be made conscious – a prerequisite for moving complex and loaded issues forward.

There is also a need to implement an awareness-raising process among the pupils (and their parents and carers). The use of personal, social and health education time in mainstream and special schools to sensitively explore what 'learning difficulty' means should yield some valuable insights and dialogue. This is an area which teachers might be a little cautious about opening up because of the scope for pupils to feel defensive – e.g. through wanting to point-score – about their own areas of learning prowess and weakness. However, this need not be an obstacle, since well-established approaches drawn from the experience of dealing with other sensitive issues such as bullying, self-esteem or sex education could be utilized.

Within already consolidated practices, such as circle time (Mosley 2005), work on what, say, mainstream pupils imagine when they think of pupils with learning difficulties, or what pupils now in special schools imagine that their mainstream peers think of *them*, might yield some very fruitful dialogue, as well as heightened self-awareness for all concerned. This approach could of course draw on already established *inclusive* settings or arrangements, enabling pupils from previously separate contexts to dialogue on the imagery that has come to the surface. Again, different techniques, using a range of game, storytelling, drama and discursive techniques could be employed, within clearly agreed rules of engagement, spending time on the language used to describe images and what they represent, where that would be fruitful (or necessary to tackle preconceptions).

The arising dialogues and any themes arising could be recorded and inform curriculum planning and policymaking. At this stage though, these proposals are *deliberately open* and consciously avoid the oft-expressed requirement by policymakers and school leaders for a justification of how this will 'improve learning outcomes' (Ray 2006). My suggestion here is that a deeper process of reflection and dialogue is needed first, without any presuppositions of where this might lead, before a policy towards inclusion which resonates with the genuine needs of all learners emerges.

Concluding remark

This chapter has attempted to open up the issue of inclusion, and the place of pupils with severe, and profound and multiple, learning difficulties within the mainstream of education, by drawing on archetypal figures from Jungian psychology. It has also suggested how a collective process of active imagination is needed to enable meaningful inclusion to take place. The application of our imagination here can perhaps provide the bridge to effective policy and practice that appears to currently elude us.

References

Allen, J. (1999) *Actively Seeking Inclusion: Pupils with SENs in Mainstream Schools*. London: Falmer.

Benjamin, S. (2002) *The Micropolitics of Inclusive Education*. Buckingham: Open University Press.

Byers, R. (1999) The National Literacy Strategy and pupils with special educational needs. *British Journal of Special Education* 26: 8–11.

Campbell, J. and Oliver, M. (1996) *Disability Politics*. London: Routledge.

Case, C. and Dalley, T. (1992) *The Handbook of Art Therapy*. London: Routledge.

Chodorow, J. (1997) Introduction. In J. Chodorow (ed.) *Jung on Active Imagination*. London: Routledge.

De Groef, J. (1999) Mental handicaps: A dark continent. In J. De Groef and E. Heinemann (eds) *Psychoanalysis and Mental Handicap*. London: Free Association Press.

DES (1978) *Special Educational Needs* (Warnock Report). London: HMSO.

DfEE (1988) *National Curriculum for England and Wales*. London: HMSO.

DfES (2001) *Inclusive Schooling: Children with Special Educational Needs*. London: DfES.

Foucault, M. (1977) Intellectuals and power: A conversation between Michel Foucault and Giles Deleuze. In D. Bouchard (ed.) *Language, Counter-memory, Practice: Selected Essays and Interviews by Michel Foucault*. Oxford: Blackwell.

Gilroy, A. (2006) *Art Therapy, Research and Evidence-based Practice*. London: Sage.

Goss, P. (2006) Meaning-led learning for pupils with severe and profound and multiple learning difficulties. *British Journal for Special Education* 33: 210–219.

Hansard (2005) Special Schools debate calling for a moratorium on closures (22 June 2005; House of Commons), www.batod.org.uk/index.php (accessed 25 April 2007).

Hillman, J. (1985) *Anima: An Anatomy of a Personified Notion*. Dallas, TX: Spring.

Hobson, P. (2002) *The Cradle of Thought: Exploring the Origins of Thinking*. London: Pan Macmillan.

Jung, C. G. (1958) The transcendent function. *The Collected Works of C .G. Jung* (Vol. 8). London: Routledge and Kegan Paul. (Original work published in 1916.)

—— (1966) The psychology of the transference. *The Collected Works of C. G. Jung* (Vol. 16). London: Routledge and Kegan Paul. (Original work published in 1946.)

—— (1968) On the psychology of the Trickster figure. *The Collected Works of C.G. Jung* (Vol. 9.i). London: Routledge and Kegan Paul. (Original work published in 1954.)

—— (1976) The Tavistock Lectures. *The Collected Works of C.G. Jung* (Vol. 18). London: Routledge and Kegan Paul. (Original work published in 1935.)

Lewis, I. (2003) *Ecstatic Religion: A Study of Shamanism and Spirit* (3rd edition). Abingdon: Routledge.

Littlewood, R. (1993) *Pathology and Identity: The Work of Mother Earth*. Cambridge: Cambridge University Press.

Marzano, R. (2003) *What Works in Schools: Translating Research into Action*. Alexandria, VA: Association for Supervision and Curriculum Development.

Moore, T. (1990) *A Blue Fire: The Essential James Hillman*. London: Routledge.

Mosley, J. (2005) *The Circle Book (Circle Time)*. Trowbridge, UK: Positive Press.

Oaklander, V. (1988) *Windows to our Children*. New York: The Gestalt Centre.

O'Hanlon, C. (1995) A comparison of educational provision for pupils with SEN in Europe. In P. Mittler and P. Daunt (eds) *Teacher Education for Special Needs in Europe*. London: Cassell.

Peacey, N. (2005) The legal framework. In G. Backhouse and K. Morris (eds) *Dyslexia? Assessing and Reporting*. London: Hodder Murray.

Ray, A. (2006) *School Value Added Measures in England*. London: OECD/DfES.

Samuels, A., Shorter, B. and Plaut, F. (1986) *A Critical Dictionary of Jungian Analysis*. London: Routledge and Kegan Paul.

Sinason, V. (1992) *Mental Handicap and the Human Condition*. London: Free Association.

Teachernet (2007) www.teachernet.gov.uk/wholeschool/sen/senglossary/ (accessed 28 January 2007).

Thomas, G., Walker, D. and Webb, J. (1998) *The Inclusive School*. London: Routledge.

Warnock, M. (1997) The keys to understanding: Interview with Baroness Warnock. *Special Magazine* November: 12.

Youell, B. (2006) *The Learning Relationship: Psychoanalytic Thinking in Education*. London: Karnac.

Chapter 4

Rousseau, childhood and the ego

A (post-)Jungian reading of *Emile*

Terence Dawson

One might be a little taken aback to find a chapter on Jean-Jacques Rousseau's treatise on education in a book about current Jungian perspectives on the place of the imagination in education today. For not only was the prickly eighteenth-century Swiss *philosophe* fiercely opposed to the stimulation of a child's imagination, especially during the formative years, but also his argument might seem to be at odds with the aims of educators who have an interest in the ideas of C. G. Jung, most of whom will be concerned with the apparently opposite goal of helping the child to recognize the importance of his or her imagination. In these pages, however paradoxical this might seem, I want to show that Rousseau's views have a great deal to contribute to Jungian theory, and that every educator should be aware of their psychological implications.

Emile, or, On Education was published in May 1762. It is divided into five sections ('books') that outline Rousseau's ideal programme for the education of a boy of average intelligence from the privileged classes. The first covers infancy, the second early childhood, the third continues until the boy is age 15, the fourth deals with adolescence and the fifth follows Emile until he is about 25. Rousseau's programme is at best bizarre, at worst, laughable. He presents it as the tale of how he would bring up Emile, an 'imaginary pupil' (Rousseau 1979 [1762]: 50) entrusted to the care of a 'governor', i.e. himself (although ideally, he would prefer the tutor to be a *young* man). He begins by laying out his conditions. Emile would answer not to his parents, but only to his governor, who would be his *only* companion until 15 and his closest friend and adviser until 25. The programme would begin with the governor putting the child in his place, and holding him there 'so well that he no longer tries to leave it' (ibid.: 91). He wants the child to feel the full implications of his dependence. And once he feels it, a curious and somewhat disturbing game begins: Rousseau watches over the boy's every development; he spies on Emile and manipulates the outcome of what the boy does; and he tells us, unashamedly, that he does this in such a way that the boy will never guess it. Until the age of 15, his entire education consists in learning from nature. At age 15, the governor enters into a contract with his charge, in which the latter willingly agrees to follow his advice until about 25. And for all these years, the governor will continue to carefully regulate Emile's behaviour, including his choice of friends, his entrance into society, his views on religion, and his first meeting with young women, whose education, he argues, should be almost solely concerned with preparing them for marriage. Today, one can only wince at such sexism, and at the advocacy of such constant surveillance and total control over his male pupil. It isn't easy to see either *how* or *why* such a text should continue to speak to us today. Nor is it an easy book to read. For, like all Rousseau's writings, it is uneven: it proceeds by unsubstantiated and categorical assertions and often irritating reiteration, and it often spins off into authorial digressions. Even so, he regarded it as his 'best' and his 'most important' work (Rousseau 2000 [1782]: 561).

The way in which Rousseau orders his material bears an obvious resemblance to Jung's distinction between the obligations of the two main stages of life. Youth, which he defines as covering 'the years just after puberty to middle life' (Jung 1969 [1931]: para. 759), is the time to establish a solidly grounded career and to start a family, whereas in 'the second half of life', which begins in one's late thirties, one has a 'duty' to invest one's life with greater depth of meaning by expanding one's understanding of one's inner world (ibid.: para. 785). The first three sections of *Emile* emphasize the child's need to develop self-reliance; they correspond to that stage of life in which Jung had not the slightest interest: childhood (although since Jung many analytical psychologists, beginning with Michael Fordham in the 1940s, have given considerable attention to childhood; e.g. Fordham 1969 [1944]). The last two sections, which span the years 15 to 25, very slowly introduce the young man to religion, to society and to women: in other words, they consist of a process of individuation unfolding not in the 'second half of life', but *during* 'youth'. The parallels are evident, but because there is space here to examine only *one* aspect of Rousseau's argument, the focus in this chapter will be on the early years, for they offer not only the more unexpected insights, but also possibly the more interesting conclusions.

Rousseau's theory of education has attracted enormous critical interest (Parry 2001: 268 provides a short bibliography). In this chapter, the first three sections of the argument he outlines in *Emile* are explored in the light of C. G. Jung's definitions of the ego and the persona. The aims are to show how Jung's terms serve to uncover an unsuspected but crucial dimension to Rousseau's text and, albeit more tentatively, to suggest a modification to Jung's definition of the ego. I shall make no attempt to disguise Rousseau's emphasis on a male child; as we shall see, however, his argument applies to all children.

Childhood and self-reliance

Rousseau's starting point is a personal assessment of society. The object of his study, he tells us, is 'the human condition' (Rousseau 1979: 42). He looks around him and does not see 'men'; he sees only creatures motivated by the most frivolous of desires. And he sees the origin of these in two equally false models of education. The first is college education which, by forcing the child to absorb before he is able to understand the underlying principles of what he learns, teaches him to value authority before his own understanding and to think that regurgitating the opinions of others is the objective of education. He regards all external influence as pernicious and detrimental to the child, but the most dangerous of all is authority, for authority deprives the child of his freedom. Moreover, as soon as the child understands the arbitrary nature of authority, he will devise means to manipulate those who exercise it. This is how his life becomes a constant exercise of deception and manipulation. Achievement becomes judged on performance. The second model is the education that a child receives from society, which produces 'double men, always appearing to relate everything to others and never relating anything except to themselves alone' (Rousseau 1979: 41). The net result of these two models is to denature human beings: human intercourse is governed by deception and manipulation.

Rousseau will have none of this. His objective is to develop an authentic individual. Traditional education serves to degenerate the species; only by seeking to develop an authentic individual can one hope to regenerate it. He wants Emile to become not a slave to the opinions of others, but a man: 'the first of all useful things,' he writes, is 'the art of forming men' (ibid.: 33). His elaboration of what he means by this is somewhat paradoxical. A father 'owes to his species men; he owes to society sociable men; he owes to the state citizens' (ibid.: 49). In other words, in Rousseau's view, one owes it *to the species* (i.e. humankind) to become a man. And by a man, he means an individual who is completely free of all the worst tendencies of society: a man whose desires are not shaped by outside pressures in his life, but come from a measured assessment of their relation to his real rather than his imagined needs.

If whatever one teaches a child contributes to his enslavement, then it follows that one must avoid teaching him anything. Rousseau describes this as his 'inactive method' (ibid.: 117). 'What must be done is to prevent anything from being done' (ibid.: 41). 'The first education ought to be purely negative' (ibid.: 93). 'The greatest, the most important, the most useful rule of all education? It is not to gain time but to lose it' (ibid.: 93). The only purpose in the early years is to guarantee the child's 'well regulated freedom' (ibid.: 92). In other words, take the child outdoors as often as is possible, ensure that he has all he needs to play creatively and leave him be. One's task is to ensure, however deviously, that he continues to play creatively and so gradually learns to better understand both the extent and the limits of his own dominion.

For Rousseau, nature shows the way. 'Do not give your pupil any kind of verbal lessons; he ought to receive them only from experience' (ibid.: 92). A verbal lesson is indoctrination. It robs a child of the opportunity to discover something for himself. A child cannot discover for himself the principles of higher disciplines. The challenges with which one presents him must be tailored to his age. 'Our first masters of philosophy are our feet, our hands, our eyes' (ibid.: 125). 'To learn to think, therefore, it is necessary to exercise our limbs, our senses, our organs, which are the instruments of our intelligence' (ibid.: 125). Leave a child outdoors; if properly guided, every moment should be a moment of joyous learning. Present him with objects that will arouse his curiosity (ibid.: 169). Let him examine 'each new object he sees for a long time without saying anything' (ibid.: 169). Let him feel it for what it is, for 'It is in man's heart that the life of nature's spectacle exists. To see it, one must feel it' (ibid.: 169).

Discuss with him only what is at hand. If you want to teach him geography, the land around his home is his school. Urge him to make connections from experience, to see, for example, the relation between the seasons and the movement of the sun. 'Let the child do nothing on anybody's word. Nothing is good for him unless he feels it to be so' (ibid.: 178). 'It is up to him to desire it, to seek it, to find it' (ibid.: 179). Help him to gradually 'Transform [his] sensations into ideas' (ibid.: 168). But be careful never to direct his thoughts. 'To make a young man judicious, we must form his judgements well instead of dictating ours to him' (ibid.: 187). 'Forced to learn by himself, he uses his reason and not another's; for to give nothing to opinion, one must give nothing to authority' (ibid.: 207). 'The goal is less to teach him the truth than to show him how he must always go about discovering the truth' (ibid.: 205).

We are now in a better position to understand Rousseau's insistence that a child's imagination should not be developed during the primary years. The child needs to learn to recognize the place that he occupies in the world, to know it, to feel it, to understand exactly how he relates to it and, above all, to recognize what pertains to him and what does not. Rousseau defines the imagination as that which 'extends for us the measure of the possible' (ibid.: 81). In other words, encouraging children to use their imagination is implicitly inviting them to imagine themselves as *other* than they are: it represents 'that false wisdom which incessantly projects us outside of ourselves' (ibid.: 79). If too much time is given to such reverie, 'We no longer exist where we are; we only exist where we are not' (ibid.: 83). We become false selves. This is why Rousseau is so hostile to book-learning. Books express the imagination of their author, not the child. For this reason, all books should be avoided, with one celebrated exception: *Robinson Crusoe* or, more accurately, the central section. Rousseau had no patience with Defoe's frame-story (how Crusoe found his way to the island and, twenty-eight years later, his way back to England); he was interested only in the episode on the island. Let the child pretend that he is Crusoe, and let him learn the skills required by Crusoe (ibid.: 185, 198). Point him toward the discovery that he too can make whatever he needs. 'Teach him what things are in themselves', as opposed to what they are in our eyes (ibid.: 187). Lead him to discover the need 'To convert to our use all that we can appropriate for ourselves and to profit from our curiosity for the advantage of our well-being' (ibid.: 192), but with this major proviso: let him learn to value 'the useful above the ornamental' (ibid.: 186).

Rousseau argues that real happiness comes from ensuring that there is no discrepancy between one's faculties and one's desires (ibid.: 81). 'The real world has its limits; the imaginary world is infinite. Unable to enlarge the one, let us restrict the other' (ibid.: 81). He sums this up in an image: 'Let us measure the radius of our sphere and stay in the centre like the insect in the middle of his web; we shall always be sufficient unto ourselves' (ibid.: 81). The somewhat disturbing image should not distract us from the importance that Rousseau gave to self-reliance, which he considered the only protection against the ups and down of the world. He was deeply influenced by stoicism. 'O man, draw your existence up within yourself, and you will no longer be miserable' (ibid.: 83).

At the end of the third book, Rousseau challenges his reader: 'Do you find that a child who has come in this way to his fifteenth year has wasted the preceding ones?' (ibid.: 208). He is undeterred by having to concede that Emile will not have learned as much as a child brought up on books. His pupil knows nothing whatsoever about history or philosophy; he knows nothing about the country in which he lives and even less about human beings, even those among which he has lived. Because he has no model for authority, 'He grants nothing to opinion' (ibid.: 207). All he knows are facts about the natural things with which he has been faced. 'Emile has only natural and purely physical knowledge. . . . He knows the essential relations of man to things but nothing of the moral relations of man to man' (ibid.: 207). He knows nothing of those sustaining fictions on which society is founded: religion, myth, models from history, models of social behaviour, and career outlines. He is not motivated by the spirit of emulation, ambition, vanity or competition. And crucially he has no *amour-propre* (self-love); that is, he is absolutely free of all fanciful ideas about himself, including ideas about his entitlement. 'He considers himself without regard to others and finds it good that others do not think of him. . . . He counts on himself alone' (ibid.: 208). But not everything is negative. Emile is also hard-working, 'temperate, patient, firm, and full of courage. His imagination is in no way inflamed and never enlarges dangers. . . . Emile has all that relates to himself' (ibid.: 208). In short, Rousseau concludes, 'Emile has little knowledge, but what he has is truly his own' (ibid.: 207).

It is hardly surprising that educators have always been uncomfortable at the idea of raising a child in complete isolation from his peers until the age of 15. This uneasiness continues to be reflected in recent criticism of *Emile*. For example, Timothy O'Hagan (1999: 59) sees it as 'part pedagogical treatise, part novel': he is uneasy that so much of it is purely speculative. Or Nicholas Dent (2005: 83), who argues that 'no crucial significance attaches to the particular chronology Rousseau gives for the emergence of each [of the issues that he identifies]'. He is equally uneasy about taking the work over-literally – and possibly rightly. Two years after its publication, Rousseau admitted that it could not be followed in practice: 'his ultimate subject was the "idea" of an education that would not corrupt the natural goodness of humanity' (Parry 2001: 250).

At a literal level, Rousseau's concern in the early years is with self-reliance. But there are good reasons for reading beyond the literal; in other words, to try to understand an 'idea' with which he might have been grappling. In the following section I want to consider one aspect of the possible psychological implications of Rousseau's argument.

The persona and the ego

Rousseau never minces his words. Traditional education, he asserts, prepares a child for a life of slavery: 'All our wisdom consists in servile prejudices. All our practices are only subjection, impediment and constraint. Civil man is born, lives, and dies in slavery. . . . So long as he keeps his human shape, he is enchained by our institutions' (Rousseau 1979: 42–43). From the moment of birth, a child is subject to the will of others: that of his nurse, his mother, his father, his teachers, all of whom are constantly telling him what to do and what not to do, telling him what to think and what not to think, imposing their wills on his in order to make him think like them; in other words, coercing him into an acceptance of their codes, their convictions, their ideology. Education is a battle of wills between the child and a small army of others whose every manoeuvre is directed toward instilling him with one or other of their own second-hand assumptions. And Rousseau is categorical about where this ends: 'As soon as one must see with the eyes of others, one must will with their wills' (ibid.: 84). A child's every view has been informed by others; he doesn't have a thought of his own. 'He will be nothing more than the plaything of others' opinion' (ibid.: 168). He will become a mindless performing monkey in a shameless materialist society that wastes its time and its efforts on frivolous activities, with the inevitable result that he will become bored and cease to enjoy the real joys of life.

Rousseau's abhorrence of the society of his time is of course excessive: we need not quibble on this score. But there can be little doubt that he touches on a point of enormous consequence when he insists that traditional education, both institutional and domestic, fosters a battle of wills between figures of authority and those entrusted to their care, and that this leads to another kind of battle in adulthood, which is dominated by competitiveness where success is measured by what today we would call performance indicators. Conflicts of power, deception and manipulation lie behind all social interactions. No one is candid; no one can be trusted; everything is performance based, and everyone changes their masks so often that it is impossible to know whether they have a true face.

Rousseau was the first person to spot that this constitutes a real problem for the individual. The society in which he lived, and the society of which he wrote, were of course very different from our own. The industrial revolution had barely arrived in France; all privilege lay in the hands of the church and the aristocracy, while the great majority of the population had to struggle to feed themselves. Yet the dominant reason that Rousseau disliked the closed, cosseted, rococo ruling class was not because it was elitist (which it was), nor because it was corrupt (which it was); it was because he felt it to be deeply *inauthentic*. And where there is inauthenticity there can be no true individuality. His central concern in Emile is the problem of authenticity.

This is why the text invites consideration from a post-Jungian perspective. One of the more neglected aspects of analytical psychology is the distinction Jung makes between the persona and the ego. The former describes 'a mask for the collective psyche, a mask that *feigns individuality*, and tries to make others and oneself believe that one is individual, whereas one is simply playing a part in which the collective psyche speaks' (Jung 1953 [1934]: para. 245). Individuals, in Jung's view, do not choose their personae; the persona suggests itself to them and they adopt it. It becomes theirs. Social life requires them to wear a persona at all times. This is normal, necessary. Because every social interaction requires a significantly different persona (the mother/father, the commuter, the doctor, the employee, etc.), every individual has several often remarkably different personae. On the one hand, because these personae reflect the collective psyche (and thus also collective assumptions) they are every bit as *authentic* an aspect of an individual as the ego. On the other hand, because they are always, and by definition, a 'mask' and all masks are collective, the persona is *not* the authentic face of the individual.

What Rousseau abhors about his fellow men is that they are not authentic. They are always pretending to be something other than they really are. His insistence on preventing *all* outside influence on a child during the early years is designed to prevent the child from *feigning individuality* before he has acquired both the maturity and the necessary objectivity to think for himself. And the aspect of the personality that feigns individuality corresponds exactly with Jung's definition of the *persona*. Seen in this light, the objective of Rousseau's programme is to ensure that the child is not absorbed by his persona (or personae) too early in life. He is the first thinker to explore the distinction between the persona and the authentic individual.

The question remains: how is one to define the authentic aspect of the personality? As I have written elsewhere (Dawson 2008), it has long been recognized that Jung's various definitions of the ego are problematic. His most frequently cited definition is that the ego is 'the centre of [the field of] consciousness' (Jung 1968 [1950]: para. 2). But envisaging the ego in terms of consciousness and of space (as a 'centre' that can be 'expanded') is an open invitation to both individual psychological inflation and a collective cult-like smugness. Jung also described the *ego* as 'a sort of complex' (Jung 1977 [1936]: para. 19), but given his insistence that complexes act like autonomous personalities, it is difficult to understand how the ego can be both a 'centre of consciousness' *and* an autonomous personality. This earlier definition is further complicated by his elaboration: one part of the ego, he continues, is turned toward the outside world, while another lies in 'the shadow-world' of unconsciousness, where 'the ego is somewhat dark, we do not see into it, we are an enigma to ourselves' (ibid.: para. 38). This too is confusing. It seems to conflate two very different modes of perception. It is intrinsically unlikely that the sense of 'I-ness' that negotiates with the outside world and which, by definition, must have a semblance of continuity is the *same* as that which lies in the unconscious, and is therefore fundamentally unstable. One would have expected a depth psychologist to distinguish between that part of the personality that responds to *outer* stimuli (whether an approaching rain-cloud, a traffic signal, verbal information, or a painting) and that part of the personality that registers a new awareness about the nature and implication of *inner* experience (whether a powerful emotion, a vivid fantasy image, an autonomous intuition, or a compulsive thought).

At age 15, it is not easy to define Emile *except* by contrasting him with his peers: unlike them, he has no personae. Although what he has 'is truly his own' (Rousseau 1979: 207), it is difficult to define exactly what this is. And this is Rousseau's point. Educational positivists of his day (e.g. Priestley and Helvétius) regarded the infant mind as a *tabula rasa* that could be imprinted with knowledge and predetermined social values. Rousseau's objective is to prevent any such indoctrination: his purpose is to provide the child with a personality that owes nothing to anyone but himself, not even his governor, and an ability to relate to others with complete candour, i.e. without *any* ulterior motive of fear or gain. At age 15, Emile 'lacks only the learning which his mind is all ready to receive' (ibid.: 208). But his mind is certainly not a clean slate: he has a much more substantial sense of himself as an individual than his peers and he has been raised to ensure that he truly understands all that he considers and not to be swayed by any form of authority.

It is difficult to identify the authentic aspect of Emile's personality with either of Jung's most frequently cited definitions of the ego. Emile is not characterized by an ego defined in spatial terms, for it has been one of Rousseau's primary objectives never to allow his pupil to have inflated ideas about himself. Nor is he characterized by an ego defined as an autonomous personality, for Rousseau's entire programme has been directed toward giving his pupil a sense of a true identity that is not going to be swayed by changing conditions. In other words, if one wants to insist that Emile's authentic sense of himself is the ego, one must modify Jung's definition.

Emile's sense of himself is not characterized by consciousness as such, for most of the time it would be dormant. It comes into play only when he is faced by new information or a new experience and has to ascertain how it relates to himself; in other words, only when he has to establish its *personal significance* for him. Understood in this way, the ego is not so much a component of the personality as a psychic mechanism that is at once constant and yet always in process of being modified as a result of the evaluations it makes about the relevance of experience to itself. Because it is engaged in evaluation, in deciding how it stands in relation to an experience, it is forever moving between an interest in otherness and deciding on the importance of this other for itself. This mechanism can be defined as the centre of the authentic individual identity, but not as a centre of consciousness. Most of our habitual conscious responses to the outer world are governed by the *persona*. The ego controls only our responses to issues pertinent to the inner world. It indicates the specific kind of *self-awareness* that comes from being connected both to one's sense of oneself and one's inner world.

Rousseau's insistence on self-reliance is the first sustained attempt to demonstrate the importance for an individual of being rooted in one's ego. Emile's entire education has been directed to strengthening his sense of his own authentic identity. But this identity does not consist of something quantifiable (i.e. that can be defined in spatial terms) so much as in his understanding of both the extent and the limits of what he knows. He is exactly what he is, including the way he understands the world in which he finds himself. He never seeks to embellish. He never pretends to be other than he is or to know anything that he has not fully understood for himself; and whatever he is faced with, his first thought is to understand its importance in relation to himself as a human being (Rousseau 1979: 168). At age 15, he embodies the ego of a young man on the threshold of his necessary entry in society.

Conclusion

All educational theory supposes a balance between *information* (from Latin *informare*, 'to shape or describe', through Middle English *informe*, 'give form or shape to', i.e. to impart knowledge or teach a skill) and *education* (from Latin *educare*, 'to lead out', i.e. to bring out and nurture a student's own *inherent* abilities: *Oxford English Dictionary*). And its purpose is to prepare a child for *life*. But what constitutes the best balance between information and education, and how one defines life is a matter of ever-changing opinion; in other words, it rests on ideological assumptions. As long as education is determined by authority and conditioned by 'reproduction' (cf. Bourdieu and Passeron 1990 [1970]), it will have far more to do with the objectives of the ruling class than with the unique individual. At the outset of the twenty-first century, these objectives are predominantly political and practical: they are dictated by a nation's perception of how it needs to meet the current economic challenges. In other words, by *life* most educational ministries mean little more than a *job*. Never has there been such widespread chatter about the needs of the individual; never have the needs of the individual been so obviously tailored to the requirements of economic survival.

Rousseau would have had two objections to this: first, that vocational concerns represent only a small, and certainly not the most important part of life; and second, because children are not ready to understand the premises underlying institutional education, they will never be able to fully engage with it: their minds will always be 'elsewhere'. Before one teaches children anything, one must first equip them with the means both to want to learn *and* to evaluate what they are learning. And this means first 'forcing' children to rely on their own resources so that they gradually discover the centre of their individual identity and then nurturing and strengthening their confidence in their own inherent abilities.

Today, most educators acknowledge that Rousseau can be credited with making two enormous contributions to educational theory. The first is the insistence that each child should develop at his or her own pace and learn by personal discovery rather than by instruction, which laid the foundation for 'child-centred' education. The second is his view that the objective of education is not to impart the presumed facts about a given subject, but to develop the child's love of learning and the 'skills' that will allow the child to learn about it in his or her own way. For both these reasons, *Emile* represents a landmark in educational thinking that deserves to be taken seriously.

In these pages, I have sought to demonstrate that Rousseau should also be credited with a third and equally significant contribution. For his argument begs a question: Who exactly – or, in Jungian terms, *which aspect* of the personality – are we educating during the school years? The persona? Or the ego? Rousseau was the first theorist to understand the importance of the ego, the authentic centre of individual identity. His argument that the early years of education should consist of preventing a child from being absorbed by his or her various personae by nurturing only his or her ego is as relevant today as it was during the *ancien régime*. For children have never been exposed to so many, such constant and such powerful outside pressures as they are today. They begin with 'blue for a boy, pink for a girl', 'say please', 'do as I tell you', and 'learn this by heart'; all-too-soon these are followed by '*x* is so-o-o cool' and 'have you seen *y*?' All children and adolescents like to think of themselves as unique individuals, but there is nothing either unique or individual about absorbing like a sponge whatever a parent, teacher or friend tells you, or about regurgitating the opinions of others, whether those of an adult or a peer group, or about preferring one branded item to another, or even about having one's personal mix of other people's wit or their views. Where exactly is the *individual* in any of these? Once children have become the plaything of ideological and market forces, they will find it extremely difficult to connect with their authentic identity. When they think they have done so, it is usually a sham for which the model is obvious.

The privileged classes assume that they have an obligation to stimulate the imagination of their children, especially during the primary years. Parents read children all manner of bedtime stories from board books to fairytales and from adaptations of Greek and Norse mythology to classics of modern children's literature. They encourage them to draw and to paint and to love music and, especially girls, to dance. But, Rousseau asks, does this really serve their best interests? He thinks not: if children develop their imagination *before* they can assess their relation to what they imagine, there is a danger that children will begin to identify with issues and values that have little to do with their own stage of development, and that, in this way, they will begin to live a false life. And from the moment they do so, it is only a short step to becoming absorbed by their personae.

Not everyone will be swayed by Rousseau's argument; indeed, very few will be able to swallow all of it. But there can be no doubt that there is more than a grain of truth in what he says. He was the first to understand that modern society places such demands on the cultivation of the persona that it is difficult not only for children, but also for adults to know how to connect with their ego, let alone remain connected with it.

But this, of course, is only the beginning. Rousseau continues, in books four and five of *Emile*, to outline the challenges that his imaginary pupil must face between the ages of 15 and 25, and what he describes is, in effect, a process of individuation. Even the way he describes his relationship with Emile reminds one of the analytical encounter. Jung the analyst, taking up the challenge *after* the damage has been done, considers that authenticity comes only from the unconscious or, perhaps more precisely, from the self. He has little time for the ego, which may explain why he is careless about his definitions of the ego. Rousseau, on the other hand, insists that authenticity can be found by following nature. And if one turns to nature to find it, and not to the spurious authority of institutional learning, there is no reason to doubt that the ego will emerge the stronger for it. And, moreover, in later years, the young adult will be in a much better position to negotiate with the inner experience of the self and therefore will stand a better chance of holding on to its authenticity for the remainder of its life. Traditional institutional education has far too little interest in, and far too few ways of helping a child to connect with its ego. Rousseau reminds us that without such a connection, we can never be more than the plaything of someone else's ideology – including, of course, in later life, when things so often go wrong, Jung's.

Emile embodies a young man who is not swayed by the fashions of the world and who will not bow or subscribe to any kind of authority that seeks to impose itself on him. In one sense, he is the antithesis of modern man; in another, he is the first truly modern individual, the first to accept and carry the burden of his own individual personality as naturally as his ancestors carried those of his tribe. Long before Darwin, Rousseau understood not only that the species had turned a corner, but also that the ruling class will do all it can to prevent the perception of this change from becoming widespread: it is much easier to control false selves than authentic individuals. As long as individuals are absorbed by their various personae, they are slaves. Hence Rousseau's paradoxical insistence, as illustrated from the beginning of *Emile* and which he repeats in *The Social Contract*, that human beings must be 'forced to be free' (1994: 141).

References

Bourdieu, P. and Passeron, J.-C. (1990) *Reproduction in Education, Society and Culture*. London: Sage. (Original work published in 1970.)

Dawson, T. (2008) The persona and the ego: *Robinson Crusoe* and modern identity. In S. Rowland (ed.) *Psyche and the Arts*. Hove, UK: Routledge.

Dent, N. (2005) *Rousseau*. Abingdon: Routledge.

Fordham, M. (1969) *Children as Individuals*. London: Hodder and Stoughton. (Original work published as *The Life of Childhood* in 1944.)

Jung, C. G. (1953) The relations between the ego and the unconscious. *The Collected Works of C. G. Jung* (Vol. 7). London: Routledge and Kegan Paul. (Original work published in 1934.)

—— (1968) Aion. *The Collected Works of C. G. Jung* (Vol. 9.ii). London: Routledge and Kegan Paul. (Original work published in 1950.)

—— (1969) The stages of life. *The Collected Works of C. G. Jung* (Vol. 8). London: Routledge and Kegan Paul. (Original work published in 1931.)

—— (1977) The Tavistock Lectures. *The Collected Works of C. G. Jung* (Vol. 18). London: Routledge and Kegan Paul. (Original work published in 1936.)

O'Hagan, T. (1999) *Rousseau*. London: Routledge.

Parry, G. (2001) *Emile*: Learning to be men, women, and citizens. In P. Riley (ed.) *The Cambridge Companion to Rousseau*. Cambridge: Cambridge University Press.

Rousseau, J.-J. (1979) *Emile, or, On Education*. New York: Basic Books. (Original work published in 1762.)

—— (1994) The Social Contract. *Collected Writings* (Vol. 4). Hanover, NH: University Press of New England.

—— (2000) *Confessions*. Oxford: Oxford University Press. (Original work published in 1782.)

Chapter 5

Education and imagination: a contradiction in terms?

Experiences from mythodramatic crisis intervention in schools

Allan Guggenbühl

To hijack the school bus was not that difficult. The bus driver was given a knock on the head. While his unconscious body was dragged away, the youngsters sneaked into the bus and filled it with explosives. Now the next, more difficult task had to be fulfilled: the bus had to crash the gates of Woodstock High School, smash into the main hall, where finally all the explosives could be ignited by remote control. The students rejoiced, as the bus blew up and debris of the building fell from the sky. Finally their plan had succeeded.

Fortunately this incident never really happened. Woodstock High still proudly demonstrates its white, impressive pillars, red brick library and meticulously trimmed green to its visitors. The students did not blow up their school and turn it into shambles. Instead they enacted a scene as part of a *mythodrama* session (Guggenbühl 2003a: 135–144). Their task was to *imagine* the end of a story, which was related to them. They were given two hours, during which they could fantasize their version of the end of a story we told them. To the bewilderment of the principal and the dismay of some of the teachers, they presented this horrid scene. Were these students out of their minds?

Myths as the key to resolve conflicts

Mythodrama is an approach in which stories and drama are used in order to help schools to deal with conflicts or violent incidents. The seven-step mythodramatic intervention is an answer to the various conflicts that schools are confronted with. It includes parents' work, counselling of the teachers and group work with the students. The method was developed by the author and is currently being employed as therapeutic tool and in conflict management by the out-patient clinic of the state of Bern, the institute of conflict management in Zurich/Stockholm, the Konohana Institute in Tokyo and a number of school psychologists in Switzerland and Germany. The core of mythodrama is the idea that our attitudes and motivations are influenced by *myths*. This term is used to point out that many generally accepted thinking patterns and explanations originate in modern myths. They function as the base of a certain society. Myths are defined as the distinct stories which emerge in societies in order to explain mysteries, problems, fears and threats. We lean on myths when we are existentially challenged and in need of answers. They help us make decisions and give us an orientation. By using the term myth, I want to indicate that these stories are also *psychic realities*. They are more than rational explanations, for they symbolise part of the soul. Myths touch us, aggravate us, enrage us, motivate us or emotionalize us. They are called great stories, because they are often adhered to by groups of people. Societies of people unconsciously submit to big stories, when seeking an answer to existential challenges or conflicts.

Modern myths behind general accusations

'Gang rape by Balkan juveniles!' proclaimed the headlines of several tabloids in Switzerland. On the television news viewers saw pictures of a school in Zurich and were told of horrific events among the students. Adolescents were accused of having drugged and raped an innocent Swiss female student. The public reacted with outrage. Discussions on television, political campaigns and heated debates among politicians and experts followed. The incident was in the headlines for several weeks. Finally, some weeks later, the police investigation revealed that only two adolescents were involved in the rape and the girl had consented. As the public interest had subsided, no one was interested in these facts. People had already identified the culprits and knew for sure what had been going on: uncivilised foreigners were abusing indigenous children. A school incident had evoked a public outcry and generated an undisputed explanation. The majority of people really believed that most of the foreign adolescents were vile, sexualised and disrespectful of Swiss laws and codes. The law had to be enforced with strictness and relentlessly. Of course, from a Jungian point of view one would also have to take psychological considerations into account. The whole debate was not just about a nasty school incident, but a myth was rehearsed. We were hearing the story of the rape of women by heinous foreign invaders. People were gathering behind an old archetypal tale. Because it is archetypal, it is embedded in our souls. Incidents, which seemingly have some resemblance to the story, can trigger powerful emotions and convictions. The collective outrage was actually fed by an archetypal disposition which emerged and temporally turned us blind. It was not just about a rape by adolescents from the Balkans, but about Attila raping our women or Genghis Khan invading Europe.

Myths often emerge in conflict situations (Guggenbühl 1996). We rely on these big stories in order to find an answer to problems and fears. Myths empower us, so we are able to confront existential challenges. Our unconscious, secret belief systems are mobilized when we feel threatened or existentially challenged. They help us make decisions, develop visions and cope with personal or professional problems.

In mythodrama a story is chosen, which depicts the myth of the group we are working with (Guggenbühl 1999). The story should reflect the issues and psychological situation of the group, in order to instigate a debate, release emotions and finally reveal their secret belief systems. The students are presented with mythology which might reflect their psychological situation. They gather in a hall – be it the gym, the music room or some other large room – and hear a story. The story is specially selected after interviews, observations and talks with the teachers, students and the parents. The psychologists, who are in charge of the mythodrama session, have to pick or create a story which reflects the challenges and complexes of the students. The story needs to have a distinct quality. It should not have a moral, political or educational message. The danger would be that students fall into the *compliance trap*. They start thinking in expected answers and anticipated solutions, instead of freeing their minds. The stories should not be neat, pacifying and politically correct, but should stir students up. What they hear might cause bewilderment, anger or irritation. In the mythodramatic interventions students are presented with violent or bizarre scenes. We want them to leave their common tracks of thinking and react psychologically on a deeper level.

Younger children are open to fairytales (Büttner 1985). We might tell them of Cinderella, dwarfs, trolls, princes and princesses. Older children and adolescents' attention can be caught, by relating *mythological themes*. Greek, Celtic or Indian myths are chosen. The young people hear of Odin, Vishnu or Baldur. These myths allow the children and adolescents to enter a world which is not coded and defined the same way as their everyday life. In some schools the intervening psychologist might address the students with *modern myths*. It could be the story of the assassination plot by the Central Intelligence Agency against Kennedy, the Wehrmacht's position during the Second World War or the childhood of Eminem. In mythodrama these stories are used as a tool to connect the students with the inner, archetypal depths.

The students never hear the stories to the end. Before a possible climax the psychologist stops and invites the students to imagine how the story might develop. What will happen after the boat capsizes? Apollo accuses Hermes of lying? A gruesome monster enters the house or the storm comes up? Lying on their backs the students imagine how the story might continue. Afterwards they work with their endings. They might draw their conclusion on a piece of paper or do a short drama in subgroups. Their drawings are then discussed, interpreted and linked to their personal challenges and situation in school. When the students chose to dramatize their endings, their performances are videotaped, viewed and connected to their specific problems and challenges. The psychologists act as interpreters. They try to make the students aware of the unconscious messages and mythic patterns, which are revealed in their dramas and drawings. What does it mean when they imagine that they confront dangers by the use of music or by engaging in a dance? What myth are they rehearsing when they dream of blowing up the school? The drama and drawings are read on a symbolical level. It is very unlikely that the students' intention is to turn their school into a shambles. By imaging a blow up, they are relating an archetypal story. The restricted, highly coded environment of their school breeds a liberation myth. They imagine themselves as heroes, scarifying themselves for freedom or fighters against evil oppressors. On a more banal level: maybe they are under the impression that the teachers are not really listening to them or are ignorant. The blow up scene shows that the students are full of anger. Be it drawings or drama, the students' endings contain valuable information on the psychological situation of the class and offer indications for what the next step could be. Imagination is possible, because the stories, the myths with which the students are confronted, contain symbols and archetypal scenes. By allowing the students to fantasize, one gets a clearer picture of the complexes, fears, myths and the group dynamics in school. Mythodrama offers a vessel for imagination. On the basis of their fantasies and endings new solutions can be sought and concrete changes implemented.[1]

Imagination and education: a contradiction?

Back to Woodstock High in Connecticut: 'If you allow students to imagine, chaos is the result,' concluded the principal of this American high school. His impression was that we have to prevent students from using their imagination unrestrictedly. If we allow students to dream up their life by themselves, they might come up with 'drugs, sex and rock'n' roll'. According to him, it is our duty as parent or teacher to safeguard our children. We have to *protect* them from their own abysmal fantasies and ideas. According to his point of view, it is naive to believe that imagination is a source of creative ideas and impulses. Psychologists might believe this fallacy, the facts of life tell a different story. Is imagination and education a contradiction?

In order to find an answer to that question we have to identify the root metaphors of education. On what ideas is education based? 'The greatest and best thoughts of man shape themselves . . . upon primordial images as a blueprint' (Jung 1966a [1943]: para. 109). Education's aim is to help children to acquire knowledge and competences. As teachers it is our duty to train the children to read, write and introduce them into traditions of our culture. Teachers need to convey to their students the *basic skills*, which are needed to survive and be successful in our society. Without education children would be helpless, disorientated and dependable. Schools inculcate children so they will develop into self-reliant, confident and capable men and women. As educators we try to help the next generation, so they can integrate into society and live a happy and fulfilled life.

The aim of education is to guide and shape the next generation. Due to the efforts of education children and juveniles obtain knowledge and competences, gain an individual profile. Education perceives students as *malleable*. Most educational approaches assert that it is education that makes us what we are. The older generation passes knowledge on and encourages the younger generation to set goals, develop ambitions and make decisions. Children and juveniles therefore have to be *led* by grown-ups, who possess knowledge and are aware of the risks of life. They have an idea what profile is desirable.

Which goals have to be achieved is decided by the schools in cooperation with the educational boards, commissions or educational specialist. It is their task to describe *goals* and *standards* and provide the students with *surroundings*, which enhances the learning process. Standards are introduced in order to define the average skills and knowledge which are expected from a student of a particular age group. Schools set the goals which students should achieve, be it understanding a reading text, writing an essay or pursuing a learning task autonomously. Such standards are often insensitive to the psychological needs of students (Mayes 2005: 98). We want the students to abide by these standards and stick to our goals. *Accountability* is a key word. With the help of curricula and test batteries schools try to increase the level of knowledge and skills among students. In some countries a national curriculum helps to clarify the goals of education and boost the level of knowledge and skills.

In order to reach these goals education tries to define *concrete objectives*. In the German speaking world, teachers and professors refer to the *Stoff* (essence, material) when they describe their endeavours. *Stoff* consists of the programme, the curricula and knowledge. It is viewed as something *factual*, more than a mental image or entity that can serve various purposes. When educators talk about *Stoff* the common association is of a heap of material which gradually accumulates in the heads of the students. The information the students are given should be understood and then piled up in an orderly way, so any item can be extracted at any time. Of course this knowledge can be obtained in various ways. Current educational approaches emphasize that the students themselves decide how they want to learn. The teacher's task is to keep the material attainable and mentor the learning process. Students will have to rely on their *Stoff* when they are confronted with the respect challenges or problems. Test batteries and standards should guarantee that students reach the defined levels. Education is founded on the idea that the process of attainment of knowledge and skills can be *manipulated* or even *controlled*. Educators have an impact on children. They can influence children's future profile and personality traits (Mallet 1987).

Because of these dictums teachers have the duty to *qualify* their students. Part of their agenda is to predict how successful a student will be and to distinguish the more intelligent from the intellectually challenged, the dunce from the genius. Knowledge and competences can be transmitted only under certain conditions. Teachers discriminate on the ground of standards: norms which define the level of quality that has to be reached in order to stay at a certain school. The purpose of standards is to make students excel. Standards and norms are of course also a power tool. Due to tests and comparisons, students can be relegated to a school or allocated to special classes. The educators are able to exercise *control* and decide the fate of students, who hold an ambivalent stance toward modern schooling. It allows them to exercise control and implement their standards, all in the name of survival in some future society.

Education is a *noble assignment*. Contrary to business people's or bankers' self-description, teachers point out that money is not their key objective. They choose to work with children because they feel it is a *valuable deed*. Students becoming teachers repeatedly affirm that they want to dedicate themselves to children, because they wish to engage in something *useful*. By choosing the teaching profession they distance themselves from the industrial, economic complex. The majority of teachers believe that they honestly care about children and their future. They define their work as a mission, more than just a job. Their work is founded on *ideals* (von Hentig 1993) and their self-image is auspicious.

Some educators might even believe they are fulfilling a *mission* – an honourable, virtuous, magnanimous assignment. Jean-Jacques Rousseau's (1985 [1762]) aim was to free children from the oppressive influence of bourgeois society. Back to nature was his message. J. H. Pestalozzi (1927) propagated the intimate, personal relationship between educator and child as a remedy against crime and depravation. Hapless children would turn into self-confident grown-ups, if they found a loving and demanding adult. Finally, Alexander Neil (1969) proposed that the abolition of authority would prevent children from becoming neurotic. The root metaphor of education is the adult, who is commissioned to induce or coerce the child or adolescent, so they will develop positively. The idea of education is based on the belief that we can turn this world into a better place if we are willing to devote time and energy to children and, of course, adhere to the right ideology (Enzelberger 2001).

The myth of the innocent child

Professions should not be reduced to competences and knowledge alone. A profession can also be the expression of a psychological attitude. The core of a profession can be a distinct *psychic pattern* which develops in interaction to the challenge or task that metier is responsible for. When we follow a vocation, we gradually incorporate that approach into our life. We begin to perceive the world and our challenges through the lens of our line of work. We set our priorities and define our values according to the blueprint of the chosen profession. We become police officers, bankers, traders, builders, soldiers or farmers. As a police officer we see culprits, felonies and people breaking the law. Right and wrong is our point of reference. We develop a sense for justice, seek clarity and try to act consistently. We might also be a bit naive and have a tendency to reduce complex issues to simple facts. In Jungian terms, the blueprint of a profession can be understood as an archetype. The archetype serves as the template of the specific profession. When we become members of a profession, we gradually immerse in its psychology and draw energy from the dominating archetype. It defines values, influences the perception and has specific myths to relate. In order to understand a profession on a deeper level, this archetypal background has to be identified. This is also important for education. Education is not just a job but also an archetypal pattern. Generally without realizing it we are loaded with the historical, ontogenetic meanings of that profession and live the myths, which its archetype produces. When we join a professional group, we unconsciously become promoters of an archetype. Its psychological background becomes personal and defines our approach to life.

By studying the wording and declared aims of education we can identify the archetypal pattern of education. By examining its rhetoric, values and goals, we might recognize the prevalent psychological complex. In education, we can observe *two tendencies*. First, as mentioned, standards, qualifications, testing, accountability and time-out are emphasized. These words indicate that performance is crucial. Schools define the criteria by which someone belongs to their institution. Their task is to draw a line. Students should comply with the goals of education. Teachers have the power to value the performances, developments and profiles of the students. It is their duty to distinguish between desired and unwanted processes. These words indicate that *controlling* is important. Education tries to constrain activities, which might get out of hand. It should exclude unacceptable tendencies. 'In the field of education . . . individuals are storage tanks for information, . . . nature (the gods) provide nothing' (Nixon 2002: 105). Order is decisive. Standards, testing, qualifications, accountability and time-out serve as tools to avoid chaos. A second observation can be made: education has an aptness for *idealistic wordings* and *settings*. Currently in education *self-management*, *the natural environment*, *self-accountability* and *personal responsibility* are key words. The student is defined as an individual who theoretically is motivated to learn and is capable of choosing the right goal. Education believes in the good. It wants to encourage students to follow their genuine calling. According to that view, if students listen to themselves, they can discover their *true* potential. Educators are responsible for the right environment and the appropriate stimuli, so as to enhance this process. This way, students might discover their true calling. Deep down they are eager to learn and are thankful for the efforts of the grown-up. The student is basically seen as a high-spirited, unspoiled being, which could be formatted by the grown-ups, if he or she is protected from bad influences and exposed to the right *Stoff*.

The archetypal pattern, on which education is based, is that of the *innocent, compassionate and obedient child*. It is the image of the child as open, genuinely interested, honest and less corrupted than grown-ups. According to this image, the child should be able to differentiate between good and bad by instinct, and has a potential to re-create and purify his or her surroundings. If the development of the child is well protected, and he or she is confronted with valuable materials, then there is hope for change in our society. The child brings us a message if we are willing to take care and protect him or her. Because of the child's attitude and profile, the child is eager to absorb our cultural legacies. We can pass on our knowledge, but of course carefully excluding unpleasant contents. Shadow issues have no place in schooling. Schools should be safe havens, where the attainment of good is possible. By following our guidance and positively engaging in the learning process, the student can develop to what he or she genuinely could be. If he or she absorbs our *Stoff* willingly, this will enhance his or her personality. Unhealthy desires, harmful drives and shady fantasies will lose their attraction. According to this myth, the student has either self-cleansed from inappropriate desires or was able to guard his or her initial innocence. Education builds on the purity and integrity of the students. It has difficulty in accepting other motives. If we study the rules and regulations which are imposed in schools in Switzerland and Germany, the tendency is clear: activities and interests which are considered normal outside the school setting are tagged and punished. Students are not allowed to use bad language, to insult each other, to be distracted, enjoy violence or express sexual fantasies. It is strictly forbidden to use cell phones in schools, because students might download pornographic pictures; if students use bad language, they are immediately punished and numerous efforts are being made in order to prevent students bullying each other, usually a prerequisite for a successful career in business or academia. Everything unwholesome should be left outside the school gates. In school itself, the student should experience an ideal model of society. Because of the image of the innocent child we are shocked when we hear of school violence or power plays (Boas 1966).

This myth has a long tradition. In 1687 the French priest Fénelon wrote a widely acclaimed essay on the purpose of education. He argued that the main purpose of education was to *protect* the innocent souls of young children. Children should be fenced off from the evil influences of society, so that they could blossom and develop their *own inner potential* (Osterwalder 2006: 155). Sensuality and worldly distraction were considered deviant. Children could become spoiled when they are confronted too much with their inner self and the joys of life. The Swiss philosopher Jean-Jacques Rousseau (1985 [1762]) argued along similar lines in *Emile ou l'education*. He proposed to insulate children. He suggested an education in a natural environment, beyond the demonic influences of bourgeois society. If children would listen to themselves, then they could identify their genuine desires. They would not be sidetracked by vile, superficial and materialistic needs.

The Reformpädagogik was founded on a similar idea. From Ellen Key's (1902) appeal to define children as artists to Paul Geheeb's (1950) dream of a society where children were educated in secluded forest schools, so they would develop into new human beings (*école d'humanité*), the prevailing idea was that education's main task was to help children develop what they genuinely are. The belief was that it was life, the vile world, which corrupted and distracted children. If we provide children with a surrounding and a well-defined setting, they could unfold their true potential. It was the educators' responsibility to protect children from bad influences. In order to enhance this natural process, the students should be confronted only with specially selected materials. Learning materials should be morally cleansed and bowdlerized.

Viewed from an archetypal perspective, the school as institution can be seen as a defence system, a fortress against the evilness of human beings. Education is an effort to hinder insane and base ideas from entering the heads of the future generation. The insistence on the correct learning material – the *Stoff* – is an attempt to control the influences children are exposed to. Educators wish to determine what enters children's minds so that their endeavours are not jeopardized. Standards turn out to be shields against the quagmire around us. Curricula are an attempt to expound what is allowed to enter.

Children need our guidance and love. It is also our duty to protect them. What the educational approach fails to realize, though, is that children carry within themselves the capability to uncover a lot more aspects of life than we imagine. They are born with the competence to *psychologize*. From early on they begin to suspect ulterior motives behind the behaviour of their parents, siblings or relatives. They fantasize about what could be behind the friendly smiles and convivial words. They suspect hidden intentions in their parent's behaviour and soon are able to decode and perform mimicry. Children are not born as tabula rasa or naive beings, but with the innate capability to interpret and see through the behaviours of their parents, spouse, relatives, friends and teachers (Plonim and Daniels 1987). Intuitively and by observation, they discover the dark side of life. They connect to the *shadow*, which we all have in ourselves and which often guides our actions. Education is therefore not just about the transmission of knowledge, competences and the good. The effects are multilayered, paradoxical, difficult to preconceive or rationally identify. Education remains a *psychological process* (Guggenbühl 2003b). The question is, though: what impact does the image of the innocent child have on children? The problem with the myth of the innocent child is that it is one-sided. The shadow is excluded. Students are not just interested in the idealized aspect of our life. Like all human beings they are intrigued by the shadow issues. They confront each other with all their complexes, dreams, fantasies and attitudes. Students realize that the image of the innocent child is a projection. The students begin to perceive education as separated from 'real life'. Children not only are a product of education, but also carry within them a blueprint. Intuitively they seek out what is in the world. Psychologically the projection of the innocent child is unbearable for them. Instinctively they realize that it is one-sided and psychologically false. When education excludes shadow issues, students try to compensate this fallacy. They do the contrary of what we tell them. We warn them about drinking and of course they begin to turn to drink as soon as they can get hold of alcohol. When we praise reading and sensible activities, they spend their time with 'ego-shooters'.

The power of imagination

Imagination detects hidden caves. We transcend the boundaries of our conscious ego-world. We envisage scenes which we consciously might not have identified. Imagination connects with unconscious topics. We sense issues which are buried in our personal or the collective unconscious (Hollis 2000). What we suppress, consider politically incorrect or filthy, is uncovered. Shadow issues are detected. Often the contents of our imaginations are obscene. We indulge in the myths and stories which lurk around us. Because imagination is basically an unconsciousness process, it presents us with perspectives which are not part of school curricula and which contradict the idealized perception of the educational process.

Students realize that education offers them a one-sided entrance into the world; psychologically they are being fenced off. They possess other powerful tools to understand and connect to the world (Gardner 1995). If we allow students to imagine, these capabilities are activated. Imagination opens up. Children can then approach their surroundings with the help of their inert *psychological faculties*. These abide by rules which are generally *not* reflected in education. They perceive the world around them, not just the way it is tagged by education, but also as perilous, obscure, threatening and full of dangerous seductions. The world around can be a source for inspirations and suspicions. Children tune into the collective unconscious and understand their fellow beings and civilization from *inside out*. They are endowed with dispositions, which allow them to construct their own version of life and see through the masquerade (Hillman 1996). These capabilities manifest themselves in spontaneous psychic activities. When they begin to imagine, their whole inner soul potential reveals itself. Imagination ignores educational standards and political correctness. The control mechanisms of education lose their power. Wanting what is correct or acceptable is not fantasized, but what is psychologically induced. When children imagine, they react to seductions, complexes, hysterias and repressed topics around them. They draw in the world around them and create images which reflect the ambiguities and monstrousness of their environment.

This capability to *imagine* is vital. By developing their own pictures and scenes, children get an in-depth perspective of what is happening in and around them. Their consciousness expands and they might even leave the restricted view that education presents to them. Small children fantasize that the big black wolf might hide under their bed. They are scared and might even scream. This reaction indicates that they are connecting into the unconscious. When parents pacify their sons and daughters and try to persuade them that the big black wolf is fiction, psychologically they are *lying*. Of course the big black wolf exists! He is a symbol of our shadow, dark motives or vicious endeavours. By imagining the wolf the child connects with a psychological reality. It creates or quotes an image, which encapsulates an important psychological insight. By imagining the big black wolf, the child gains consciousness and psychological insight.

Education follows a different agenda. It is an attempt to design the world according to idealistic concepts and goals. What students intuitively connect to through their capacity to imagine *threatens* the school setting. Students might lose their innocence and fail to comply with standards. Psychological realities have to be ignored, because they might irritate the educational undertaking. Ideals, standards, the *Stoff* and goals serve as defence mechanism. Students of course sense this orientation immediately. They realize that in order to be successful in an educational environment they need to turn a blind eye to nonconforming realities and fascinations. One should not be perturbed by alternative insights, is what any educational setting conveys. Students are successful when they identify with this school complex. An extraverted, sensations-based attitude is the best way to cope with the presented tasks (Neville 2005). If analytical thinking is demanded, then the successful student rehearses critical thinking; if knowledge is wanted, then the student acquires a scholarly attitude; and if social competences are on the list, then the intelligent student chooses the right words. Inappropriate, unwanted drives and dreams have to be repressed. The majority of students abide by these rules. They adapt to the system, keeping their drives and dreams to themselves. In order to attain a favourable position in society or just to be let alone, they close themselves in. Imagination, which might uncover embarrassing insights and ideas, is certainly not on the agenda. Because imagination might lead to dark caves and unpleasant scenes, it is wise to ignore it. Adaptation to the system is the key word. The bizarre ideas and images which imagination produces, might lead to confusion.

Conclusions

In our mythodramatic crisis interventions, it became apparent that regular schooling and imagination contradict each other. When students are allowed to imagine, this brings an uncontrollable element into the school complex. Especially when students envisage obscene or violent scenes, this was considered as dangerous and threatening by the teachers. According to our experience, their identification with the core myth of the innocent and immaculate child hindered them from recognizing the psychological value of bizarre images. The images which the students produced were understood literally. When they were fantasizing about and playing at hijacking a school bus in order to blow up their school, the majority of the teachers were shocked. They feared that they were witnessing a heinous schema or that the students were given bad ideas. Most teachers did not read the scenes on the symbolic level, but understood the playing and the fantasies of their students concretely. It was difficult to persuade the teachers that the imagined scenes were an attempt by the students to connect to ubiquitous fear and anger. The students were not preparing an attack, but trying to cope with a psychological dimension in their lives. Their imaginations were an *antidote* to the safe environment that educators want to create and to the image of the innocent child. By imagining horror, the students were trying to initiate themselves into the abyss. They were trying to connect to complexes which they felt belonged to our lives.

Instead of hindering students from imagining, schools should offer vessels, where imagination is possible. As imagination connects us with deeper, even archetypal realities, it might lead to places which are unknown to us. Jung wrote that *Katabasis*, the descent into the underworld, is necessary for psychospiritual maturation (1966b [1932]: para. 213). All energy 'can only proceed from the tension of the opposites' (Jung 1966a [1943]: para. 34). According to our experience and the scientific evaluation of the crisis interventions done in Sweden, Switzerland and the United States, imagination can even be a tool to solve conflicts. Imagination makes the psychological background of conflicts accessible. The detour into a virtual world can help students to be psychologically grounded. Imaging horror and working through horrifying scenes can be a relief, because the shadow is not excluded. When students express their fantasies in a civilized way, it helps them to understand themselves. They connect to the shadow, which is paramount, influencing their thoughts and behaviour. They relate to the matrix, which breeds socially inappropriate emotions and fantasies. Imagination should not be understood literally, but has to be interpreted on a *symbolic level*. The students' products often contain hints on how a sensitive issue or a difficult situation in school can be tackled. By producing inappropriate, appalling scenes the students were unconsciously appealing to the teachers, to help them integrate and relate to the complexes, which the school setting is trying to shut out.

A child sees in front of his inner eye how his teacher attacks the class with an axe. Even though this attack is unlikely to occur, it might still contain some truth. The image conveys a psychological message. It might be an indication that the teacher is suppressing her anger. The child develops an image for the aggression that he unconsciously senses in the teacher. Although the image at first glance seems absurd, reading it psychologically it contains an important message. It helps the child to connect with an emotion or complex that lurks in the room.

Note

1 As part of a three-year research project founded by the Axel Johnson Foundation in Stockholm, mythodramatic crisis intervention was performed in the United States, Sweden, Switzerland and Liechtenstein, which were confronted with violence and aggression. Among the schools chosen for intervention was Woodstock High in Connecticut (Guggenbühl et al. 2006).

References

Boas, G. (1966) *The Cult of Childhood*. Dallas, TX: Spring.

Büttner, C. (ed.) (1985) *Zauber, Magie und Rituale: Pädagogische Botschaften in Märchen und Mythen*. Munich: Kösel.

Enzelberger, S. (2001) *Die Sozialgeschichte des Lehrerberufs*. Munich: Weinheim.

Gardner, H. (1995) *The Unschooled Mind*. New York: Perseus.

Geheeb, P. (1950) Rede zur Eröffnung der Odenwaldschule. In U. A. Carrirer (ed.) *Die Idee einer Schule im Spiegel der Zeit – 40 Jahre Odenwaldschule*. Heidelberg.

Guggenbühl, A. (1996) *The Incredible Fascination of Violence*. Woodstock, CT: Spring.

—— (1999) *Das Mythodrama*. Zurich: Edition IKM.

—— (2003a) Mythodrama. In D. W. Rhea and R. Stallworth-Clark (eds) *Healing the Social Disease of Violence*. Boston: Custum.

—— (2003b) *Die Pisa-Falle*. Freiburg I. B.: Herder.

Guggenbühl, A., Hersberger, K. R. T. and Boström, P. (2006) *Helping schools in crisis: A Scientific Evaluation of the Mythodramatic Intervention Approach in Swiss and Swedish Schools*. Zurich: Edition IKM.

Hillman, J. (1996) *The Soul's Code*. New York: Random House.

Hollis, J. (2000) *The Archetypal Imagination*. College Station, TX: Texas A&M University Press.

Jung, C. G. (1966a) On the psychology of the unconscious. *The Collected Works of C. G. Jung* (Vol. 7). London: Routledge and Kegan Paul. (Original work published in 1943.)

—— (1966b) Picasso. *The Collected Works of C. G. Jung* (Vol. 15). London: Routledge and Kegan Paul. (Original work published in 1932.)

Key, E. (1902) *Das Jahrhundert des Kindes*. Berlin.

Mallet, C.-H. (1987) *Untertan Kind*. Munich: Huber.

Mayes, C. (2005) *Jung and Education: Elements of an Archetypal Pedagogy*. Lanham, MD: Rowman and Littlefield.

Neil, A. S. (1969) *Summerhill: A Radical Apporach to Child Rearing*. New York: Hart.

Neville, B. (2005) *Educating Psyche: Emotion, Imagination and the Unconscious in Learning*. Greensborough, Victoria: Flat Chat Press.

Nixon, G. (2002) Education as a mythic image. *Spring* 69: 105.

Osterwalder, F. (2006) Die Sprache des Herzens: Konstituierung und Tranformation der theologischen Sprache der Pädagogik. In R. Casale, D. Tröhler and J. Oelkers (eds) *Methoden und Kontexte: Historiographische Probleme in der Bildungsforschung*. Göttingen: Wallstein.

Pestalozzi, H. (1927) Wie Getrud ihre Kinder lehrt. In A. Buchenau (ed.) *Pestalozzi's sämtliche Werke*. Berlin.

Plonim, R. and Daniels, D. (1987) *Genetics and Experience: The Interplay between Nature and Nurture*. Thousand Oaks, CA: Sage.

Rousseau, J.-J. (1985) *Emil oder Ueber die Erziehung*. Paderborn.

Von Hentig, H. (1993) *Die Schule neu denken*. Munich: Hanser.

Chapter 6

Storytelling, socialization and individuation

Raya A. Jones

Once upon a time in the middle of the twentieth century, a folklorist called J. Barre Toelken stayed with a Navaho family who lived far from any roads in Montezuma Canyon, Utah. They spent the evenings of a severe winter sitting in the large hogaan around the fire, listening to the head of the family, Little Wagon, tell tales, legends and yarns. One night, a family travelling on horse-back stopped with them. It was snowing outside, and one of the travellers' children asked why it snows. Little Wagon told a long story about an ancestor who found a piece of beautiful burning material and guarded it for several months. When some spirits came to claim it, the man asked whether he could keep a piece. They refused, but agreed to do something for him. He had to perform several complicated tasks which tested his endurance. In recognition of his merit, the spirits promised that each year, when cleaning their house, they would throw the ashes from their fireplace down into Montezuma Canyon. Sometimes they forgot, sometimes they threw too much, but overall they turned their attention regularly towards the inhabitants of Montezuma Canyon ever since. After a moment of respectful silence, the boy pointed out that it was snowing also in Blanding, and asked why that was. Little Wagon replied at once, 'You'll have to make up your own story for that.' After they left, the old man reflected sadly that the boy did not understand stories, and blamed the 'deadly influences of white schooling' for that (Toelken 1969: 213).

Toelken ascertained that Little Wagon did not regard the traditional tale as an etiological story, nor believed in any way that this was how snow originated. Rather, if the story was 'about' anything, it was about moral values and the development of a young man whose actions showed an appropriate reciprocal relationship between him and nature. This meaning of Navaho tales was often overlooked by earlier collectors, whose interpretations suffered distortions due to what Toelken (1969) called cultural myopia; namely, our culture's tendency to see things in terms of its own categories. Extending that point, Little Wagon's condemnation of 'white education' could be taken as a cautionary tale about importing other cultures' fairytales, myths and legends into the curriculum. Cultural attitudes are communicated not only in the contents of stories, but also in how the stories are contextualised. For instance, a teacher from Arizona reports on how she combined sky-related legends, myths and folktales with astronomy curriculum: as the sixth-grade students heard different explanations regarding how celestial objects came to be, they realized that 'cultures respond in different ways to natural phenomena, and that while their interpretations are often different, the need to create explanations is universal' (Cañizo 1994: 31). Aside from projecting the motivations driving modern science onto indigenous storytelling, the positive multicultural awareness that Cañizo hoped to instil in her students might be offset by the juxtaposition of scientific and mythological accounts. If the scientific account is asserted as true, the myths are implicitly positioned as false.

Educators and Jungian analysts alike tend to put fairytales in one basket with myths and legends, though may do so for different reasons. It should be borne in mind, however, that those types of narratives were sharply differentiated in their indigenous contexts. In his fieldwork, Malinowski (1971 [1926]) observed that the people of the Trobriand Islands distinguished among stories which they told with different labels and different sets of performance practices. Myths, or sacred tales, played 'a most important function . . . closely connected with the nature of tradition, with the continuity of culture, with the relation between age and youth, and with the human attitude to the past'; legends too entered 'deeply into the tribal life of the community' (ibid.: 91). Both myths and legends were distinguished from the 'mere fireside tale', which they told for amusement in social gatherings. This chapter concerns chiefly the 'mere fireside' kind of stories, which has been referred to variously as fairytales, folktales, wonder tales or *märchen*. Little Wagon's tale falls into this category.

As seen in the anecdote about Little Wagon's storytelling, such tales were seldom understood by their tellers as causal explanations of natural phenomena. Caduto and Bruchac (1988) make a similar point in their Teacher's Guide. They stress that Native American storytelling was, and still is, a communal activity. The stories do not seek to explain the world as it is. 'Is it possible that . . . a huge bird can make the wind with its wings?' they ask rhetorically, referring to a well-known Abenaki story, and answer: 'Asking the question is similar to asking if the beanstalk in the famous story of Jack really did grow up to a land in the clouds where a giant had a magical goose' (ibid.: 11). Rather, such tales create a world that 'mirrors and draws upon our own' and 'may show us important things about the world we live in, teach us ways to behave' (ibid.: 11). A major exponent of the Jungian approach to fairytales, Marie-Louise von Franz (who originally presented her studies in lectures during the 1950s) made a convergent point, though with a twist. Noting that the hero in fairytales has the function of reminding us of the 'right way of behaving', she ponders: 'But what is the "right" kind of behaviour? This is one of the difficulties in fairytales'; in some tales, heroes 'may just sit over the stove and yawn and apparently achieve nothing, but they end in marrying the princess, while others may have to overcome brigands and witches, etc.' (von Franz 1980: 19). Von Franz concludes that the 'right way' of behaving, which fairytales show us, 'does not conform to the ordinary civilian's standards'; instead, it is 'in accordance with the totality of the human being' (ibid.: 19, 21). In Jungian psychology, the totality of the Self and its unfolding, the process of individuation, are construed in ontological opposition to the socializing function which educators and developmental psychologists may attribute to storytelling.

'In myths and fairytales, as in dreams, the psyche tells its own story', claimed Jung (1980 [1948]: para. 400). Hearing the story that the psyche tells by means of fantasies may help us to understand ourselves better. Jungian psychology posits the existence of fairytales, myths, etc., as an expression of individuation. Whereas in non-Jungian parlance, individuation usually means taking one's place as an autonomous member of a social group, in the Jungian context the term means the integration of the psyche or Self through the resolution of inner conflicts. It implies a lifelong process, based in our biologically given constitution and its configuration into a 'collective unconscious', which occurs despite the person's adaptation to a social-cultural milieu and its moral codes: 'Individuation is a natural necessity inasmuch as its prevention by a levelling down to collective standards is injurious to the vital activity of the individual' (Jung 1973 [1921]: para. 758). To echo Toelken's observation of cultural myopia, there is also intellectual myopia, manifest in the tendency to study phenomena of human life in terms of the categories, concerns, issues and practical goals which define a particular field of study. When educators recommend using fairytales, myths and legends in the classroom – or when some social commentators warn against exposing children to fairytales – they do so for different reasons than the reasons motivating Jung and Jungian analysts to study such stories. The Jungian interest is implicitly guided by the therapeutic goal and is ultimately driven by the quest for self-understanding.

What, if anything, could Jungian ideas contribute to educational discussions about engaging children with storytelling? Before considering the relevance of Jungian insights, it would be apt to consider the discourses with which the Jungian perspective must compete.

On fairytales and children

Fairytales were not originally meant for children, and historically were considered as unsuitable for children. Some tales were passed down in community storytelling, and the oral tradition remained strong in some European communities well into the twentieth century (see, e.g., Skjebred 2001, on Sámi storytellers in the late 1990s), but the most famous tales in the modern western world were created by literary writers who modified motifs from folklore (see, e.g., Hohr 2000 on Cinderella). Inventing fairytales became fashionable among European upper classes during the sixteenth and seventeenth centuries (Zipes 1997, 1999). Clergymen and educators regarded those as too dangerous for children, for the stories lacked Christian teaching, did not represent the moral values of the time, and were too 'stimulating'. Nineteenth century writers, such as the Grimm brothers and Hans Christian Andersen, started to write stories that met criteria of suitability for children so as to please middle-class and aristocratic *adults*, as Zipes (1999) notes. The Grimms deliberately changed the oral tales which they collected. In the twentieth century, the genre became commodified, culminating in the Disney films and similar adaptations. The history of fairytales in Europe thus became split, for the oral tradition persisted (at least in some communities) in parallel to the rise of the commercial genre. The late twentieth century renaissance of storytelling in the Anglophone world could be understood as 'a reaction to the commodofication of folk culture in a world of technology' (Zipes 1997: 11).

Among other things, that renaissance has manifested in enthusiasm about storytelling in the classroom, which is communicated in resource books for teachers. The aforementioned guide by Caduto and Bruchac (1988) is one example. Another one is Grainger's (1997) excellent guide for using fairytales in the primary classroom. Grainger lists a host of benefits: activities involving fairytales can promote spoken language competence, knowledge about language, language learning through story-drama, oral communication skills such as a sense of audience and active listening, knowledge of story structure, holding visual images in the mind, creativity in writing, and reading fluency.

Educators and various commentators have always been concerned about the cultural values that fairytales might communicate. Voicing feminists' objections to the type of fairytale embraced by Anglo-American culture, Lieberman declared in 1972: 'It is widely accepted that stories like Cinderella, Snow White, and Sleeping Beauty have had a damaging effect on masses of children' because they 'serve to acculturate women to traditional social roles . . . and perpetuate the myth of the happy-ever-after marriage' (quoted in Westland 1993: 238). The reality might be more complex and nuanced, however. When Ella Westland investigated whether 11-year-old British students identified with the protagonists of well-known fairytales, she discovered that the girls almost unanimously said that they would not like to be a princess, whom they perceived as having unattractively restricted lives. In contrast, most of the boys said that they would like to be a prince, a position which they associated with wealth, power and being able to do what they want. Westland concludes, 'On this evidence, we should be worrying about the effect of fairytale stereotype not upon on our daughters, but upon our sons' (ibid.: 245). The fact that children learn what fairytale princes and princesses ought to be like does not necessarily mean that they apply similar criteria to how they themselves ought to be. It could be opined that the participants in

Westland's study were too old and world-wise for fairytales. Bronwen Davies (1989) found that preschool children 'resisted' the subtext of non-traditional tales. For instance, regarding a story in which the prince is kidnapped by a dragon and is rescued by the princess (who outwits rather than slays the dragon), the children maintained that the passive prince was heroic, while regarding the princess as not being like a 'real' princess, because she was sooty and wore a paper-bag after the dragon burned her castle. Whether or not their attitude reflects an indoctrination into stereotypical gender identities, as assumed by feminists (Davies included), such responses clearly attest to the fact that young children learn canonical narrative formats.

Gender aside, debates regarding the suitability of fairytales have often centred on the brutality and cruelty that some tales depict. Whereas more recent debates about the effects of violence in films and video games tend to concern the influence of negative role models, historically the concern was about the distress to the child. There was a tendency to eliminate distressing elements in tales adapted or created for children, which was contested by psychoanalysts (Zipes 1999). The psychoanalysts viewed the violence and conflict in fairytales as a symbolic expression of fundamental instinctual aspects of the psyche, and contended that it is important for children to engage with those in the course of personal development. Bruno Bettelheim (1991 [1975]) submitted that the imaginary world of the fairytale allows children to deal with their anxieties. The tale provides a 'safe' space where fears of abandonment, death and danger can be symbolised and consequently dealt with, and in this way helps the child towards autonomy. The tale presents the darker side of life to the child in a simplified form, and 'works' through the child's identification with the hero. The fact that children sometimes become inexplicably attached to tales that terrify them, wanting to hear the tale over and over, might indeed attest to a deep psychological significance. Orbach et al. (1993) noted two contradictory psychoanalytical explanations for children's fascination with frightening tales. One explanation is based on Freud's tension reduction model, and posits a therapeutic cathartic effect of stories such as Hansel and Gretel. Freud submitted that either an excessive excitation of the instincts or the deprivation of needs may cause tension which has to be discharged, and is experienced as anxiety. The subsidence of the tension or anxiety results in the experience of satisfaction and pleasure. Based on that, some psychoanalysts (e.g., Bettelheim) view the fairytale 'as a stimulator of instinctual energy which turns into anxiety, which is then discharged' (ibid.: 379). Such stories not only mirror the child's unconscious conflict, but also provide mechanisms for its resolution and the release of pent-up tensions, a relief that is experienced as pleasure. The other explanation is based on Freud's repetition compulsion model, according to which 'noxious' stimuli and inner anxiety set off a process that leads to an unpleasant accumulation of tension, rather than its release. The person is repeatedly driven to seek similar stimuli in the hope of mastering anxiety.

Repetition compulsion is regarded as an uncontrolled, unconscious process that operates regardless of factors such as a happy ending or how many times the child heard the story. Orbach and his associates carried out an empirical study with children aged 6–9. The results suggest that the theories are not mutually exclusive. Rather, whether catharsis or repetition compulsion is activated depended on the type of story.

The extent to which children's story attachments are explainable by reference to Freudian mechanisms depends on whether or not the Freudian framework is accepted in the first place. Lately, with little or no acknowledgement of psychoanalytical theories, several developmental psychologists have investigated storytelling in families (e.g., Fiese et al. 1999; Petraki 2002; Chang 2003; Wang and Fivush 2005; Bohanek et al. 2006). Their focus is typically on reminiscence, that is real-life rather than imaginary stories, and how storytelling practices and styles interact with the child's autobiographical memory and identity construction. To my knowledge, the work done by Peggy Miller and various collaborators is unique in examining also fictive stories in that context (Miller et al. 1990, 1993; Alexander et al. 2001). Irrespective of the nature of stories in focus, most researchers build upon a sociocultural standpoint commonly associated with Lev Vygotsky (though going beyond his ideas). The basic assumptions could be summarized after Miller et al. (1993) as follows. Families are organized in ways that bring children and parents together for recurrent activities. These activities are mediated by particular forms of discourse or conversational exchanges. The routine participation of children in the socializing practices of their family has social and psychological consequences for the child. These consequences depend on how messages are packaged in discourse. Personal stories constitute an important means by which young children reconstruct and revise their experiences of self in relation to other. Children are exposed to personal stories in three ways: they hear stories *around* them when hearing people tell each other things; stories *about* them when the adult tells someone about the child in the child's presence; and stories told *with* the child as a co-narrator. To those, Miller et al. (1993) add fictive stories to which the child forms a strong attachment.

Miller became intrigued by children's story attachment when overhearing her 2-year-old son tell himself *The Tale of Peter Rabbit*, originally written and illustrated by Beatrix Potter in 1902 (Miller et al. 1990, 1993). Miller recorded her son's subsequent retellings, and analysed how the story was progressively altered as he told it. Specific troubles and conflicts in the original tale were changed by the child, until by the fifth recorded retelling all the conflicts were resolved, resulting in a different story altogether. He stopped telling it after that. Miller linked those conflicts to her son's real-life experiences at the time. The fact that children's story attachments cannot be predicted and replicated experimentally hinders the scientific investigation of this phenomenon. As deHart (1993) notes, Miller's case study does not tell us whether her son's reactions to an emotionally charged story are typical of children of that age. Children may retell stories for various reasons, and it is not known how frequently or commonly the retelling involves working through emotional issues. It is also not clear from Miller's case study whether her son's reworking of the dilemmas in the story actually played a critical role in his development, nor is there evidence that there was an interaction with his sense of self. A study by Miller and other collaborators, in which several mothers kept diaries, describes more systematically how stories become personally meaningful to children (Alexander et al. 2001). They found that story attachments occur within a mix of multiple narrative worlds, evoke a complex mix of emotions, and are supported by variable parental involvement and responses. Despite presenting a more elaborated picture of children's story attachments, the study by Alexander et al. (2001) does not demonstrate a necessary link between children's story attachments and sense of self. Such a link depends not only on how specific findings are interpreted, but also on how 'the self' is defined.

If the self is defined as contingent on having a story about oneself, then young children's increasing capacity for autobiographical memory could be equated with the construction of a self or (sometimes interchangeably) identity. The conception of the self as narrative or narrative-like overlaps the Jungian concepts of the ego-complex and the persona, to do with conscious self-concept and adaptation to one's social milieu. In Jungian psychology, the Self (capital S) is a broader theoretical construct, referring to the totality of the psyche – conscious and unconscious, innate and acquired elements combined. Closely following Jung, von Franz (1996) submitted that all fairytales describe one thing, the Self. Because we cannot know the Self directly, 'hundreds of tales and thousands of repetitions . . . are needed until this unknown fact is delivered into consciousness; and even then the theme is not exhausted' (ibid.: 2). Recurrent motifs such as the Great Mother, Trickster, Wise Old Man, Hero's Journey, Rebirth and more, which can be readily found in fairytales, are believed to express various stations in the course of individuation. When particular stories happen to captivate us – in the way that *Peter Rabbit* captivated Miller's son – it could be that their archetypal imagery resonates with our inner state at the given time. Jung's concept of *projection* could be useful as a stepping-stone towards explaining story attachments. Whereas in Freudian theory, projection is a defence mechanism which has negative connotations like repression and denial, in Jungian theory it is a necessary and positive mechanism towards individuation. An unconscious element of one's personality is brought to consciousness only when seen in other people and is recognized as a projection, as opposed to regarding it as a trait of the other person (Jung 1951). It could be hypothesized that story attachments both in children and adults reflect a similar process of projection; and that this process is aided by one's recognition that the protagonists and their adventures are make-believe.

The indirect message to teachers and parents might be that children should be permitted to explore fairytales so as to get in touch with their inner world, but this message ought to be treated with caution. Simply making 'archetypal' material available would not mechanically trigger projections or aid individuation. The psychological process has to be already ongoing within the child. Jungian theory is neither grounded in child observation nor informed by developmental psychology. Rather, it concerns more directly the *adult's* 'inner child', and views fairytales as naive spontaneous products of a dreamy childlike state of consciousness. Since at least the 1940s, some Jungian analysts have expanded analytical psychology to account for development in early childhood, but I don't know of any who examined fairytales in this context.

When turning to Jung's own work, we turn away from discourses about children, child development, and education as such, and enter a discourse within which the child features like an archetypal 'container' for adults' romantic yearnings. Those yearnings perpetuate an idealized notion of childhood that emerged in nineteenth century romanticism – an age that is 'almost invariably understood as a liberator of the imagination' (Sky 2002: 363). As Sky notes, 'the German Romantics prized the products of the imagination, of fantasies and dreams'; consequently the genre of the fairytale was identified with the 'spontaneous, innocent, untutored mind – with children and unsophisticated, ordinary, even primitive people' (ibid.: 363). That conception underpins Jung's view on fairytales, reviewed next.

A close-up on the Jungian position

Whereas the discourses of education and developmental psychology typically concern the *effects* of stories, Jungian theory concerns chiefly the *existence* of fairytales and similar fantasies; or, more precisely, of certain motifs embodied in them. In developing his ideas, Jung drew upon a view that was widespread in his intellectual milieu; namely, that human consciousness evolved in stages analogous to the intellectual development of a modern child: 'It is true that primitives are simpler and more childlike than we' (Jung 1964 [1931]: para. 112). Traditional fairytales were commonly regarded as the products of childlike primitives and simple rustic folk. To Jung, this has justified examining such material in the context of mapping out the archaic foundations of modern consciousness. 'Being a spontaneous, naïve, and uncontrived product of the psyche, the fairytale cannot very well express anything except what the psyche actually is,' claimed Jung (1980 [1948]: para. 432).

Jung's characterization might seem naive, a fairytale about fairytales, for the tales that we hear or read are hardly free of contrivance. They are told and retold, their themes remoulded by storytellers with their own slant. This point did not elude von Franz (1996: 1), who shared Jung's premise that fairytales are 'the purest and simplest expression of collective unconscious psychic processes'. She alludes to two contrasting processes that are at play in the formation of specific fairytales. On the one side, there is a universalizing process. A story which comes into being as a local legend – an anecdote of something extraordinary or inexplicable that happened to someone – eventually loses the details that pin it down to a particular time and place. Von Franz (1980) illustrates this with a documented account of how a certain folktale was traced back to a real family's record of an event that subsequently became a local legend. At the same time, despite the absence of specific names and places, and similarities such as references to witches, helpful animals, etc., fairytales are 'not quite purified of specific factors', because the setup of the story would be quite different in Native American versus European tales, for instance (ibid.: 13). Thus, on the other side, there is a localizing process: a tale takes on local colouring as it migrates across settings. The folklorist Valdimir Propp (1958 [1928]: 11) gives this example: a tale of a dragon kidnapping the king's daughter is transformed so that the dragon becomes a whirlwind, devil, falcon or a sorcerer; the daughter becomes a sister, bride, wife or mother; the king becomes a prince, peasant or priest; and abduction may be replaced by vampirism or 'any other means by which disappearance is effected in folktales'. Propp's main point was that the functions of the *dramatis personae* – villain, victim, rescuer, etc. – remain constant throughout the tale's transformations, and constitute its plot-axis. The Jungian point (implicit in von Franz's discussion) is that the elements which remain constant are those that strike a chord with all storytellers and their audiences; and those strike a chord because they invoke universal aspects of the Self.

Whereas folklorists typically seek to document and classify tales as found in the field, and are attuned to the tales' diversity and variability (even when charting thematic similarities), Jungians typically seek to understand *why* certain themes recur, and are attuned to similarities even when drawing upon diverse tales. The recurrence of similar motifs in the productions of ostensibly unrelated cultures is presumed to lend support to the Jungian hypothesis of an innate, biologically given, collective unconscious. That hypothesis was brought to bear on the study of fairytales as an *a priori* assumption, and fostered indifference towards the actual history of particular tales. Whereas folklorists may understand the 'why' question, concerning the origin of a particular tale or theme, as inviting an account of its history, Jungians may understand it as inviting an account of its psychological function, hearing the 'why' as concerning why human beings spin tales in the first place.

Unlike the folkloristic endeavour to classify tales collected in the field in terms of their motifs, Jung and his followers selectively harvest fairytales collections for convenient illustrations so as to back up Jungian claims about the archetypal configuration of the psyche. A case in point is Jung's (1969 [1948]) most explicit work on fairytales, an essay titled 'The phenomenology of the spirit in fairytales'. Jung labours to show that fairytales concretize an archetypal notion of 'spirit' (*Geist*) chiefly in the motif of the Wise Old Man. The typical role of an old man character in tales is that of mentor or guide. He 'represents knowledge, reflection, insight, wisdom, cleverness, and intuition on the one hand, and on the other, moral qualities' (ibid.: para. 406). Furthermore, the old man 'always appears when the hero is in a hopeless and desperate situation' (ibid.: para. 405). Compelled to seek opposites, Jung also points out the Old Man as 'an ambiguous elfin character . . . the wicked magician who, from sheer egoism, does evil for evil's sake' (ibid.: para. 413). When Jung says that the (good) Wise Old Man represents moral values, he is not interested in *which* moral values specific tales impart. Rather, he is interested in what the existence of the motif reveals about the dynamics of individuation; for example, a need for a mentor or guide that arises at some point. Jung attributes the existence of motifs such as the Old Man to an 'autonomous primordial image which is universally present in the preconscious makeup of the human psyche' (ibid.: para. 396); the term *primordial image* is synonymous with *archetype* in Jung's usage. In his preamble, Jung describes how it struck him upon investigating patients' dreams that 'a certain father-complex has a "spiritual" character . . . the father-image gives rise to statements, actions, tendencies, impulses, opinions, etc.' (ibid.: para. 396). Subsequently, he seeks a similar constellation in fairytales; namely, the Old Man motif. When critically evaluating Jung's position, the attribution of specific motifs to psychological processes should be separated from the attribution of those processes to an innate structure. The commonality of some aspects of human life may account for the recurrence of certain motifs across innumerable retellings in unconnected cultural settings, and in individuals' dreams as well as collective productions at the level of the social group. From a non-Jungian standpoint, the father-complex could be understood as a person's internalization of the attitudes, values, and behaviours typically associated with the Father role in patriarchal societies. The role is reflected in the stories produced by such societies, and, because the stories mirror a recognizable social world, are retold and reinvented. While such account does away with innatism, it does not invalidate Jung's observation of similar thematic constellations at the level of both the individual and social group.

In his essay, Jung (1969 [1948]) drew upon fairytales from all over the world to illustrate the universality of the Old Man. His examples attest to the fact that the motif can indeed be found worldwide, but do not inform us as to how common it might be in comparison with other motifs either within or across cultures. Nor does the commonality of the specific motif suggest that it has anything to do with notions of spirit(s) that informed indigenous storytellers. Curiously, the role that spirits play so conspicuously in Native American tales does not enter Jung's considerations of the *spirit* (singular) in fairytales. As seen, Little Wagon's tale was about a pact between man and spirits (plural), and yet does not contain the Old Man motif (although, incidentally, in Toelken's anecdotal account Little Wagon himself is portrayed as a wise old man). In contrast, folklorists interested in representations of spirits would most probably seek to classify the ways in which those entities actually feature in tales, and would be unlikely to regard wise old men as relevant, for indigenous cosmologies draw a sharp distinction between humans and spirits (see Jung's 1980 [1948] explanation for the belief in spirits). Jung should not be chastised for not doing 'proper' folkloristic research, for such research was not his aim. To ask whether Jung's reading of the Old Man motif as symbolizing spirit is true, in some scientific sense, is like asking whether it is true that snow falls because spirits throw down the ash from their fireplace. Jung could be described as addressing the question, why do human beings tell fairytales, with a story about necessary reciprocal relationships between various elements of the experiential realm. Experiences of evil, the feminine, redemption, and more, find expression in fairytales (e.g., von Franz 1972, 1974, 1980). Estés (1992) has extended this insight to the experiential realm of womanhood through her interpretations of world fairytales. Kawai (1988) applied it to the Japanese psyche through his analyses of Japanese fairytales. None of these analysts places their subject matter in relation to child education. They seek to uncover the psyche which tells its own story in fairytales.

The story we may hear

Jungian psychology was made possible by the historical and cultural conditions associated with early modernity and the rise of national identity in the German speaking world of Central Europe. Some of Jung's claims about archetypes and the collective unconscious – which, as seen, bear on his approach to fairytales – make sense only if we accept a characterization of 'primitive man' which was invented in the late nineteenth century. Following a history of ideas that began with Herder in the eighteenth century, leading figures of romanticism extrapolated a Darwinian model of evolution from the biological to the cultural sphere, describing myths as evincing the 'irrationalities that revealed the childhood of human thought' (Lincoln 1999: 70). In Lincoln's account, this reflected and legitimized the burst of colonial expansion by supplying a narrative in which the 'savages' lacked, 'not the Christian gospel, but reason and/or history' (ibid.: 70). Viewing nations, cultures or Völker (ethnic groups) as 'primordial, bounded, unproblematic entities and that myth is the equally primordial voice, essence, and heritage of the group', those scholars embraced myth partly as their rejection of Enlightenment values, and partly towards finding it 'useful to yoke this newly lionized category to völkisch and nationalist projects' (ibid.: 210). Jung (e.g., 1964 [1931]) further legitimized the portrayal of the 'primitive' by clothing it with a putatively authoritative account of primitive mentality. Although he partially subverts the colonial thrust by locating primitive irrationalities deep within the soul of the modern civilized adult, much of what he says about archetypes and the collective unconscious is entrenched in that late nineteenth century discourse. Thus, some of Jung's specific claims are 'answers' to common preoccupations in his milieu – preoccupations which nowadays have ceased to matter (if they ever did) in developmental psychology and education in the Anglophone world.

A parallel development within the same milieu as Jung's was *Völkerpsychologie* or ethno-psychology (e.g., Danziger 1983). In his variant of *Völkerpsychologie*, Wundt (1916) divided human history into epochs associated with the emergence of particular art forms. Based on material that anthropologists, explorers and missionaries collected from living hunter-gatherer societies, he posited the *märchen* as the oldest, most primitive, form of literary production. He regarded a subcategory, the 'märchen-myth', as an early precursor of the heroic myths and sagas of later ages (e.g., the Norse sagas). Wundt (1916) illustrated his point with a legend from the Pawnee tribe in North America, which tells of a young man who went alone into the forest and returned with a buffalo cow who became his wife and bore him a buffalo calf. When they entered his hut, they were transformed into human beings. Later some misfortune caused the child and mother to change back into buffalo. The man went with them into the forest, where he too became a buffalo and lived with the herd. Then he returned home, a man again. He learned from the buffalo how to lure them forth in order to hunt them, and imparted this secret to his tribe. The tale was recounted by the Pawnees when they wished the buffalo to appear for the hunt (ibid.: 273–274). Yet, some tales have no heroic connotations: 'The most primitive märchen . . . recounts an event without any discernible purpose or without bringing the action to any natural conclusion' (ibid.: 272). Wundt illustrates this kind with an Australian aborigine tale about women who went to gather grass seed. A magpie offered to watch their children, and they leave the children in its care. When they return, the children are gone. The magpie had hidden them in a hollow tree. The women hear the children crying, but do not know where they are, and return home without them (ibid.: 272–273). Commenting on this tale's 'lack of aim', Wundt contrasted it with the 'markedly superior' mythic tales that 'gradually develop a closer connection between the events', such as the Pawnee buffalo legend (ibid.: 273).

Far from being pointless, the magpie tale seems to me to communicate a universal maternal anxiety about wicked babysitters. It poignantly imparts a warning about leaving one's child with a stranger. Wundt's failure to appreciate that meaning could be attributed to cultural myopia. Some recent explanations of the origin of storytelling may likewise suffer myopia, although nowadays the biases reflect the zeitgeist of the Information Age. In preliterate societies, stories were (and still are) a fundamental vehicle for passing on vital information. This was seen in the wake of tsunamis in the Indian Ocean. As noted by Nowak (2006), most people on the Indonesian island of Simeulue lived near the coast close to the 2004 earthquake epicentre. Tipped off by stories that were passed down the generations, they fled to the hills when the sea retreated, and only 7 out of a population of 78,000 died. Similarly in Thailand, the Moken people knew to flee. In contrast, many of the Moklens, who are integrated into mainstream Thai society and have lost their traditional stories, perished on the beach. Arguing from a neo-Darwinian standpoint, Sugiyama (2001) speculated that the capacity for storytelling was naturally selected because the ability to transmit information in a concise and memorable form conferred survival advantages in the ancestral environment. Sugiyama concedes that some stories seem at odds with that explanation theory. For example, a certain anthropomorphic tale provides 'accurate and useful' information for predicting armadillo burrows, but it also tells of a mare-roping contest, which makes sense only if the characters are imagined as human: 'Neither foxes nor armadillos hunt horses, nor do they challenge each other to contests of strength' (ibid.: 232). Sugiyama suggests that the tale might nevertheless contain information about interspecies interactions – an arguably contrived explanation, reflecting an intellectual myopia. Surely, it would be better to acknowledge that some stories impart useful knowledge about the natural world, while other stories employ people's familiarity with the natural world so as to create symbolic representations of the subjective realm. When asking why human beings are compelled to hold a distorted mirror to their experiential realm, we enter the domain of Jungian interest.

Many 'mere fireside' tales told in preliterate societies contain moral messages. Consider the following humorous tale, attributed to the Nupe of Nigeria, which first appeared in Leo Frobenius' *Volksmärchen und Volksdichtungen* in 1924:

> A hunter found a human skull in the forest and asked, 'What brought you here?' The skull answered, 'Talking brought me here.' The hunter ran off and told the king that he had found a skull that talked. The king did not believe him and sent a guard to see if his story was true, with orders to kill him if it was not. All day long the hunter begged the skull to speak, but it remained silent and the hunter was killed. When the guard had left, the skull asked, 'What brought you here?' The hunter's head replied, 'Talking brought me here.'
>
> (Bascom 1977: 274)

Bascom documented forty-three versions in all, including the above, gathered by various researchers. In African American versions, dated to the days of slavery, the king is replaced with a white master. In some versions, the skull is replaced with a talking or singing animal. Sometimes the discoverer is merely punished. Often the message is 'don't tell lies'. But sometimes the skull talks to the man's executioners, who realize that they have killed him for nothing. As told by the Yoruba of Nigeria, the skull speaks to the executioner, who then tells the king, who sends others with the guard to verify the story; again the skull refuses to talk, the first guard is killed, the skull talks to his executioner;

and so it repeats, until some appropriate ritual of atonement is performed. While the moral message differs, all versions of the talking skull story tell some lesson about proper conduct. They communicate their lesson in a humorous – hence memorable – manner.

There is a spurious similarity between the above and the motif of a talking head or skull that appears in Inuit and Siberian tales related by von Franz (1972, 1996). In those tales, a young unmarried woman finds a disembodied male head, who speaks to her, and she takes it in as a secret partner; she is typically banished when her parents find out. Von Franz interpreted the skull motif in such tales as a representation of the animus, that is, the masculine in the female psyche. Clearly, the African motif does not lend itself to the archetypal interpretation that seems appropriate in the circum-arctic tales. Like an alphabet that can be used to write very different things, a staple imagery may communicate quite different messages. If we seek only the archetypal motifs which Jungian theory prompts us to seek, we might fail to recognize other images and meanings in the tales. If fairytales are snapshots of a social-moral world as subjectively experienced, and we are attuned only to echoes of the 'archaic man', we might remain deaf to the socializing voices in the here-and-now of *telling* the story.

Storytelling and liminality

Irrespective of whether the story is a traditional fairytale from far away or a personal anecdote, it would be told by someone to someone for some purpose. In a similar vein, Day and Tappan (1996) assert that stories structure the ways in which action choices are made, make possible re-evaluations of action, as well as place moral values in relation to an audience, time and place. Towards developing their narrative approach to moral development in childhood, Day and Tappan invoke a neo-Vygotskian idea of moral action as 'mediated' action: 'moral action always occurs in relation to other persons' (ibid.: 70). Earlier research by Day suggests that moral life is characterized by a multiplicity of 'voices' (or viewpoints) both at the level of the individual and the level of the community; other people become an internalised 'moral audience' of imaginary or real, dead or alive others (ibid.). Generally, developmental psychologists tend to regard the development of the self as contingent upon the child's integration into a social world. In that context, storytelling is often viewed as serving functions such as moral instruction, building a consensus through shared evaluations, and fostering a sense of community or *communitas*, which implies comradeship and communion.

The anthropologist Victor Turner (1974) contrasts 'communitas' with societal structure. Communitas too has a social structure, but it is a structure of symbols and ideas which emerge in states of liminality (from *limen*, Latin for threshold). Turner's concept of liminality builds upon Arnold van Gennep's description of rites of passage in tribal societies. In such rites, between a ritualistic separation from the community and the subsequent reintegration into the community, there is a liminal phase, when 'the state of the ritual subject ... becomes ambiguous, neither here nor there, between and betwixt all fixed points of classification' (Turner 1974: 232). Turner notes that, whereas tribal societies provided for this emergence in their rituals, in modern societies there is little or no structural provision for liminality. Therefore, the retreat from societal structure often appears 'to take an individualistic form – as in the case of many post-Renaissance artists, writers, and philosophers' (ibid.: 260). Indeed, Jung's individualistic psychology – with its core metaphor of the (lone) hero's journey – could be classed as a similar consequence of modernity.

In contrast with the emphasis on social integration, the perspectives typically expounded in Jungian, existentialist and humanistic psychologies regard personal development as a journey towards self-actualization or self-discovery. Such a journey entails 'removing' oneself from the social normative order so as to discover one's true self; or, put another way, transcending the mask-like identity or persona which has been acquired in the adaptation to one's milieu. Viewed thus, an active creative engagement with the imagination fulfils the special function of facilitating a state of liminality. Such a function of creative storytelling is glimpsed in Jung's (1977 [1932]) foreword to 'The Tale of the Otter' in a collection of literary fairytale written by Oscar A. H. Schmitz. Jung writes: 'I happen to know how the tale came to be written. It ... was never even thought out, but flowed unconsciously from his pen' (ibid.: para. 1717). Its content 'clothed itself in fairytale form not with the secret pretence of being an allegory, but because in this guise it could find the simplest and most direct access to the reader's heart' (ibid.: para. 1716). In the fairytale:

> The utterances of the heart – unlike those of the discriminating intellect – always relate to the whole. . . . What the heart hears are the great, all-embracing things of life, the experiences which we do not arrange ourselves but which happen to us. All the pyrotechnics of reason and literary skill pale beside this, and language returns to the naïve and childlike.
>
> (Ibid.: para. 1719)

Powerful words indeed; but, before getting swept away in the sentiment, it would be circumspect to listen to the silent story. The distinction between 'utterances of the heart' and 'discriminating intellect' reflects and reinforces a separation between *logos* and *mythos* drawn in modern western cultures. A pitfall of dichotomizing logos and mythos is a tendency to viewing it as a case of 'either/or', which means sliding from one pole to the other. Someone or some viewpoint is heard being for logos and therefore against mythos (or vice versa). The resistance to the dominance of logos in our societal milieu is sometimes expressed in a polemical rejection of the boundary. In effect, everything becomes 'mythos'; science is denied its logos. Such polemics are associated, not only with New Age Jungianism, but also with the nostalgic rhetoric of the postmodern narrative movement in the human sciences. The antidote would be to view both these modes of conception as fundamental and irreducible to each other, like sides of a coin (Jones 2007).

The liminality of creative writing cannot be mechanically induced in the classroom. The personal compulsion to write, which fires the literary writer, is not necessarily kindled simply by requiring schoolchildren to write a creative story. Furthermore, in so far as different developmental tasks are typically negotiated in childhood (and different age groups) as opposed to adulthood, what 'works' towards individuation later in life might not 'work' earlier.

Conclusion

So what could the Jungian position contribute to the pedagogical discourse? The answer depends on what one takes from Jung. If fairytales are viewed as expressing the archaic, the primal and original, within us (as Jung believed), an enthusiastic conviction in their value for children might be a projection of our own yearning for the 'child within'. Ironically, while the classical Jungian framework offers the most incentive to study fairytales in a psychological framework, its message to teachers and parents might be trite, little more than a 'romantic' plea to let children freely explore fairytales and perchance encounter there projections of their own inner world. It is at bottom a down-graded version of the adult-centred therapeutic goal, and its applicability to children ought to be questioned.

Fairytales not only reflect cultural values, but also instruct in the canonical narrative structures, or 'story schemas', of one's culture. Such structures influence what is actually remembered (Bartlett 1967 [1932]), how real-life events are told and explained (Bruner 1990) and set criteria for self-narratives and personal accounting (Gergen 1994). As Bruner (1996: x) put it, culture 'provides us with the toolkit by which we construct not only our worlds but our very conception of our selves and our powers'. A post-Jungian perspective attuned to the origin of meaning in cultural activity may make a stronger case for engaging children with fairytales and similar creative stories. It would take into account the socializing function of storytelling. An awareness of both the socializing and individuation potential of fairytales may guide teachers in selecting suitable material for use in the classroom, and thus providing children with part of that indispensable toolkit.

References

Alexander, K. J., Miller, P. J. and Hengst, J. A. (2001) Young children's emotional attachments to stories. *Social Development* 10: 374–398.

Bartlett, F. C. (1967 [1932]) *Remembering*. Cambridge: Cambridge University Press.

Bascom, W. (1977) African folktales in America: I. The talking skull refuses to talk. *Research in African Literatures* 8: 266–291.

Bettelheim, B. (1991 [1975]) *The Uses of Enchantment*. Harmondsworth: Penguin.

Bohanek, E. G., Marin, K. A., Fivush, R. and Duke, M. P. (2006) Family narrative interaction and children's sense of self. *Family Process* 45: 39–54.

Bruner, J. S. (1990) *Acts of Meaning*. Cambridge, MA: Harvard University Press.

—— (1996) *The Culture of Education*. Cambridge, MA: Harvard University Press.

Caduto, M. J. and Bruchac, J. (1988) *Keepers of the Earth: Teacher's Guide*. Golden, CO: Fulcrum.

Cañizo, T. L. (1994) Legends and myths of the sky. *Science Scope* 17: 31–33.

Chang, C.-J. (2003) Talking about the past: How do Chinese mothers elicit narratives from their young children across time? *Narrative Inquiry* 13: 99–126.

Danziger, K. (1983) Origins and basic principles of Wundt's Völkerpsychologie. *British Journal of Social Psychology* 22: 303–313.

Davies, B. (1989) *Frogs and Snails and Feminist Tales: Preschool Children and Gender*. Sydney: Allen and Unwin.

Day, J. M. and Tappan, M. B. (1996) The narrative approach to moral development: From the epistemic subject to dialogical selves. *Human Development* 39: 67–82.

DeHart, G. B. (1993) Placing affect and narrative in developmental and cultural context: Comments on Miller et al. In C. A. Nelson (ed.) *Memory and Affect in Development*. Hillsdale, NJ: Lawrence Erlbaum.

Estés, C. P. (1992) *Women who Run with the Wolves*. London: Rider.

Fiese, B. H., Sameroff, A. J., Grotevant, H. D., Wamboldt, F. S., Dickstein, S., Fravel, D. L. et al. (1999) The stories that families tell: Narrative coherence, narrative interaction, and relationship beliefs. *Monographs of the Society for Research in Child Development* 64: 1–162.

Gergen, K. J. (1994) *Realities and Relationships*. Cambridge, MA: Harvard University Press.

Grainger, T. (1997) *Traditional Storytelling in the Primary Classroom*. Leamington Spa: Scholastic.

Hohr, H. (2000) Dynamic aspects of fairy tales: Social and emotional competence through fairy tales. *Scandinavian Journal of Educational Research* 44: 89–103.

Jones, R. A. (2007) *Jung, Psychology, Postmodernity*. London: Routledge.

Jung, C. G. (1951) Aion. *The Collected Works of C. G. Jung* (Vol. 9.ii). London: Routledge and Kegan Paul.

—— (1964) Archaic Man. *The Collected Works of C. G. Jung* (Vol. 10). London: Routledge and Kegan Paul. (Original work published in 1931.)

—— (1969) The phenomenology of the spirit in fairytales. *The Collected Works of C. G. Jung* (Vol. 9.i). London: Routledge and Kegan Paul. (Original work published in 1948.)

—— (1973) Psychological types. *The Collected Works of C. G. Jung* (Vol. 6). London: Routledge and Kegan Paul. (Original work published in 1921.)

—— (1977) On the tale of the otter. *The Collected Works of C. G. Jung* (Vol. 18). London: Routledge and Kegan Paul. (Original work published in 1932.)

—— (1980) The psychological foundations of belief in spirits. *The Collected Works of C. G. Jung* (Vol. 8). London: Routledge and Kegan Paul. (Original work published in 1948.)

Kawai, H. (1988) *The Japanese Psyche: Major Motifs in the Fairy Tales of Japan.* Dallas, TX: Spring.

Lincoln, B. (1999) *Theorizing Myth: Narrative, Ideology, and Scholarship.* Chicago: University of Chicago Press.

Malinowski, B. (1971) *Myth in Primitive Psychology.* Westport, CT: Negro Universities Press. (Original work published in 1926.)

Miller, P. J., Potts, R., Fung, H., Hoogstra, L. and Mintz, J. (1990) Narrative practices and the social construction of self in childhood. *American Ethnologist* 17: 292–311.

Miller, P. J., Hoogstra, L., Mintz, J., Fung, H. and Williams, K. (1993) Troubles in the garden and how they get resolved: A young child's transformation of his favorite story. In C. A. Nelson (ed.) *Memory and Affect in Development.* Hillsdale, NJ: Lawrence Erlbaum.

Nowak, R. (2006) How a lullaby can warn of an approaching tsunami. *New Scientist* 191.2562 (29 July): 14.

Orbach, I., Vinkler, E. and Har-Even, D. (1993) The emotional impact of frightening stories on children. *Journal of Child Psychology and Psychiatry* 34(3): 379–389.

Petraki, E. (2002) The play of identities in Cypriot-Australian family storytelling. *Narrative Inquiry* 11(2): 335–362.

Propp, V. I. (1958 [1928]) *Morphology of the Folktale.* Bloomington, IN: Indiana University Press.

Skjebred, A. H. B. (2001) 'These stories will not lead you to Heaven': An encounter with two Sámi narrators. *Folklore* 112: 47–63.

Sky, J. (2002) Myths of innocence and imagination: The case of the fairy tale. *Literature and Theology* 16: 363–373.

Sugiyama, M. S. (2001) Food, foragers, and folklore: The role of narrative in human subsistence. *Evolution and Human Behaviour* 22: 221–240.

Toelken, J. B. (1969) The 'pretty language' of Yellowman: Genre, mode and texture in Navaho coyote narratives. *Genre* 2: 211–235.

Turner, V. W. (1974) *Dramas, Fields, and Metaphors.* Ithaca, NY: Cornell University Press.

Von Franz, M.-L. (1972) *Problems of the Feminine in Fairytales.* Dallas, TX: Spring.

—— (1974) *Shadow and Evil in Fairytales.* Dallas, TX: Spring.

—— (1980) *The Psychological Meaning of Redemption Motifs in Fairytales.* Toronto: Inner City Books.

—— (1996) *The Interpretation of Fairy Tales* (revised edition). Boston: Shambhala.

Wang, Q. and Fivush, R. (2005) Mother–child conversations of emotionally salient events: Exploring the functions of emotional reminiscing in European-American and Chinese families. *Social Development* 14(3): 473–495.

Westland, E. (1993) Cinderella in the classroom: Children's responses to gender roles in fairy-tales. *Gender and Education* 5(3): 237–249.

Wundt, W. (1916) *Elements of Folk Psychology.* London: George Allen and Unwin.

Zipes, J. (1997) *Happily Ever After: Fairy Tales, Children, and the Culture Industry.* London: Routledge.

—— (1999) *When Dreams Come True: Classical Fairy Tales and their Tradition.* London: Routledge.

Chapter 7

Literary individuation

A Jungian approach to creative writing education

Madeline Sonik

> Man struggles with his inborn needs and fulfillment. New unfoldings struggle up in torment in him, as buds struggle forth from the midst of a plant. Any man of real individuality tries to know and to understand what is happening, even in himself, as he goes along. This struggle for verbal consciousness should not be left out in art. It is a very great part of life. It is not superimposition of a theory. It is a passionate struggle into conscious being.
>
> (D. H. Lawrence 1950: viii)

Creative Writing pedagogy is characterized by an inherent paradox. Even as academic programmes in the subject proliferate, and universities and colleges enthusiastically introduce or expand their offerings in what has in recent years become an immensely popular, even fashionable, area, the academy still adheres to the belief that Creative Writing can not really be taught. And to make this situation even more paradoxical, the most committed adherents of this cliché are often none other than the instructors themselves. The inevitable consequence of this mindset is that Creative Writing programmes unintentionally belie their name by playing down the 'creative' side of the discipline. Rather they focus on teaching students technical or craft aspects of writing: considerations of literary form and structure, effective use of point of view, diction, dialogue and description, ways to render character and construct plot. What cannot be taught, many instructors would insist, is the other, more elusive side, the side which has to do with the quality of the work, with talent, the side that falls under the broader heading of 'Art' and emanates from what we might consider the inner dimensions of the writer. Customarily, this internal dimension is not addressed in the vast majority of educational settings, and, if acknowledged at all, is generally considered out of the standard jurisdiction of the teacher. The teacher is not trained to deal with the student's psyche, and some have even gone as far as to suggest that it might be dangerous for instructors to engage with what goes on in the inner reaches of our students' souls (Bell 1997). The act of Creative Writing, however, has as its goal self-expression, which naturally and conspicuously draws upon the writer's inner world. Currently, Creative Writing instructors have no vocabulary to address this most important dynamic, let alone any method for facilitating it in their students. If, however, we consider the teaching of Creative Writing through a Jungian lens, not only could the independent reality of the inner world be acknowledged, but also specific Jungian concepts could provide tools to assist students and teachers in gaining access and understanding. In the following pages, I hope to offer some preliminary thoughts about how the paradox might be resolved.

Towards the concept of a 'literary individuation'

Perhaps a good starting place would be to outline the Jungian concept of 'individuation' as it speaks directly to the interplay of conscious and unconscious, of outer and inner worlds. Jung theorized that people are naturally propelled towards wholeness, that we exist in a constant state of becoming who we are, and that all things we do in life (and indeed, all things life does to us) are attempts to facilitate this process. When this process is conscious, it is called 'individuation'. Jungian analysts seek to assist the course of 'individuation' by having analysands acknowledge and relate to the unconscious. Stein (1982: 36) writes that analysis assists the analysand in 'establishing a more vital and aware relationship' between the unconscious and consciousness. Besides a 'host of small adjustments of ego-attitude that take place in analysis', there are also 'deep changes' (ibid.: 39). One of these deep changes is perceptual. Once the analysand's ego is aware of the unconscious, it no longer can see itself as the controlling centre of the analysand's life, but must relocate this function in relation to the emerging 'Self'. As Hall (1986: 42) puts it, 'in individuation the center of the personality moves from the ego toward the Self, establishing a new center of the psyche somewhere between the two'. Jung saw the 'Self' as an 'archetypal image of man's fullest potential and the unity of the personality as a whole' (Samuels et al. 1986: 135). It is experienced by consciousness 'as a transpersonal power which transcends the ego' (Hall 1983: 121) and embraces both conscious and unconscious.

For writing students, the perceptual shift that occurs in discovering this larger entity as the nucleus of creation can be extremely beneficial. Not only are their egos freed from the impossible responsibility of generating stories and the debilitating anxiety that sometimes surrounds that, but also the approach they will then take to their writing becomes consciously relational. One strives then not to 'create' but rather to attune oneself to the expression of the unconscious, to establish, as Stein (1982: 39) characterizes it, a 'fluidity' between the ego and unconscious. According to Stein, this flow in analysis 'brings with it an influx of energy and vitality' as well as 'more creativity' (ibid.: 31). 'There seems to be a continual give and take. The conscious cannot write without inspiration from the unconscious, the unconscious cannot formulate in a bearable form without the help of the conscious' (Hannah 1971: 215).

Instructors can utilize Jung's ideas about the individuating psyche and assist students in experiencing the larger entity of the 'Self'. This expanse of consciousness can lead to greater psychological depth in the student writer which is an important (albeit, currently ignored) consideration in Creative Writing teaching. Like Jungian analysts, Creative Writing instructors can learn ways of assisting students in observing and reflecting upon their inner worlds – ways that will enhance their natural literary unfolding and will lead to greater creativity and the ability to produce deeper, richer writing. The process of literary individuation will be more effective if student writers understand what is involved and, as a first stage, become familiar with specific Jungian terms and methods, and how these can be applied directly to their work.

The ego

Jung saw the ego 'as the complex factor to which all conscious contents are related', and claimed that 'It forms, as it were, the centre of the field of consciousness; and, in so far as this comprises the empirical personality, the ego is the subject of all personal acts of consciousness' (Jung 1969 [1951]: para. 1). The Creative Writing instructor might explain the ego, then, as that part of us that we identify as us – the part of me that I identify as 'me'. In the process of individuation, the ego must first accumulate 'ego strength', which can be achieved through increasing consciousness. The act of writing itself, when exploratory, can promote ego strength. Ego strength grows as student writers uncover facts and perspectives of which they were previously unaware. As it increases, writers will find a more fluid connection forms with the unconscious, and as this occurs, the greater access they will have to the larger unexplored dimensions of the psyche. Stephen Minot (1993) points out in *Three Genres: The Writing of Poetry, Fiction, and Drama* that there is both a simple and a sophisticated kind of writing. 'Essentially, sophisticated works "do" more in the sense that they suggest more, imply a greater range of possibilities, develop more subtle shadings of meaning, than simple works do' (ibid.: 135). Student writers, striving towards 'literary individuation', who consciously work to build ego strength, may be better able to access this full sophisticated spectrum than might students who ignore or disregard their inner processes.

The instructor could present, as an example of ego dynamics and their functioning in the process of writing, the general condition of ego rigidity. Rigid ego positions initially formed through defence mechanisms or simply through collective conventions can affect behaviours, self-perceptions and worldviews. We may experience a rigid ego position on the question of what is 'right' or what is 'wrong', or what is 'true'. In analysis we may discover that rigid ego positions hamper our psychological development by discounting the possibilities we need to explore in order to grow. Similarly, in our efforts to write creatively, rigid ego positions can hamper us. At their most basic level, rigid ego positions can impose concretized ways of seeing and experiencing the world that are not spontaneous personal responses but rather unreflective, undifferentiated duplications of what is predominant in the collective. In other words, the rigid ego position will prevent the writing student from writing in original ways. Consider, for instance, student writers who wish to describe a sunset or a mountain range. The students can learn various writing techniques to assist with the task; they can look at the works of other authors and see how these techniques have been successfully used. But, ultimately, it is the students' perceptions that will dictate the writing. The sunset and the mountain range that students see in their imaginations and thus depict in their writing may well be the same sunset and mountain range that exists on a million postcards. With character, plot, dialogue and all of the other elements of writing we could list, it could be similarly the case. If student ego perceptions of characters, situations and conversations exist in a rigid, undifferentiated collective way, no matter how brilliant the technique, their writing will fall flat because although they can accurately render the contents of their vision, it is the vision itself that presents the problem.

Many books on Creative Writing stress the importance of the writer being able to present material in unique and original ways, but few if any give more than abstract advice on how this is to be done. Student writers who learn first to acknowledge their ego consciousness as an entity existing alongside a greater unconscious and who learn to promote their ego's growth actively are more likely to see, experience and imagine the world in original ways.

The persona

Jung defined the persona as a 'functional complex that comes into existence for reasons of adaptation or personal convenience' and is 'exclusively concerned with the relation to objects' (1971 [1921]: para. 801). It is the mask we wear, a front we develop, that acts as a mediator between ego consciousness and the external world, that allows us to appear consistent, and that aids us in our interactions with others. It is also what pigeon-holes us to our occupations and roles. 'The absent-minded professor', 'the happy homemaker', 'the mad scientist', 'the crazy artist' – all these superficial and stereotypic labels can be seen as related to the persona. 'Politicians, movie stars, and sports figures all have "public personas" behind which hide their "private lives" ' (Hopcke 1995: 6). 'Everyone knows what is meant by "putting on official airs" or "playing a social role".' Jung noted, 'Through the persona a man tries to appear as this or that, or he hides behind a mask, or he may even build up a definite persona as a barricade' (1953a [1928]: para. 269). The persona is deceiving, for it appears to be separate and personal, but is in fact a collective construct. 'Fundamentally, the persona is nothing real; it is a compromise between individual and society' (Hopcke 1995: 13). Interestingly, the persona is both a psychic and a physical manifestation. We discover it not only in the behaviour of individuals, but also in the way they dress and speak, and in their body language. A cowboy's drawl and stance, for example, along with his boots and hat, identify him as such. The aim of individuation is to 'divest the self of the false wrappings of the persona on one hand, and of the suggestive power of the primordial images [of the collective unconscious] on the other' (ibid.: 15). In Jungian analysis, 'in its scrutiny of one's personal unconscious', there is often

> a dissolution of the persona and . . . the relativization of the ego. Analysis increases one's awareness that one is not all one seems to be nor is one's conscious self-image, or ego, coextensive with the contents of the entire unconscious self. The dissolution of the persona in analysis usually ushers in an emergence of one's real or essential self, or, as Jung put it, one's true individuality.
>
> (Ibid.: 15)

Student writers who have some familiarity with this psychic component and can recognize it as an aspect of a character's make-up will benefit in a number of significant ways. Perhaps one of the greatest advantages will be in the realization that there is more to stereotypic characters than one may originally identify or express. The tough cop, for example, or the hooker with the heart of gold – two clichéd stereotypic characters in student writing – might be explored and transformed through an understanding of persona. Students may be directed to find what exists beneath these masks. They might be encouraged to consider how these stereotypic masks fit. Is the character comfortable in the mask? When does the mask create problems for the character? Does the mask confine the character? Does the mask liberate the character? Is the mask functional or dysfunctional? How does the character use the mask? Conversely, a student's work may contain a character who is completely inauthentic through inconsistency. In this instance, the writer may also wish to explore the possibility of an appropriate persona for this character. Does the character, in fact, have a persona? Is the inconsistency of character caused by this failing? If so, is this failing integral to the character or does the character require a persona?

The student writer who works with the concept of persona, even when not fully knowledgeable about its dynamics, will soon become aware of the many ways in which this aspect of the personality can influence plot. For instance, a persona that is constricting to the character's ego will create a particular set of conflicts and tensions for that character. Characters devoid of a persona will have great difficulty in dealing with the people and situations in their world. Jung describes those without personas as blundering from one social solecism to the next, perfectly harmless and innocent, soulful bores or appealing children, or . . . spectral Cassandras dreaded for their tactlessness, eternally misunderstood, never knowing what they are about, always taking forgiveness for granted, . . . hopeless dreamers . . . blind to the reality of the world, which . . . has merely the value of an amusing or fantastic playground [to them].

(Jung 1953a [1928]: para. 318)

Characters whose personas do not fit into their collective milieu will become outcasts and ostracized. Characters whose personas are weak will struggle to keep them intact, and characters with overly strong personas may find they become fully identified with them and must struggle to regain their genuine selves.

The shadow

Jung's concept of the 'shadow' could also benefit writing students. Working with the shadow can assist in strengthening the ego, accessing the inner world, and translating its contents more efficiently into writing. Instructors could introduce students to this term by presenting the dream that Jung (1963) related about the shadow in his work *Memories, Dreams, Reflections*. In the dream, Jung found himself in a windstorm carrying a small flickering light while being pursued from behind by a dark, overwhelming creature. On waking, he wrote:

I realized at once that the figure was my own shadow on the swirling mists, brought into being by the little light I was carrying. I knew too that this little light was my consciousness, the only light I have. Though infinitely small and fragile in comparison with the powers of darkness, it is still a light, my only light.

(Ibid.: 87–88)

Instructors could explain how Jung developed the term 'shadow' as a metaphor for that part of the unconscious psyche that resides just beyond one's ego consciousness. The shadow is composed of those negative qualities and traits that an individual has rejected. The collective also has a shadow. In the collective shadow, those things that have been deemed inappropriate in a particular society or culture reside; greed, rage and hatred, for example, inhabit our collective shadow (Zweig and Abrams 1991). From an early age, children in our society are taught consciously to repress these feelings and behaviours and try to cultivate their opposites. These attitudes, behaviours and feelings that we sever from consciousness do not actually disappear, though to our eyes they do not appear as parts of our selves any more. According to the Jungian model, the unconscious shadow content regresses and gains a particular kind of strength in the psyche, which can overwhelm or 'possess' consciousness when consciousness is weak. For example, when we are tired or run down, we may become moody, irritable or pessimistic, in spite of our best efforts to maintain more collectively acceptable attitudes and behaviours. James Hall (1986: 37) writes: 'what is developmentally cast into the shadow might just as well in different circumstances have become ego. Much of the shadow can be reworked in adult life and add dimension and contrast to the ego.'

There are many examples of the human shadow that instructors could point to in literary fiction. One of the classic stories often cited to illustrate the extreme workings of shadow possession is R. L. Stevenson's (2003 [1886]) *The Strange Case of Dr. Jekyll and Mr. Hyde* in which a quiet, mild-mannered doctor, whose conscious objective is to help humankind, becomes a lascivious, murdering beast. The instructor could point out that there is a particular authenticity in this fiction, for although Dr Jekyll and Mr Hyde, as they exist in Stevenson's text, do not exist and never could have existed in the world, the story conveys a particular psychological dynamic. This is the very dynamic that Jung identifies and labels as shadow possession (von Franz 1980 [1978]: 95–121).

Another classic work of fiction in which the human shadow is rendered is Oscar Wilde's (1998 [1880]) *The Picture of Dorian Gray*. In this instance, the dynamic is shadow projection, rather than possession, a process in which the unacknowledged shadow is projected upon an object, an individual, or a group of individuals (von Franz 1980 [1978]). The shadow is projected before it can be integrated back into consciousness. One may, for example, consider the individual who takes the last piece of cake at a birthday party as 'greedy', until one acknowledges one's own hitherto unacknowledged greed for that same piece of cake. The greed appears in another when we refuse to see it (or are incapable of seeing it) in ourselves. We label the other as 'greedy' because we ourselves want the last piece. In the case of Dorian Gray, his shadow is projected onto his portrait. It is his own image that carries all the dark and unacceptable qualities of personality that he does not wish to acknowledge. At the end of the story, his desire to destroy the portrait results from a final denial to carry his shadow.

In certain individuals who have, for various reasons, become identified with collectively negative traits, the shadow can harbour more conventionally positive qualities and can likewise possess or be projected. In Charles Dickens' (1991 [1843]) *A Christmas Carol*, for example, the miserly Ebenezer Scrooge after a night of ghostly visitations finds his positive shadow in possession of his person, while the captain in Joseph Conrad's (1950 [1912]) *The Secret Sharer* projects the positive shadow quality of decisive action upon his doppelganger Leggatt.

By teaching student writers about the shadow, the Creative Writing instructor can assist them in enlarging their own ego consciousness, while at the same time give them new methods of exploring the psychology of the characters they write about. The understanding that a character possesses an unconscious shadow will invite student writers to produce more 'psychically authentic fiction'. In psychically authentic fiction, no matter how seemingly unrealistic or disconnected from the author's conscious life and world, the story resonates as a true account of a character's authentic human psychic action and interaction. Besides the standard works already mentioned, many other classic fictions in which the incredible is made credible come to mind: Franz Kafka's (1996 [1915]) *Metamorphosis*, for example, in which the main character, Gregor Samsa, awakes one morning to find he has become a bug, and Bram Stoker's (1997 [1897]) *Dracula*, in which an innocent and unassuming clerk, Jonathan Harker, is imprisoned in a vampire's castle. We know that people literally do not turn into bugs and that there are no such things as human vampires of the literal kind, yet the characters in these works respond to their unbelievable predicaments and worlds in such humanly authentic ways that we cannot help but acknowledge these stories as credible, even if we know they could not have taken place in the 'real' world. In these two instances, we can discern the psychological mechanics of shadow possession and projection, though they are not quite as obvious as they are in the other examples. We did not know Gregor Samsa prior to the possession of his devolved insect-like shadow, and the story of Dracula does not make the implicit connection between Jonathan Harker and Dracula as his shadow projection. But by approaching all of these works with an understanding of the human shadow and its workings, we can better see the numerous and diverse ways this specific psychological concept and mechanism can be employed to produce a psychically authentic situation in fiction.

Student writers can use this understanding of the shadow and its workings not only as a starting place for constructing stories but also as a means of assisting with character and plot development once a story has begun. For example, they may find themselves writing about a character who is the archetypal 'good daughter'. It would be useful to explore the unconscious of this character, in order to know all the things she thinks herself not to be, and how these things may unconsciously play themselves out. Patterns, when unconscious, prevent the genuine expression of an individual. Without even thinking, the good daughter may act in compliance with the mother, and often it is possible only after the mother is dead that the daughter can begin to question her responses and develop a stance of her own uninfluenced by her mother's taste, values and attitudes. These kinds of psychological points can be investigated idiosyncratically, depending on the student's piece.

In technical aspects of Creative Writing, we can consider this concept in relation to points of view. A conventional first-person point of view (or what we might call 'the ego's point of view') will always be immediately open to the strong influence of the narrator's shadow, since what the character presents to the reader in the narrative is only ever what he or she is consciously aware of. An omniscient third-person narrator, on the other hand, what we might call 'the Self's view point', possesses a broad and diffuse field of consciousness that can include that of the many characters rendered. The 'shadow story' of the narrator, therefore, is absent, while that of the characters themselves may become more prominent.

As one works with the shadow, it is important that one does not allow consciousness to thoroughly direct the course of the story, but instead allows it simply to inform the unconscious, taking a position toward the story as a listener rather than a self-conscious creator. As Jung tells us (1963: 326), 'just as the unconscious affects us, so the increase in our consciousness affects the unconscious'. The concept of a writer 'listening' to the story as it unfolds, rather than consciously directing the story's unfolding, is fundamentally opposed to what is taught in a conventional Creative Writing curriculum, where story outlines, plot graphs and the like are used as methods for story construction.

The process of rendering by 'listening', and specifically in this instance by listening to the character's ego and the shadow content of a developing work, must be undertaken with an active consciousness. I therefore call this writing process technique 'conscious listening'. 'Conscious listening' can be seen to work along the same lines as the 'observer effect' in quantum physics and the idea that 'vigilance operating through continual observation actually alters the physical atomic world' (Wolf 1994: 70). In the instance of a literary work, continual observation through conscious listening subtly delineates a story's development – and it is the spontaneity that this subtlety produces that is of most value in this approach. The feeling, then, in writing, becomes not so much one of consciously directing an outcome as of having witnessed the outcome and its inevitability and simply reported it, to the best of our technical ability. If we try to consciously direct the movement of the story, it is unlikely that the outcome can in any way be a revelation. If the work holds no revelations for the writer, it also is unlikely to hold any revelations for the reader. The 'predictable' story is one in which new consciousness has not emerged.

In short, the shadow is a useful concept for the writer of fiction because it provides a deeper understanding of the working of the human psyche and thus allows the rendering of even the most fantastic tale to resonate with 'psychic authenticity'. When the concept of the shadow is coupled with the writing process technique of 'conscious listening', the unconscious is able to supply the story's necessary organic movement, presenting solutions and resolutions to literary pieces that are at once inevitable, yet at the same time revelatory.

An understanding of the workings of the ego and the shadow immediately presents natural, psychologically authentic points of character conflict and interaction. Writing exercises in which students are asked to explore the workings of a character's ego and shadow can be interesting for students and can yield richer results than the conventional character sketch. Students will discover how just by entertaining the concept of the shadow complexity is added to good and evil characters. Often, student writers struggle to render 'believable characters' and think that this obviates the possibility of 'villains' and 'heroes'. Working with the Jungian conception of the shadow in one's writing can be like working with the colours black and white on an artist's palette. Very dark villains and very bright heroes can still be 'believable characters'.

Projection and possession

'Possession' and 'projection' are two further Jungian concepts to aid student writers in improving the authenticity of their work and developing greater psychological maturity in themselves. Once students have a basic understanding of the ego, the persona and the shadow, a more detailed acquaintance with how Jung saw the functioning of the unconscious will allow students to incrementally build upon their knowledge of the inner world. Jung believed that contents of the unconscious do not just lie dormant, awaiting integration, but can be projected outwards, or can overwhelm ego-consciousness and take possession of an individual. In the first instance of projection, there are many avenues the instructor might encourage students to explore. One could begin, for example, by considering literary settings within the context of projection.

Conventional books on writing inform us that setting helps to orient the reader: it 'fixes a work of fiction in place and time' (Minot 1993: 219). Setting 'is intended to reflect a character's personality, create a mood, or provide a contrast with another scene' (ibid.: 221). Unhappy characters, for example, will see their world in a bleak way. When they look outside the living room window of their suburban home, they will not notice the beautiful sunset or the daffodils in the garden, but may instead see the dead cherry tree, the scraps of garbage on the lawn, the peeling paint on the house across the street. Student writers will most probably be familiar with the idea of setting as a potential reflection of a character's inner turmoil or simply as a reflection of the character's personality. Consider, for example, the following dialogue between Adrian, Sebastian, Antonio and Gonzalo in William Shakespeare's (1998 [1623]: 29) *The Tempest* and what it tells us of their characters. They have just escaped drowning and are on an island looking for the king's son:

Adrian: The air breathes upon us here most sweetly.
Sebastian: As if it had lungs, and rotten ones.
Antonio: Or as 'twere perfumed by a fen.
Gonzalo: Here is everything advantageous to life.
Antonio: True; save means to live.

Sebastian: Of that there's none, or little.
Gonzalo: How lush and lusty the grass looks! How green!
Antonio: The ground indeed is tawny.

Although all characters are commenting on the same place, each, depending on his level of pessimism or optimism, sees it differently.

James Hollis (1998) writes:

> All projection occurs unconsciously, of course, for the moment one observes, 'I have made a projection,' one is already in the process of taking it back. More commonly, we only begin to reclaim our purchase on consciousness when the Other fails to catch, hold, reflect our projection. If there is a central law of the psyche, it is that what is unconscious will be projected.
>
> (Hollis 1998: 35)

From the outset, writing students who understand the subjectivity of human consciousness – those who know that every character, depending on his or her personal nature, will perceive the world in a different way and will project upon it in a different way – will be in a much better position to render authentic fiction than those who hold notions of universally objective perceptions.

The Jungian concept of projection can expand the student writer's understanding of subjectivity, for now the external world is not only a reflection of a character's conscious struggles or personality but also a projection of unconscious contents. The unconscious content can belong to a single character, to a group of characters, or simply to a situation. Furthermore, unlike reflection, projection is implicitly dynamic. It requires, and persists in attempting to achieve, a conscious reconciliation of dispersed contents.

Possession, on the other hand, exists when unconscious contents overwhelm our ego consciousness, making us behave in ways we do not consciously control. When we act hastily, in a passion or destructively, we are often acting in a possession. When we believe ourselves to have 'acted out of character' or when, upon later reflection, we are stunned by our former actions, it is likely that we have been 'possessed'. Possession, like projection, works to integrate unconscious content by making us question our behaviour. For example, a character may believe she is a good mother. She is conscious of loving her children totally, of wanting only the best for them, and the thought of harming them in any way is something she would never contemplate. One day, however, when one of her children arrives home from school with a low mark on her report card, the mother becomes irate and shouts and spanks the child. On later reflection, she regrets her action and feels embarrassed by it. She realizes that she was acting out of control and that the low mark could not justify her reaction. At this point, she has an opportunity to integrate the unconscious content that possessed her by coming to understand that she is not entirely 'the good mother' she believes herself to be. By investigating her actions, she may have to face the fact that perhaps there is a dark side to this 'good mother'; perhaps there is a side which exploits her children's abilities and talents in order to feed her own self-esteem. Perhaps there is also a strong will to have power over her children, to have them reflect her and her unlived potentials, instead of her encouraging them to live their own lives. By consciously acknowledging these negative qualities of herself, qualities which influence her mothering, she gains more control over the contents that possess her; the next time her child shows her a low mark on the report card, she may feel the possession bubbling up inside of her, but because she now knows that what she is really responding to is her own needs, it is much easier for her to take control of the feeling and stop it from doing harm. Often, however, people do not gain consciousness from their possessions. Instead, they either attempt to justify or deny them, or only go so far by excusing them as some form of temporary insanity. If possessions are not investigated, they continue and often worsen. For the student writer, understanding how the characters and the situations they write about might be experiencing and expressing such dynamics can be both mind-expanding and creatively empowering. Besides possibly gaining personally by investigating their own thoughts and responses, students will find that even the dullest, clichéd and superficial characters become infused with an internal energy and conflict when these psychological concepts are considered.

The archetype

Exceptional literary art is capable of transforming the reader. Even when it is fanciful or fantastic, it deals with problems and patterns of humanity and of the human soul; it gives us expansive insights into these, without ever giving us reductive answers. Exceptional literary art has the capacity to extend into the human psyche, and through an imaginal encounter bring about psychological change. Consideration of universal human patterns and the way they emerge in literature might greatly benefit students of Creative Writing and could be explored through Jung's conception of 'archetypes'. According to Jung, there is a 'personal unconscious' composed of unknown, disowned and unregarded content of a 'personal nature'; and there is also, beyond this, a collective unconscious, which is a 'deeper layer' that contains universal content, the 'modes of behaviour that are more or less the same everywhere and in all individuals and thus constitutes a common psychic substrate of a suprapersonal nature which is present in every one of us' (1959 [1954]: para. 3). He writes:

> Great poetry draws its strength from the life of mankind. . . . Whenever the collective unconscious becomes a living experience and is brought to

bear upon the conscious outlook of an age, this event is a creative act which is of importance for a whole epoch. A work of art is produced that may truthfully be called a message to generations of men.

(Jung 1966 [1950]: para. 153)

It is the contents of the collective unconscious that Jung called the archetypes. According to Samuels (1985), Jung's self-analysis as well as his work with patients demonstrated that

> imagery fell into patterns, that these patterns were reminiscent of myth, legend and fairytale, and that the imaginal material did not originate in perceptions, memory or conscious experience. The images seemed to Jung to reflect universal human modes of experience and behaviour.

As explained by Samuels et al. (1986), in *A Critical Dictionary of Jungian Analysis*,

> archetypes are recognisable in outer behaviours, especially those that cluster around the basic and universal experiences of life such as birth, marriage, motherhood, death and separation. They also adhere to the structure of the human psyche itself and are observable in relation to inner or psychic life. . . . Theoretically, there could be any number of archetypes.
>
> (Samuels et al. 1986: 26)

The archetype is 'essentially an unconscious content that is altered by becoming conscious and by being perceived, and it takes its colour from the individual consciousness in which it happens to appear' (Jung 1959 [1954]: para. 6). In itself, it is irrepresentable. However, 'archetypal images allow us to perceive it' (Jacobi 1971: 35). The 'archetypal images' have great power. They have 'a tremendous impact on the individual, gripping him and holding him in a grip, often . . . with an accompanying feeling of mystery and awe' (Samuels 1985: 29). A person who finds himself in the grip of an archetypal image will find it impossible to remain unaffected by it. Significantly, the images can appear in dreams and visions.

The archetypal image, because it can be conceptualized as a 'transcultural constant' existing outside of culture and history, can be an anathema in some disciplines. In Creative Writing, however, that very figurative location works to allow writing students to report upon the cultural and historical enmeshments of their own ego. In other words, finding a ground outside of one's culture and history, while at the same time acknowledging one's participation in it, extends the field of consciousness in the writer without a positive or negative judgement, and, ultimately, allows the written product to reflect this larger, more discerning awareness.

In Jungian analysis, the analyst attempts to assist the analysand in 'integrating' powerful archetypal contents, which are incorporated when they are 'divested of their power and autonomy' and 'rendered intelligible on the personal level. . . . If this happens, if the [analysand's] ego can manage such integration, then the personality is enriched' (Samuels 1985: 29) and there occurs in the analysand a transformational experience towards greater wholeness. Similarly, both the writing and reading of literature, activities which involve us in archetypal and imaginal realms, can transform us towards greater states of wholeness. As Hillman (1983: 47) writes, 'it is the imagination that can recover our sense of wholeness by evolving these [archetypal] images as they emerge from our psyche'. The writing and reading of literature, like therapy, revives 'the imagination and exercises it. . . . "Word-images" . . . are free from the perceptible world and free one from it' (ibid.: 47). Stories motivate our psychic and emotional participation. And like an alchemical vessel, a story can contain our feelings, allowing for a transformation in consciousness to occur.

John Allan and Judi Bertoia (1992: 3) found that children and adolescents were able to 'transform some very negative emotions and painful experiences' as well as 'gain new understanding of themselves and their world and . . . make substantive changes in their perceptions, cognitions, and behaviour' through writing. Literary artists often do precisely the same thing. However, what distinguishes one form of writing from the other and what distinguishes Creative Writing from personal therapy is the ability of the literary artist to image this personal process, which wells from the unconscious, in such a way that others can partake of the experience too. The more complete the experience for the reader, the more successful the writing students have been in engaging with and translating their own experiences.

Creative Writing students who seek to create meaningful and transformational literature can be taught first to identify and then to render the archetype intelligible. They can be given direction in translating the archetype for the collective as well as for themselves. As Bettina L. Knapp (1989: 3–4) writes, 'great Creative endeavours must be looked upon . . . not merely as personal expressions, but as revelations; not simply as individual offerings extracted from their author's depths, but as an indication of what lies hidden "behind the scenes" for the collective'. Identification of the 'archetype' would offer a concrete locus in the abstract domain of what has been, up to this point, an unidentifiable component in the making of great literature. It would allow Creative Writing instructors to embrace consciously the role of midwife to their students' unconscious content, with a greater understanding of the potential risks, hazards and benefits. Ultimately, evolving the archetypal image could assist student writers to mature both as artists and individuals, while at the same time assure the production of deeper and more collectively meaningful works.

The complex

Once the writing student understands the concept of archetype and begins to grasp the ways the unconscious can be projected or can overwhelm consciousness, an introduction to the notion of the complex will further aid the comprehension of these psychological dynamics. James Hall (1986: 30) offers a useful definition of a complex: 'In Jungian theory [it] is a group of related images having a common emotional tone and formed about an archetypal core'. Hall gives the example of images that may form around the mother archetype, such as one's personal mother, a grandmother, or a female teacher. These, he says, can 'shade' into figures from collective consciousness, such as certain actresses, perhaps the queen of England. All of these figures will have 'a maternal meaning in relation to the ego' (ibid.: 30); thus, we may speak of a mother complex. 'Complexes are formed as experiences cluster about archetypal determinants. It is as if the archetypes form a magnetic field that differentially attracts and orders experiences' (ibid.: 30). In spite of popular misconceptions, complexes are not in themselves negative and are not things to rid oneself of; rather, 'they are normal building blocks of the mind . . . [which] determine to a great degree how we experience ourselves and others' (ibid.: 32). Jung considered the ego itself a complex, but different from other complexes in that consciousness is attached to it. Jung saw the 'Self' as both the centre of the psyche and as the archetypal core of the ego complex.

> Every complex consists primarily of a 'nuclear element,' a vehicle of meaning, which is beyond the realm of the conscious will, unconscious and uncontrollable; and secondarily, of a number of associations connected with the nuclear element, stemming in part from innate personal disposition and in part from individual experiences conditioned by the environment.
>
> (Jacobi 1971: 9)

The complex, once activated, can break away from ego consciousness, acting like an 'animated foreign body in the sphere of consciousness' (ibid.: 9). As Hall (1986) elucidates:

> Each complex has the potential of organizing an entire personality of greater or lesser complexity, analogous to the way in which each cell of the body contains the genetic information *in potentia* for the creation of an entire human organism. Of course, the complex is constrained to function as a part of the total organism, just as human body cells in the healthy state behave as orderly parts of a body. A cell unregulated to serve the good of the body as a whole becomes cancerous; a complex unrelated to the organization of the psyche (including both

conscious and the unconscious) can lead to neurosis or (in the worst case) psychosis.

(Hall 1986: 34)

As one grows older, complexes can change, 'particularly in cases of pathological complexes, compensating forces in the psyche work towards transformation' (ibid.: 34). The complex possesses an individual by overwhelming ego consciousness. In the hold of a complex, an individual finds his or her stable personality can vanish and it is as if one has assumed another personality. As Hall points out,

> If one can imagine that the complex has a rudimentary consciousness of its own, it is then possible to imagine that it has its own particular purpose. The complex may, in fact, form its viewpoint, feel that it knows what is best for the psyche as a whole.
>
> (Ibid.: 34)

For the student writer, an understanding of psychological complexes can assist in both plot and character development in literary work. By recognizing disparity in fluid conceptualizing, the writer is better able to take an explorative approach to subject matter. The writer can become less concerned with creating continuity and more involved in examining the fragmented, as experienced by the story's characters.

Anima and animus

Through his clinical practice and his own self-exploration, Jung hypothesized that every man has an inner female aspect (which he termed the 'anima') and that every woman has an inner masculine aspect (or 'animus'). Both, according to Jung (1959 [1954]), are archetypes of the collective unconscious. They can express both personal and collective components that contain functions, traits and characteristics opposite to one's conscious personality; they can also carry a particular collective character. When undeveloped, these characters, according to Jung, behave with the worst collective and cultural traits of each sex. The animus and anima can both possess and be projected as well as be integrated into consciousness. Much of the focus of Jungian writing has been on the negative impact of the undeveloped animus and anima, which Jung found caused women, for example, to be opinionated and men to be moody. When these aspects are developed, however, Jung saw them as acting as a bridge for feeling in men and intellect in women. He saw them as figures who would play 'a vital role in analysis in connecting the person as he or she is (ego) with what he or she may become (self)' (Samuels 1985: 212). In the words of Marie-Louise von Franz (1999: 311), the 'anima embodies all feminine psychic qualities in a man – moods, feelings, intuitions, receptivity to the irrational, his personal capacity for love, his sense of nature and most important of all, his relationship to the unconscious'. If a man has experienced his mother in a negative way, and as a result the anima 'bears the stamp of his mother's character', then 'his anima often takes the form of depressive moods, irritability, perpetual malcontent, and excessive sensitivity' (ibid.: 311). The animus, according to Jung, is 'the deposit . . . of all woman's ancestral experience of man' (1953a [1928]: para. 336). The animus can express himself as 'sacred convictions' (von Franz 1999: 319). He can be 'something in her that is cold, stubborn, and completely inaccessible' (ibid.: 319). When developed, however, the animus is expressed positively as 'initiative, courage, objectivity and intellectual clarity' (ibid.: 23).

The concept of anima and animus has been the focus of much extension and revision as well as much critical discussion among post-Jungians. The assignation of a biological gender to collective psychological characteristics and the binary approach have tended to dominate post-Jungian debate. 'Jung's descriptions of gender fall, over neatly, into two mutually defining and mutually exclusive modes: the anima collapses into woman, feeling, Eros, relating, the feminine, while the animus stresses thinking, Logos, spirit, creating and, hence, the masculine' (Rowland 2002: 54). As Andrew Samuels (1985: 215) writes: 'Jung's approach to gender and sex was affected by both his personal situation and the context in which he lived, and also by his whole cast of thought, his *conceptual bias*'. June Singer (1976: 28) suggests that 'the behavioural models of the past are not viable models for where the boundaries of the soul are today. Man is no longer as unconscious of his anima as he used to be, or woman of her animus'. If these reservations are taken into account, however, the notion of the anima and animus, when considered as the contrasexual embodiment of 'something *other*, strange, perhaps mysterious, but certainly full of possibilities and potentials [of each sex]' (Samuels 1985: 212) is a useful concept for student writers to reflect upon. It is also useful for student writers to grapple with ideas of psychic and physical nature and their literary and metaphoric embodiment in a character's sexuality. They might consider, for example, the contrasexual characters in their own work. Do these characters, in some way, express the unconscious contents of the author? Do they express something of the collective unconscious? What is the interplay between masculine and feminine characters in a particular work? How does one serve as a bridge for the other's consciousness and psychological development? Further, one might consider the way particular cultural biases of gender may affect the contrasexual components of characters. These kinds of questions further one's understanding of the characters one finds inhabiting one's writing as well as adding to one's self-understanding, which in turn promotes psychological growth and maturation.

As noted previously, the anima and animus can both possess us and be projected onto others. Anne McNeely writes: 'it is all but impossible not to project the contrasexual archetype. It is a natural response in relationships'

(McNeely 1991: 13). Romantic love, for example, is thought to occur when the anima and animus become projected. Similarly, strong feelings of any kind, positive and negative, attach to the outer world carriers of these internal figures. This conception is theoretically useful for student writers in the unearthing of character motivations, and it can also assist them in establishing more productive relationships with their own writing practices. As McNeely (1991) points out, because these contrasexual figures can play such a large part in creative processes, it is often the case that problems one experiences in writing can come about through animus or anima issues. She has found that her own writer's block arises through possession by the negative animus:

> Even when writing supports the positive animus, the discouragement appears to be sparked by the negative animus. It takes such forms as: 'That has already been said,' 'It is not worth the trouble,' and a number of corollaries, such as, 'It won't be read,' or 'It will meet with nothing but criticism,' and the most deadly of all: 'It's impossible to put all that into any meaningful form.'

(Ibid.: 15)

The anima can be equally thwarting in the writing process. According to Marie Louise von Franz (1999), the negative anima

> will endlessly whisper within a man: 'I'm nothing,' 'It doesn't make sense anyhow,' 'It's different for other people,' 'Nothing gives me any pleasure,' and so on. . . . She constellates a general sense of gloom. Troubled moods like these can intensify to the point of temptations to suicide; thus the anima can become a demoness of death.

(von Franz 1999: 311)

Both negative anima and animus can possess student writers, whispering evil in their ears, denouncing their efforts as inferior and futile, and making the task of writing painful if not completely impossible. Acknowledging the inner voice of the negative manifestation, and discerning, through investigation, that this negative voice is not one and the same as the ego's can assist a great deal in a student writer overcoming common obstacles to writing. Indeed, the concept of 'the inner critic' as discussed by Natalie Goldberg (1990) and others is an attempt to demonstrate the discrepancy between two conflicting polarities in the writer. As one aspect moves to create, the other moves to destroy. The ego, until it begins to pay attention, believes itself to be the voice of both. By paying attention to one's animus or anima and its responses to one's creative efforts, one can eventually evolve the more 'negative critic' into the 'helpful editor'. Also, negative anima and animus can be projected onto others.

The Creative Writing teacher as well as fellow classmates may become the carriers for a student's negative and positive projections. Students who are the same sex as their teachers and classmates may project shadow qualities onto them, while opposite sex students may find in their instructor and classmates a convenient hook on which to hang their animus or anima projections. In the Creative Writing workshop, such a state of affairs can cause all kinds of interesting and distorted situations, which, in many instances, may prevent the constructive functioning of the class. Having some idea of these archetypal components can assist student writers as well as instructors in all aspects of teaching and learning.

Active imagination

Active imagination is a technique that necessitates the interaction of an analysand's ego consciousness and the unconscious. Learning about the Jungian concept of 'active imagination' can assist student writers in developing this essential interplay that is necessary in the production of literary art. Active imagination finds that middle place between dreams, which are the spontaneous expression of the unconscious, and fantasies, which are a person's ego-directed imaginings. With active imagination, the ego engages with the unconscious by interacting with the images that spontaneously arise. As James Hall (1986: 105) writes: 'When situations or persons other than the imaginal-ego react to the ego in active imagination, they must be permitted to react with no interference whatsoever from the ego.' This practice is a difficult one, as our egos tend to want to revise and fix. If we ask a question of our inner characters and they give us responses we do not like or understand, we may be inclined to use our ego's fantasy-making abilities to put the words we would rather hear into their mouths. Active Imagination, as a practice, will assist student writers in developing a trusting relationship with their unconscious. They will discover how they can approach the inner world and, with a little probing, find a depth and breadth of meaning their ego consciousness had no awareness of previously.

The combination of unconscious and ego-consciousness gives rise to what Jung called 'the transcendent function' (1953b [1943]: para. 121). June Singer (1972) in her *Boundaries of the Soul* succinctly outlines its workings:

> This third element . . . belongs neither to the ego sphere nor to the unconscious and yet possesses access to each. It stands above them, participating in both. . . . The transcendent function's emergence grants autonomy to the ego and also to the unconscious by relating to both of them independently, and in doing so, unites them.
>
> (Singer 1972: 333)

One simple and practical way for student writers to work with 'active imagination' in the production of literature is by dialoguing with their characters (as well as their characters' shadows and contrasexual components) and allowing them to respond without ego interference. Again, such work can greatly enhance the student's trust in the larger vision of the unconscious and create a greater fluidity between the two. While such dialogues will most probably never be used in the literary work, the process itself adds depth and dimension to the writing.

Conclusion

While the preceding is by no means a comprehensive approach to a Jungian method of Creative Writing instruction, it does demonstrate how Jungian concepts that alert us to the workings of the inner world can be potentially beneficial in both the process and the product of Creative Writing. They can help to resolve the paradox outlined at the beginning, since through their application the 'creative' component of the discipline can, in a very real sense, be taught.

Writing technique, the main thrust of current Creative Writing pedagogy, will always be important in refining expression and rendering the most complete picture of what the student writer sees. But a Jungian approach promises to offer much more. Student writers, by gaining access to unconscious dimensions both in themselves and in their literary products, can also gain a more expansive, complex and original way of seeing. They will gather greater ego strength as they consciously observe the evolving connection between their outer and inner worlds, and discover that 'creation' cannot occur by the ego's dictates alone. Because greater creative vistas will open to student writers who are given a theoretical framework and language to support entry and exploration into unknown psychic terrain, the literary projects they embark upon will take on the dynamism of discovery. They will, in fact, have been taught to write creatively.

References

Allan, J. and Bertoia, J. (1992) *Written Paths to Healing: Education and Jungian Child Counseling*. Dallas, TX: Spring.

Bell, M. S. (1997) *Narrative Design*. New York: Norton.

Conrad, J. (1950) *The Secret Sharer*. New York: Signet. (Original work published in 1912.)

Dickens, C. (1991) *A Christmas Carol*. New York: Gramercy. (Original work published in 1843.)

Goldberg, N. (1990) *Wild Mind: Living the Writer's Life*. New York: Bantam.

Hall, J. (1983) *Jungian Dream Interpretation*. Toronto: Inner City Books.

—— (1986) *The Jungian Experience: Analysis and Individuation*. Toronto: Inner City Books.

Hannah, B. (1971) *Striving towards Wholeness*. Boston: Sigo Press.

Hillman, J. (1983) *Healing Fiction*. Barrytown, NY: Station Hill Press.

Hollis, J. (1998) *The Eden Project: In Search of the Magical Other*. Toronto: Inner City Books.

Hopcke, R. H. (1995) *Persona: Where Sacred Meets Profane*. Boston: Shambhala.

Jacobi, J. (1971) *Complex/Archetype/Symbol in the Psychology of C. G. Jung*. Princeton, NJ: Princeton University Press. (Original work published in 1959.)

Jung, C. G. (1953a) The relations between the ego and unconscious. *The Collected Works of C. G. Jung* (Vol. 7). Princeton, NJ: Princeton University Press. (Original work published in 1928.)

—— (1953b) On the psychology of the unconscious. *The Collected Works of C. G. Jung* (Vol. 7). Princeton, NJ: Princeton University Press. (Original work published in 1943.)

—— (1959) The archetypes of the collective unconscious. *The Collected Works of C. G. Jung* (Vol. 9.i). Princeton, NJ: Princeton University Press. (Original work published in 1954.)

—— (1963) *Memories, Dreams, Reflections*. New York: Vintage.

—— (1966) Psychology and literature. *The Collected Works of C. G. Jung* (Vol. 15). Princeton, NJ: Princeton University Press. (Original work published in 1950.)

—— (1969) Aion. *The Collected Works of C. G. Jung* (Vol. 9.ii). Princeton, NJ: Princeton University Press. (Original work published in 1951.)

—— (1971) Psychological types. *The Collected Works of C. G. Jung* (Vol. 6). Princeton, NJ: Princeton University Press. (Original work published in 1921.)

Kafka, F. (1996) *The Metamorphosis*. New York: Norton. (Original work published in 1915.)

Knapp, B. L. (1989) *Machine, Metaphor, and the Writer: A Jungian View*. University Park, PA: Pennsylvania State University Press.

Lawrence, D. H. (1950) *Women in Love*. New York: Viking. (Original work published in 1920.)

McNeely, D. A. (1991) *Animus Aeternus: Exploring the Inner Masculine*. Toronto: Inner City Books.

Minot, S. (1993) *Three Genres: The Writing of Poetry, Fiction, and Drama*. Englewood Cliffs, NJ: Prentice Hall.

Rowland, S. (2002) *Jung: A Feminist Revision*. Cambridge: Polity.

Samuels, A. (1985) *Jung and the Post-Jungians*. London: Routledge.

Samuels, A., Shorter, B. and Plaut, F. (eds.) (1986) *A Critical Dictionary of Jungian Analysis*. New York: Brunner-Routledge.

Shakespeare, W. (1998) *The Tempest*. New York: Signet. (Original work published in 1623.)

Singer, J. (1972) *Boundaries of the Soul: The Practice of Jung's Psychology*. New York: Doubleday.

—— (1976) *Androgyny: The Opposites Within*. Boston: Sigo Press.

Stein, M. (1982) The aims and goal of Jungian analysis. In M. Stein (ed.) *Jungian Analysis*. London: Open Court.

Stevenson, R. L. (2003) *The Strange Case of Dr. Jekyll and Mr. Hyde*. London: Hesperus Press. (Original work published in 1886.)

Stoker, B. (1997) *Dracula*. New York: Signet. (Original work published in 1897.)

Von Franz, M.-L. (1980) *Projection and Re-collection in Jungian Psychology*. London: Open Court. (Original work published in 1978.)

—— (1999) *Archetypal Dimensions of the Psyche*. Boston: Shambhala.

Wilde, O. (1998) *The Picture of Dorian Gray*. New York: Modern Library. (Original work published in 1880.)

Wolf, F. A. (1994) *The Dreaming Universe*. New York: Simon and Schuster.

Zweig, C. and Abrams, J. (eds) (1991) *Meeting the Shadow: The Hidden Power of the Dark Side of Human Nature*. Los Angeles, CA: Jeremy P. Tarcher.

Chapter 8

The dialectical mind

On educating the creative imagination in elementary school

Austin Clarkson

> Go through the door of your imagination
> And see the world through the eyes of your heart.
> As you dance to the music of your dreams,
> Fly free in your world!!!
>
> (Girl, age 10)

> I learned that you close your eyes and let your imagination run free.
> I can do anything with my imagination.
>
> (Boy, age 10)

The ruling metaphor of Shakespeare's *A Midsummer Night's Dream* is the marriage of the Reason and the Imagination. The rationalistic Theseus, Duke of Athens, insists that the imagination does nothing but delude 'cool reason'. He derides the poet whose imagination 'bodies forth the forms of things unknown' and gives 'to airy nothing a local habitation and a name'. For him the magical events of Midsummer's Eve are 'more strange than true'. Hippolyta, Queen of the Amazons, disagrees:

> But all the story of the night told over,
> And all their minds transfigur'd so together,
> More witnesseth than fancy's images,
> And grows to something of great constancy;
> But, howsoever, strange and admirable.
> (*A Midsummer Night's Dream*,
> Act 5, Scene 1)

For Hippolyta the events are true because they had observable effects on the lives of the young lovers. Moreover, the transformations will endure, for the couples are to be married. What more proof is needed than that each discovers his or her truth? Although Theseus had conquered the Amazons and won Hippolyta by force of arms, they celebrate their nuptials with the prospect that the Reason and the Imagination will 'eternally be knit'. The entente between Reason and Imagination did not last long. Reason divorced the Imagination during the Enlightenment in order to get rid of superstition and the taboo against experimental science, and they did not resume relations until the nineteenth century.

Rejecting the 'mechanical philosophy' of the Enlightenment, William Blake insisted that matter lies beyond Newton's compass and should be consumed in 'the "Fire" of the dialectical imagination' (Woodman 2005: 88). Samuel Taylor Coleridge sought a standpoint that would comprehend both the Imagination and the Reason:

> Grant me a nature having two contrary forces, the one of which tends to expand infinitely, while the other strives to apprehend or *find* itself in this infinity, and I will cause the world of intelligences with the whole system of their representations to rise up before you.
>
> (Quoted in ibid.: 19)

The imagination, he said, is 'the distinguishing characteristic of man as a progressive being, . . . it ought to be carefully guided and strengthened as the indispensable means and instrument of continued amelioration and refinement'. He complained that 'modern systems of education' place too much emphasis on 'the judgment', and insisted that, 'We should address ourselves to those faculties in a child's mind which are first awakened by nature, and consequently first admit of cultivation, that is to say, the memory and the imagination' (Coleridge 1950: 401–402). The discovery of the unconscious reinforced the idea that it is not enough to educate the intellect alone, and concern for creativity, symbolic thinking and the child's self-directed maturation lay at the heart of the educational reforms of John Dewey, Arnold Gesell, Maria Montessori, Rudolf Steiner, Lev Vygotsky and Heinz Werner.

Cognitive science, stimulus-response behaviourism, the computational model of the brain and the exigencies of the Cold War reasserted the dominance of 'scientific thinking'. Following Jean Piaget (1962: 289), educators viewed the 'magical thinking' of children as a passing phase on the way to mature cognitive processes that should be relatively free of symbolic representations. In the 1960s and 1970s the domains of feelings, values and the creative imagination were promoted in so-called 'confluent education' (Frye 1963; Jones 1968), but the movement made limited inroads. Howard Gardner's widely distributed theory of multiple intelligences is based in cognitive science and follows from the premise that intelligence is confined to specific cognitive domains (see Gardner 2006). While the theory has been beneficial in broadening the concept of intelligence, it does not admit an intelligence of the imagination. Cognitive psychologists interested in the child's imagination concern themselves with its re-creative and reproductive rather than its creative and productive functions (Harris 2000; Currie and Ravenscroft 2002). They now admit magical thinking into mature thought as 'a natural by-product of the adaptive functioning of the mind' (Nemeroff and Rozin 2000: 19–20), but are not interested in authentic, spontaneous expressions of the creative imagination.

Educators committed to cognitive models of development fail to appreciate what depth psychologists know beyond the shadow of a doubt, namely, 'that the unconscious mind contains potential meaning' (Modell 2003: 161) and is a vital source for the individual's meaningful engagement in education. Kohn (2004: 9–10) cites research that demonstrates the value of actively involving students in designing their own learning and of stimulating intellectual exploration and creativity. The roster of educators who value imaginative, holistic and depth psychological approaches is growing: Egan (1992), Greene (1995), Miller (1996), Kessler (2000), Efland (2002), Eisner (2002), Mayes (2005) and Neville (2005). The Imaginative Education Research Group founded by Kieran Egan at Simon Fraser University in British Columbia (see www.ierg.net) has developed research programmes, teacher training curriculum, community initiatives, teaching strategies and lesson plans for elementary and secondary schools to show that the imagination is a vital adjunct to learning in many subject areas. But advocates of the imagination in education need to keep in mind the difference between the reproductive (re-creative) imagination and the productive (creative) imagination.

C. G. Jung was dissatisfied with approaches that explain fantasy images in terms of past experience alone, for he found that the fantasy also has a prospective, goal-directed tendency. He pointed to the fact that in everyday experience we accept that a person's opinion is not simply a product of previous opinions expressed by others, but is a statement of that individual's aims and intentions. Thus a teleological standpoint is introduced into an explanation of the opinion. If this is the case for conscious contents, then there is no reason not to apply a goal-oriented perspective to the explanations of fantasy and the contents of the unconscious, for the unconscious can be shown to supply knowledge that compensates for the limited perspective of the conscious attitude (Meier 1984: Ch. 1). And so Jung defined the fantasy both causally and purposively: 'Causally interpreted, it seems like a symptom of a physiological or personal state, the outcome of antecedent events. Purposively interpreted, it seems like a symbol' (Jung 1971 [1921]: para. 720). Jung investigated both the causal meaning of the fantasy and the prospective meaning of symbols that emerge spontaneously from the creative imagination. Particularly interested in the latter, he developed a method for stimulating the imagination to produce symbolic images, for he found that such images can be the highest expression of a person's individuality and 'may even create that individuality by giving perfect expression to its unity' (ibid.: para. 714). He advised patients to start with any image, 'contemplate it and carefully observe how the picture begins to unfold or to change'; and to note these changes and 'eventually step into the picture yourself' and interact with the images (Jung 1973 [1947]: 460).

Jungian psychoanalysts continued to practise active imagination. Marie-Louise von Franz (1983: 125–128) outlined four steps:

1   Empty one's mind from the trains of thought of the ego.
2   Let a fantasy image from the unconscious come into the field of inner attention.
3   Give the fantasy some form of expression in writing, painting, dancing, etc.
4   Confront the ethical implications of whatever has been produced.

The last step ensures that the individual does not identify with their emergent images and feelings, but feeds them into the dialectic between the reason and the imagination. Several other therapeutic disciplines practise varieties of active imagination, for example, psychosynthesis and neuro-linguistic programming. Bernard Neville (2005: 93–117) provides a survey of these and other methods in his valuable handbook for classroom teachers. The challenge is to find ways of activating the creative imagination safely and responsibly in the general classroom.

The programme for elementary school children that I shall describe arose from a university course that was given during the 1980s and 1990s to undergraduates in fine arts. 'Foundations of Creative Imagination' was based on Jung's concepts of the creative imagination and the transcendent function, the analysis of myths and fairytales, archetypes and psychological types, the creative process and the ritual process, the symbolic attitude and individuation. The team of instructors included specialists in visual art, movement, drama, music and the psychology of Jung (Clarkson 2003, 2005a). One of the unintended consequences of the course was the formation of an ongoing community of artists, poets, teachers and therapists that has given public shows of their creative work together with workshops on creativity for adults and children. In 2002 a community arts organization sponsored the artist-teachers of the group to provide a programme for classes of children from local elementary schools. 'Exploring Creativity in Depth' was warmly received and has continued with funding from municipal and provincial agencies. The findings reported here are based on the following documentation: evaluations of each programme (separate forms for children, parents and teachers), interviews with teachers, follow-up questionnaires given to selected classes several weeks after the programme, photographs of artworks and video-taping of the programme. The programmes of 2005–2006 were the subject of an assessment (Gee 2006).

Exploring creativity in depth

Some 1700 children came through the programme during its first five years. Of these, 60 per cent were 9 and 10 years of age (grades 4 and 5), 20 per cent were 11 (grade 6) and 10 per cent were 12 and 13 (grades 7 and 8). The remaining 10 per cent consisted of secondary school art students and youth with special needs. At the core of the programme is an exercise for activating the imagination while viewing a work of visual art, the making of original pictures and creative writing based on that experience, and discussion of the pictures and writing in small groups. The active imagination exercise was first developed in the university course and then adapted for both children and adults in an interpretive exhibit for an art museum. The exercise was tested with focus groups, recorded on a compact disc, and installed in 1993. Many thousands of visitors of all ages, educational backgrounds and nationalities have sat in a booth, put on a headset and listened to the exercise while gazing at a landscape canvas a few feet away. Some 1500 of them left 'share-your-reaction' cards on which they wrote words and drew sketches that indicated that the exercise had facilitated an intensely meaningful engagement with the painting (Clarkson and Worts 2005).

The programme for school children begins when a class of between twenty-five and thirty-five students, the teacher, and one, two or three parent-volunteers arrive at the art centre. They are welcomed, given a description of the day's activities, and invited to enter the gallery and view the artworks in the show. After a few minutes a guide's voice comes over the public address system asking them to choose an artwork and sit down in front of it. She says that this is a time for discovery and adventure, a time to open a door in the mind and enter the world of your very own imagination:

> You can do this exercise in your own way . . . there is no right or wrong way of doing it . . . you may imagine a lot of things or only a few . . . you may have lots of feelings or only a few . . . be patient and let your imagination do its job . . . everyone's imagination is different . . . be relaxed and enjoy going into your imagination.

She gives a brief relaxation exercise based on the breath and then says that she is going to ask them to look at the artwork in a special way. They scan the artwork all over slowly, shut their eyes, imagine there is a TV screen behind their eyelids and that they can see the artwork on that screen. The scanning and imagining sequence is repeated. They open their eyes, locate a place in the artwork that attracts them, and imagine going to that place. They look around from there, sense the temperature, feel the textures, listen for sounds, and go for a walk and explore. They choose a colour, focus on that colour and note the feeling that the colour brings. They choose a shape, imagine being that shape and moving around as that shape. The exercise ends with a minute of silence during which the imagination is free to play.

Activating the imagination transforms the artwork from a passive object into an active participant in the aesthetic experience. Users of the museum exhibit reported that the painting at first looked dull and boring, but that the viewing exercise evoked a strong energy field that made it seem to 'come alive'. Several made two drawings, one of before the exercise showing the painting as was, and one of after the exercise, showing the painting trans-formed by the imagination. Some remarked on how the exercise reduced and even eliminated the distance between the viewer and the painting (Clarkson and Worts 2005: 268–269). In ordinary consciousness the invitation to 'go into' an artwork seems incongruous, but when the attention is focused and the imaginal bond is well established, viewers have no difficulty imagining that they are 'in the painting' and following the other directions. Children remark that now that they have discovered how to 'go into a picture', they will do it on their own with other paintings.

John Dewey (1958 [1934]: 267) spoke of merging with the artwork as a procreative act, as 'when varied materials of sense quality, motion, and meaning come together in a union that marks a new birth in the world'. Suzanne Langer (1942) distinguished between presentational and represen-tational states of mind, where representational meaning derives from the relation between a signifier and a referent and presentational meaning emerges directly from the expressive medium itself. Harry T. Hunt (1995) describes the condition as one of 'presence-openness'. Felt meaning emerges as the result of an experiential immersion in the expressive pat-terns of the symbolic medium 'in the form of potential semblances that are "sensed", polysemic and open-ended, and so unpredictable and novel' (ibid.: 42). In this state the imagination combines feelings, sensations, memories and intuitions in symbolic images that are experienced as ori-ginal, personal and deeply meaningful. The experience may involve body, mind and spirit so fully and meaningfully that participants describe the experience as spiritual, a communion, an epiphany (Clarkson and Worts 2005: 271–272).

Activating the imagination brings the secondary process of conscious, ego-awareness into contact with the primary process of the unconscious. Jung (1958) referred to this state as the 'transcendent function', because it tran-scends consciousness and the unconscious. The psychiatrist Silvano Arieti (1976) coined the term the 'tertiary process' for this state:

> The tertiary process, with specific mechanisms and forms, blends the two worlds of mind and matter, and, in many cases, the rational with the irrational. Instead of rejecting the primitive (or whatever is archaic, obso-lete, or off the beaten path), the creative mind integrates it with normal

logical processes in what seems a 'magic synthesis' from which the new, the unexpected, and the desirable emerges.

(Arieti 1976: 186)

The Jungian psychoanalyst Nathan Schwartz-Salant (1989: 107) described the 'imaginal couple' that forms in the therapeutic encounter as occupying a transitional area between the space-time world (where processes are characterized as an interaction of objects) and the infinite pleroma, and that in its creative form the imaginal couple has a numinous quality that can be the source of healing. The psychologist Henry Reed (1996a, 1996b) leads groups during which participants seated in pairs intend silent communication with each other. Participants report experiences of mutually imagined energy forms and intense felt meanings while in the 'liminal zone of imaginal communication' (Reed 1996b: 220). Similar exercises between pairs of musicians who intend musical communication with each other in silence result in imagined synaesthetic energy forms and reciprocal musical and gestic play (Clarkson 2005b: 19–20). Functional magnetic resonance imaging shows that the wilful act of forming the mental image of an object with the eyes closed selectively activates the same place in the brain as seeing that object with the eyes open; and further, that the information reaching the brain from the outside world is conditioned by the mental state of the viewer (Schwartz and Begley 2002: 336–337). Psychiatrist Jeffrey Schwartz studied the effects of sustained meditation practices on stroke patients and concluded that mental states contribute to the final perception even more powerfully than does the stimulus itself (ibid.). Furthermore such mental effort over considerable spans of time has observable effects on brain development. The mental and spiritual force that sustains attention in meditation and other reflective practices can produce 'plastic and enduring changes in the brain and hence the mind. *Intention is made causally efficacious through attention*' (ibid.: 360; italics added).

Children unused to sitting still and focusing their attention sometimes have difficulty with the exercise, but most are delighted with the results. Asked what they learned about their imagination, they write: 'It can take you anywhere'; 'I found out how to go somewhere without moving'; 'I could do things that I don't ever think about'; 'I learned that my imagination never ends and to never stop thinking.' They remark on the relaxed atmosphere and the ability to work quietly on their own: 'We had the chance to seat by ourselfs [*sic*] and think, act, feel, draw different.' They understand the benefits of persistence and patience: 'I never knew art was this hard but my work is what I'm proud of'; 'I learned about art that it's all up to you and you never have to stop.' Neville (2005: 95–96) affirms that repeated exercises for activating the imagination can markedly change the student's self-image, attitudes and behaviour, that it is not particularly difficult to script guided visualizations around curriculum content, and that focusing exercises assure students 'of their inner knowledge and their ability to find their own direction'.

After the exercise in the art gallery the children go to the studio and sit at tables provided with cartridge paper, oil pastels and paper towelling. They pick a colour like the one they chose in the gallery and cover the sheet of paper with that colour. Prompts reinforce the association of colours with feelings: 'How does the colour make you feel – happy or sad, peaceful or anxious, brave or scared, loving or angry, hopeful or lonely?' They choose a second colour, outline the shape that they focused on, and fill in the shape with that colour. They scrub the two colours together with the towel or their fingers to make new shades and textures. More prompts encourage them to go with the flow of the imagination:

> You are making your very own, original picture, not a copy of the art-work in the gallery . . . let your imagination guide you . . . there is no right or wrong way . . . it doesn't have to look like anything you've seen before . . . you don't have to like what you are making . . . what you think is a mistake may be a chance to do something different . . . you can even scribble.

After about thirty minutes they are asked to think of words that describe the feelings and images in their pictures. They turn the paper over and write on the back – separate words, a poem, a story. They return to the gallery with their pictures and sit in groups of six to eight, each led by a guide who asks them what attracted them to the artwork they chose, what happened during the imagination exercise, how they made their pictures, and what they see in them. They discuss the meanings and feelings of the colours and forms, what features make each picture unique and what they have in common. The children are invited to read their poems and stories to the group. Some children prefer not to share what they wrote, and the guides do not insist. If a child's material is particularly troubling, the guide may bring it to the attention of the teacher.

The guides emphasize that the artworks are not being viewed critically and judgementally, but rather as gifts of new and fascinating images and feelings that are being shared with the group. Children appreciate the small group discussions and some say that what they like most about the programme was learning more about their friends. Teachers remark that group discussions are difficult to handle in the school environment and that 'the small groups take away pressure' and give 'opportunity to share and celebrate successes'. They are impressed by how well the children share their thoughts and feelings: 'It helped the students to reflect upon the artwork and express those thoughts in their artwork.' And they note the effect on mutuality and reciprocity: 'Students learned how to encourage others to foster love for art'; 'Great way for debriefing, sharing and receiving feedback'; 'Developed courage to try and self-esteem from the effort and feedback'.

After lunch the children assemble in the gallery, where the guides show samples of their artwork and talk about how they became artists. The children enjoy getting to know 'real artists'. During the lunch period the pictures from the morning are placed on the floor beside the tables in the studio. The children return to the studio and do the focusing exercise again, this time while looking at their own pictures. They make a second picture as before, write on the back, and return to their groups to discuss how the second picture came out of the first and how the two pictures differ. They fill out evaluation forms, have popsicles, and board the bus back to school. Activating the imagination with their own pictures and taking the creative process through a second phase greatly reinforces its impact.

The cycle of the creative process

The programme follows in general the model of the creative process first enunciated by Graham Wallas (1926: 87). Taking his cue from William James' idea of subliminal consciousness, Wallas collected reports from scientists, philosophers and poets on their experience of the creative process. His model is notable for giving as much importance to the unconscious stages of incubation and illumination as to the conscious stages of preparation and verification. The 'preparation' phase consists of the children selecting an artwork in the gallery. During the 'incubation' phase the imagination is activated to engage with the imagery of the artwork, and during the 'illumination' phase images and feelings flow into conscious awareness. The incubation and illumination phases continue in the studio while they make pictures and write about them. The 'verification' phase concludes the process with discussing the pictures in the groups and filling out the evaluation forms at the end of the programme. Wallas's model is criticized by cognitivists, who deny the existence of the unconscious and regard creativity as a matter of rearranging already known contents in novel ways. They devised experiments to demonstrate that the incubation phase does not require the participation of the unconscious (Weisberg 1993: 42–50).

Making a second picture based on the first enables children to experience the transformative potential of the creative imagination. Jung used the term 'enantiodromia' to describe 'the emergence of the unconscious opposite in the course of time' (1971 [1921]: para. 709). As a rule, the second picture depicts images and feelings that are strongly contrasted to the first. If the first picture is a jumble of disparate elements, with feelings of sadness, loneliness or anger, the second picture is likely to be a symmetrical or mandala-like design with feelings of peace and love, happiness and joy. The first picture will usually contain imagery from the artwork in the gallery, while the second will be completely original. If the first picture is of solitude in a dark forest, the second may be of a family picnic by the sea. If the first picture is a scene of battling monsters and erupting volcanoes, the second may show those energies contained in a powerful Self-figure. Taking the creative process

Plate 1

Plate 2

Plate 3

Plate 4

Plate 5

Plate 6

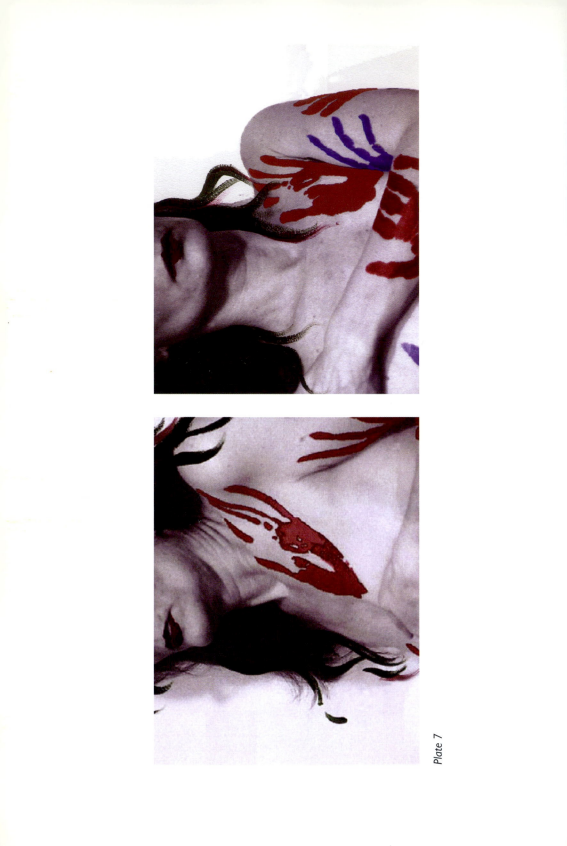

Plate 7

through two phases in succession brings the ego more fully into contact with the Self – a term that signified for Jung the unity of the personality as a whole. Jung identified symbols that unify the opposites as the circle, square and cross, etc. (ibid.: para. 790). Similar totality symbols that appear spontaneously in the children's pictures include the t'ai chi sign, the rainbow, the peace sign and the sun and the moon on opposite sides of the picture. The second picture is usually a marked transformation of the first, with heightened focus on a numinous central image that is completely original. The Self-portrait may be a large, centrally placed sun or moon, butterfly or flower, heart or tree, mountain or island, or, with boys, some image from their favourite sport. Such pictures are metaphors for the totality of the personality that James Hollis describes as 'that mysterious and dynamic purposefulness in each of us' (Hollis 2000: 105).

Seven children

A 9-year-old girl (Girl 1) chose a painting in the gallery of several brilliant goldfish swimming against a dark background, and her first picture was of two goldfish facing each other with three air bubbles above (Plate 1). On the back of the picture she wrote: 'Exploring something new . . . A whole new world under the sea . . . It's a whole new world if you don't think of boundaries.' Her experience of going into the picture was of discovering a wonderful, liberating and boundless world. After the focusing exercise with the first picture, she made a second that was completely original: instead of fish in the sea, it was a twelve-petalled, happy-faced sunflower radiating beams of light (Plate 2). On the back she wrote: 'Only you hold the key of happiness for yourself. Nothing can stop you when you're happy. Happiness will find a way. So be happy! Go ahead and spread some sunshine.' Her first picture referred to the painting in the gallery as it ushered her into the realm of the imagination, while the second tapped into the Self-system, flooding her with feeling and the recognition that she should acknowledge her happiness and share it with others. On the evaluation form she wrote that the workshop made her more confident in her work and that she 'found the artist inside me'. About six weeks later she wrote on the follow-up questionnaire that she learned from the workshop that she had a big imagination and that all she had to do was use it.

Hundreds of children reported that they had no idea that their imagination was so huge, wild, amazing, free and powerful; that they can now travel anywhere they want in their imagination; that the imagination is even better than TV and video games; that their first picture surprised them because they didn't know they could draw so well; that they used to think art was dull and boring, but now it's 'cool' and 'more fun'. The workshop changed positively the children's attitude to art, and a remarkable 76 per cent said that they would like to take further courses in the arts (Gee 2006: 10). A surprising number said that now they would like to become artists. Discovering the artist within indicates that the ego-system has come in contact with the Self-system.

Activating the imagination induces a state of reverie in which mental energy flows from conscious ego awareness to the liminal zone of imaginal cognition. In this meditative state children lose their inhibitions about working and playing in expressive media, and teachers are amazed that children who generally resist projects in art and writing have so much success. A grade 5 boy (Boy 1) was one of the few visible minority students in his class and had the darkest skin. The artwork he chose in the gallery was the portrait of a black man in the uniform of a postman, and the wall card gave his name as 'Ismail'. The boy's first picture mirrored the frontal view and smiling features of Ismail, while 'Toronto Rapotors' (properly, 'Raptors') names the local professional basketball team (Figure 8.1). Although he invested the portrait with the power and glamour of his sports heroes, on the back he wrote a story about a boy who was being bullied:

> Once upon a time there was a boy named Lucaleshish. He was different from other kids. He used to get bullied by a kid named N. He always beat on Lucaleshish and one day Lucaleshish ran away. The End.

The boy's name was of Arabic origin, and there was a Caucasian boy in the

Figure 8.1

class named N, so it is likely that Boy 1 was indeed telling his own story. His second picture was a complete transformation: a hill or mountain flanked by trees on each side, a flock of birds forming an arch overhead, and a small animal at the base of the mountain. The symmetrical design is flooded in golden light (Figure 8.2). On the back he wrote: 'A place you can stay. A place you can be when you are alone. A place you'll be safe. A place you can grow.' He had created a beautiful, secluded refuge where he could be in safety and develop in peace. On the evaluation form he wrote that his first drawing surprised him because he didn't know that he could draw so well and that he now realizes he is good at making art. Several weeks later he wrote on the follow-up questionnaire that what he remembered best about the field trip was the picture of the man named Ismail, that he learned that art is really fun, and that now he can travel in his imagination and show it on the paper. When asked about the effects of the programme, the teacher singled out this boy. She said that he was very extraverted, did not follow instructions, gave up easily, and had not finished a single art project all year. She was amazed by his pictures and that he was so proud of them. The programme, she said, 'allowed him to be in his own material'. This boy was typical of many who were liberated by discovering the imagination and by learning how to express themselves in art.

A 10-year-old girl (Girl 2) chose the painting of a house, and her first

Figure 8.2

picture was of that house with a prominent front door. During the afternoon exercise, she imagined going through that door into a magical world. She drew the doorframe at the centre of her second picture and surrounded it with concentric swirls of flowers, a leaping dolphin, the sun and moon, and energy spirals (Figure 8.3). On the back she wrote: 'Go through the door of your imagination and see the world through the eyes of your heart. As you dance to the music of your dreams, fly free in your world!!!' Her words capture her ecstatic feelings at discovering that the imagination provides a blissful, liberating experience of the inner world. The disparate elements in her picture whirl about in a round dance, a mandala-like image of the infinite pleroma. On the evaluation form she said that the workshop had changed her idea about art, because now she likes 'to imagine unexplainable things'. On the follow-up questionnaire she wrote that the most valuable part of the programme was the exercise for looking at an artwork and 'using our imagination to figure out what we think is going on'. She learned how the imagination can go wild, that no one else has 'the exact same imagination', and that 'all imagination is right'. The teacher said that this girl was one of the youngest in her class and usually felt left behind, but that she had blossomed in the workshop and had gained greatly in self-confidence. Discovering her gift for painting and poetry encouraged her to participate in school with more confidence.

Figure 8.3

The children may indicate on the evaluation form that they are interested, happy and excited at the beginning of the programme, but engaging the creative process in depth allows them to express whatever may be bothering them. And going through the creative process a second time enables them to gain another perspective of the situation. A 10-year-old boy (Boy 2) called his first picture 'Confusion', because a welter of images had appeared 'out of nowhere' – ugly faces, evil eyes, animals, fish, question marks, and in the lower right-hand corner, a quiet place with two trees (Figure 8.4). He wrote: 'My picture is really confusing. I did that so I could see the different things that might appear out of nowhere and get me thinking about other things. I call it confusion. It gets me asking questions.' He recognized that the purpose of the confusion was to raise questions. The second picture provided the answer (Figure 8.5). He wrote:

> This is a picture about my anger. I fight with my brothers, but I still love them. I drew this picture to express my anger. In the picture it looks like me and my brothers fight. But it's a giant frog and a giant fish fighting. The setting takes place in the sea.

He symbolized his conflict between loving his brothers and fighting with

Figure 8.4

Figure 8.5

them as a struggle between a giant frog and a giant fish deep in the sea. The stronger frog seems to be the aggressor, while the weaker fish appears to be on the defensive. Depicting the conflict as a struggle between powerful protagonists deep in the unconscious, the boy was identifying a difficult life situation and trying to bring it into consciousness. He wrote on the evaluation form that his first drawing surprised him because he didn't know that he could draw so well, but that he liked his second picture better because 'my artwork got more detailed'. On the questionnaire some weeks later he said that what he learned was that 'you close your eyes and let your imagination run free. I can do anything with my imagination.' He had gained confidence in his imagination as a resource in which he found strength and support.

Jung's theory of the compensatory function of the unconscious plays out time and again in the twofold structure of the programme. When the first picture is placid and realistic, the second picture is likely to be more abstract, intense and problematic. Or if the first picture is fearful and anxious, the second picture usually depicts a scene of peace and happiness. Many children are oppressed by images of conflict and violence, and their concerns come through in their artworks. The first picture by a 13-year-old girl (Girl 3) is of a lonely figure looking out on a dark scene of thunderclouds and bolts of lightning (Plate 3). She wrote:

The whole world has turned its back on me, so I sit here alone watching. I look outside my window and I see people dying! No one comes to help. Everyone just watches, so I sit here alone watching.

Her second picture transforms the despair and loneliness in a mass of large and small energy spirals that whirl about in a field of warm pinks and mauves (Plate 4). She wrote:

This picture is about happiness. There is [*sic*] so many things in life that put us down but we still have to continue living! We have to live every moment of life and enjoy it!

The feelings of abandonment and helplessness were answered by an influx of happiness and the desire to live life to the full in spite of the things that put her down. On the evaluation form she wrote that she was surprised by all the human qualities that appeared in her pictures.

A 13-year-old boy (Boy 3) experienced a similar reversal. His first picture is of a sad face floating in a sea of blue. On the back he wrote in capital letters: 'FEELING ALONE / FEELING ALONE' (Plate 5). His second picture is bilaterally symmetrical around an enormous sun over a tropical island, a place of paradisal beauty (Plate 6). He wrote: 'It is a beautiful day in an island. An island nobody knows about.' The pervasive blue of the first picture is now contained by the square patches of the sea and the circular clouds. Though still alone, he is now blissful and at peace. On the evaluation form he said that he learned about the association between colours and feelings: 'My feelings seem to mix in with the drawings. Now I know that I should use a lot of colours to change the mood of the painting.' The boy discovered the power of colour to symbolize his feelings, and then realized that making a picture was a means of working through those feelings. We often see pictures in which the children have written the names of the feelings beside the colours, so that a single picture may depict many different feelings. Of course, the particular correspondence between colours and feelings varies from child to child.

Teachers and parents note the effect of the programme on self-esteem. A 10-year-old boy (Boy 4) drew a picture of a small star inside a ring, with a larger, brighter star outside the ring and wrote a story about a star enclosed in a ring that wanted to be as bright as the other stars. The ring told him that it didn't matter if he was not as bright as the other stars. He shouldn't care what others think because he is a star. His teacher said that the boy was good at drawing from life but had no confidence in drawing from his imagination. Indeed, he wrote on the feedback form that he didn't think he was any good at making art 'from his head', but that the workshop had shown him that his imagination was creative. The teacher remarked that this boy had suffered from low self-esteem, but that he now accepted the fact that others thought he was a really good artist. He felt he had succeeded and now felt proud of his pictures.

These seven children, who were selected to illustrate particular themes, are typical of many hundreds who made two artworks that were strongly contrasted in imagery, design and feeling tone. Undergoing the deep structure of the creative process twice in close succession illustrates Jung's principle of enantiodromia, for the second picture as a rule brings forth images and feelings that provide a fresh insight and helpful perspective on the initial condition. Through creating, experiencing and sharing artwork in this way children discover that they have within themselves the transformative potential for furthering the individuation process.

The gender gap

The 284 students surveyed for the assessment were about equally divided between boys and girls, but their respective responses showed a few notable differences (Gee 2006: 18–22). The first question on the evaluation form asked the children to tick off words that described how they felt at the beginning of the workshop. The great majority selected the positive adjectives – 'excited', 'happy', interested' – but the few who ticked the neutral or negative adjectives – 'nervous', 'uninterested', 'scared' – showed differences according to gender. Of the 22 per cent who felt nervous, there was no statistical difference between boys and girls, but among the 12 per cent who were 'uninterested' there were four times as many boys as girls, and of the 7 per cent who were 'scared' there were nearly 2.5 times as many boys as girls. Thus, among the relatively few children who arrived with some resistance to the programme, boys greatly outnumbered girls.

The third question asked whether they were surprised by their first picture and to explain why; 30 per cent of the girls and 25 per cent of the boys were positively surprised by their first picture: 'It surprised me because I thought it would turn out horrible, but it turned out looking great' (girl, grade 5); 'It did surprise me because I was just working and all of a sudden I saw a beautiful picture' (girl, grade 5); 'It surprised me so much that it opened a world of happiness in my imagination' (boy, grade 5); 'It was the most good thing' (boy, grade 5). Among the 7 per cent who were negatively surprised, there were 2.5 times as many boys as girls: 'The first picture did not have good colours' (boy, grade 5); 'I thought I would have done better' (boy, grade 5); 'Cause it was horrible' (boy, grade 5); 'It was worse than I expected' (boy, grade 5).

Question four asked which of their two pictures they liked better. Among the 65 per cent who preferred the second picture there were slightly more boys than girls. Question five asked what they liked most about the programme and question six asked what they didn't like about the programme; 65 per cent of the girls and 50 per cent of the boys said they liked everything about the programme. This suggests that the boys who began with some resistance became more positive during the day. The seventh question asked what they learned about their imagination. Only 8 per cent said that they learned nothing about the imagination, but in that group there were four times as many boys as girls. Gee (2006) concluded that though the number of children who did not have a positive experience of the programme was very small, there is concern that many more boys than girls fell in this category. She recommended that more should be done to ensure that all boys have a good experience in the Exploring Creativity in Depth programme (ibid.: 22).

Art and imagination

Educators who subscribe to the cognitive model of development regard creativity as a product-oriented, outer-directed and expert-assessed activity. They think of art as the intentional and rational rearrangement of already known contents and of artworks as having explicit, discursive meanings that have been established by critics. The effects of this attitude are evident in children who come to the Exploring Creativity in Depth programme saying that they are no good at art because art has to be perfect.

Question eight on the evaluation form asked whether the programme changed their ideas about art; 67 per cent answered yes, and most of the rest explained that they answered no because they already liked art. Further comments about art: 'First I thought art was hard, now I feel good about it' (girl, grade 3); 'I thought you had to be neat in art' (boy, grade 4); 'I have learned more ways to do art' (boy, grade 5); 'Art is like imagination, it also has no limits' (girl, grade 5); 'Now I don't worry about what other people think of what my art turns out like'. About art and feelings: 'I learned I could use shapes and colours to experience my feelings' (boy, grade 5); 'I never knew you could draw what you felt' (girl, grade 5); 'Now I realize that art is anything you do to express yourself' (girl, grade 5); 'Now I am going to draw things in my life and what I feel like' (girl, grade 5). About interpretation: 'Now I see more in art than I did before' (girl, grade 5); 'It helped me expand my art ideas and the way you see it' (boy, grade 5). About empowerment and self-concept: 'I liked most when we experienced our talents' (boy, grade 4); 'I noticed that I am a good artist' (boy, grade 4); 'I have more confidence . . . I got to prove to myself how good I am at art' (boy, grade 5); 'It made me feel better about myself' (boy, grade 5); 'I learned to believe in yourself' (girl, grade 5); 'If you want to do something, you go for it' (boy, grade 5). To the ninth and last question, which asked whether they would like to take more courses in the arts, a remarkable 76 per cent said yes (Gee 2006: 9–14).

Learning about the imagination, hands-on experience of the creative process, and discovering that the interpretation of an artwork can vary from person to person shifts the attitude to art. When children realize that their imagination is unique and that they can give form to what they imagine, then art becomes a fascinating and powerful medium for aesthetic experience and meaningful communication. Removing the fear of making mistakes does not diminish the value of art as a core subject in the school curriculum. For the developing child the arts provide the richest possible medium for self-expression. When art instruction enables children to experience for themselves and share with others who they uniquely are, then, as Gee (2006: 10) observed, 'Art becomes something that students do for *their own substantial benefit.*'

Discovering the imagination

Nearly all the children (92 per cent) said that they learned something about their imagination (Gee 2006: 40), and their comments convey the importance of this discovery: 'I learned that I have an imagination because before I thought I didn't have one' (boy, grade 4); 'I learned that my imagination can go wild and it's not the same as anyone else's' (girl, grade 5); 'Your imagination has a world' (girl, grade 5); 'We can find stuff we never knew' (boy, grade 5); 'I learned that imagination literally has no limits' (girl, grade 5) (ibid.: 12).

The most remarkable finding of the programme is that children experience the imagination as a capacity of the mind that is distinct from rational cognition. The 9- and 10-year-olds said: 'The imagination can really open up to what you want if you open up too'; 'The imagination makes you think your picture is real'; 'I found out I know more than I knew I knew'; 'I learned that your imagination is a mind of its own'; 'That things that come out of your mind don't also have to be what you think'; 'The imagination can do more than we thought'; 'I learned about the imagination that I can go beyond "the box".' The 12- and 13-year-olds show a more sophisticated understanding of the relation of the imagination to directed thinking: 'I learned I have a lot of things stored up in my imagination waiting for me to imagine them'; 'What you think you see when you look at a painting isn't always what your mind and imagination and soul see.' They recognize that this new-found capacity of the mind is so valuable that they should take responsibility for it: 'My imagination can open doors for all kinds of arts and it's my job to use it'; 'I have many ideas and thoughts in my head that I should let out once in a while'; 'Your imagination will take you anywhere you want to go and you shouldn't be afraid to show that.' They understand that it is necessary to let go of normal directed thinking in order to liberate the creative imagination: 'I learned that I can do anything and to let my hand take over instead of my mind'; 'I learned a new method to start painting and that you can draw from your emotions'; 'I learned that our minds can construct things that we could never have thought of – this part of the programme was to go into the depths of our thought.' They learn that the imagination brings them in touch with their feelings: 'My imagination is crazy but has a lot of feelings and that I have a lot of love'; 'I found out the place I should go in my imagination when I'm sad, mad'; 'I learned that you can let all your feelings out and it can make something good.' They discover that their pictures provide a glimpse of their authentic selves: 'I never thought my imagination was so deep. I found out my artwork symbolizes me'; 'I found out that my ideas are really good and if I look into them I will be good.'

Discovering the creative imagination gives children the ability to mediate between the unique reality of their inner world and the consensual reality of the outer world. Subsuming inner and outer reality in a more comprehensive standpoint gives confidence and boosts self-esteem, for it enables the child to affirm his or her authentic self-hood in the face of the collective.

The dialectical mind

The philosopher Richard Kearney (1988, 1995) asserts that it is ever more urgent to educate the imagination in the postmodern world, saturated as it is with endlessly mutable and replaceable images. Kearney models the relationship between the individual and the other on the bond between the narrator of a personal story and the listener. 'The ethical imagination bids man to tell and retell the story of himself. And it does so not to shore up the illusion of self-sufficiency, but out of fidelity to the other' (Kearney 1988: 395). Telling and listening to personal stories transforms personal identity into the identity of the community. We must continually tell our stories as they unfold. 'The narrative relation of self to other – which imagination recollects from the historical past and projects into the historical future – is a story which cannot be brought to an end' (ibid.: 395–396). Telling and listening to authentic stories prevents us from falling into empty imitation. Kearney (1995: 91) calls for a 'hermeneutic dialectic between a critical *logos* and a creative *mythos*'. Understanding our personal myths is the basis for understanding the myths of community. 'For hermeneutic imagination, to be inside tradition is to be simultaneously outside. To imagine ourselves as we truly are is to imagine ourselves otherwise.'

The dialectic between creative mythos and critical logos is a crucial consequence of educating the creative imagination. After children recognize that the creative imagination affords a truthful and meaningful experience of their world, they learn to translate its symbolic language into the propositions and facts of critical, directed thinking, and vice versa. The effect of educating the creative imagination can be explained in terms of the model of the dialectical mind as described by the Jungian psychoanalyst Wolfgang Giegerich (2005). To begin with, the child experiences the 'I' as fixed, self-consistent and unitary; he or she sees no alternative to the 'I', and hence thinks that the 'I' is identical with itself. During the creative process the imagination throws up images and feelings that are surprising and captivating, authentic and meaningful. The 'I' experiences them as though they come from some 'not-I'.

The children say: 'I didn't know that that's what I would come up with', or, 'Our minds can construct things that we could never have thought of.' This leads to the recognition that the 'I' is not unitary, self-consistent, and identical with itself. During the sharing in the groups the children inquire into the meaning of their pictures, stories and poems. While discovering what the 'not-I' says about the 'I', the dialectic moves to the third stage in which the 'I' and the 'not-I' are subsumed in a more differentiated, inclusive, and resilient conscious standpoint. As Giegerich states, the 'realized Self is that status of consciousness that consciously exists as the complexity of this logical relation, but relation not in the sense of a static structure, but as the fluidity of a dialectical movement, as process and performance' (ibid.: 183). The increase in confidence and self-esteem that parents and teachers observe and that children themselves express suggests that the 'I' and the 'Other' are participating in an expanded concept of the Self. One child answered the question whether his ideas of art had changed, with 'Yes, I have a new perspective on things in life.' It would seem that he found a cognitive standpoint that comprised both the reason and the imagination. The programme had widened his mind's horizon.

Kearney (1995) points out that the dialectic between critical logos and creative mythos has an effect on the ethical imagination. Many children respond to the programme with the urge to reach out to others in friendship, kinship and love. Large, centrally placed hearts, flowers, trees, peace signs, rainbows and images of family make frequent appearances. The responses of the three girls discussed above are typical of many who express strong feelings for community. Arnold Modell (2003: 175) points out that the capacity for identifying with others rests on a paradox: 'that one is similar to the other and yet one remains oneself'. The relation to the other person is thus modelled on the paradox of the 'I' and the 'Other' that is encountered during the creative process. Modell (2003) affirms that the cognitive capacity to empathically know other minds relies on an unimpaired faculty for metaphoric thought: 'The acceptance of paradox assumes a capacity for metaphor – a cognitive capacity that allows for the play of similarity and difference' (ibid.: 176). The dialectic between the 'I' and the 'Other' within has consequences for the relationship between the 'I' and the 'Other' without.

Closing thoughts

Duke Theseus may still object to taking time away from educating 'cool reason', but Queen Hippolyta will continue to insist that 'the forms of things unknown' inform the child of his or her particular truth, and that the results 'grow to something of great constancy'. Moreover, she should add, it is not a zero-sum game, for we have seen that educating the imagination enhances the child's capacity and desire for learning. So let us urge Theseus and Hippolyta to renew their marriage vows and resume a lively partnership. The need is palpable. Nine out of ten teachers who bring their classes to the Exploring Creativity in Depth programme say that they would like to learn how to apply the techniques in their own classrooms. Moreover, they have asked us to adapt the programme for children as young as 6 and 7. They also indicate that they would like to apply the programme in literature, social studies, science and mathematics.

Although the Exploring Creativity in Depth programme has not been the subject of a formal study, the anecdotal evidence from five years of operation supports the finding that activating the creative imagination, engaging the deep structure of the creative process, and expressing the experience in artistic media has important benefits for children in elementary school. It seems that it is beneficial for children already in the primary years to be shown how to negotiate between outer reality and inner reality, the known and the unknown, the I and the Other, critical logos and creative mythos. As we continue to provide the programme in coming years, we hope to increase our knowledge of how to cultivate in children the dialectical mind.

References

Arieti, S. (1976) *Creativity: The Magic Synthesis*. New York: Basic Books.

Clarkson, A. (2003) A curriculum for the creative imagination. In T. Sullivan and L. Willingham (eds) *Creativity and Music Education*. Toronto: Canadian Music Educators' Association.

—— (2005a) Educating the creative imagination: A course design and its consequences. *Jung: The e-Journal of the Jungian Society for Scholarly Studies* 1(2) www.thejungiansociety.org (accessed 18 December 2007).

—— (2005b) Structures of fantasy and fantasies of structures: Engaging the aesthetic self. *Current Musicology* 79–80: 7–34.

Clarkson, A. and Worts, D. (2005) The animated muse: An interpretive program for creative viewing. *Curator: The Museum Journal* 48: 257–280.

Coleridge, S. T. (1950) The education of children. In I. A. Richards (ed.) *The Portable Coleridge*. Harmondsworth: Penguin.

Currie, G. and Ravenscroft, I. (2002) *Imagination in Philosophy and Psychology*. Oxford: Clarendon Press.

Dewey, J. (1958) *Art as Experience*. New York: Capricorn. (Original work published in 1934.)

Efland, A. D. (2002) *Art and Cognition: Integrating the Visual Arts in the Curriculum*. New York: Teachers College Press.

Egan, K. (1992) *Imagination in Teaching and Learning: The Middle School Years*. Chicago: University of Chicago Press.

Eisner, E. W. (2002) *The Arts and the Creation of Mind*. New Haven, CT: Yale University Press.

Frye, N. (1963) *The Educated Imagination*. Toronto: CBC Publications.

Gardner, H. (2006) *Multiple Intelligences: New Horizons*. New York: Basic Books.

Gee, J. (2006) *Arts Education for the Whole Child: An Assessment*. Toronto: Milkweed Collective.

Giegerich, W. (2005) Jung's thought of the self in the light of its underlying experience. In *The Neurosis of Psychology: Primary Papers towards a Critical Psychology* (Vol. 1). New Orleans, LA: Spring Journal Books.

Greene, M. (1995) *Releasing the Imagination: Essays on Education, the Arts, and Social Change*. San Francisco, CA: Jossey-Bass.

Harris, P. L. (2000) *The Work of the Imagination*. Oxford: Blackwell.

Hollis, J. (2000) *The Archetypal Imagination*. College Station, TX: Texas A&M University Press.

Hunt, H. T. (1995) *On the Nature of Consciousness: Cognitive, Phenomenological, and Transpersonal Perspectives*. New Haven, CT: Yale University Press.

Jones, R. M. (1968) *Fantasy and Feeling in Education*. New York: Harper and Row.

Jung, C. G. (1958) The transcendent function. *The Collected Works of C. G. Jung* (Vol. 8). Princeton, NJ: Princeton University Press. (Original work published in 1916).

—— (1971) Psychological types. *The Collected Works of C. G. Jung* (Vol. 6). Princeton, NJ: Princeton University Press. (Original work published in 1921.)

—— (1973) *C. G. Jung Letters* (Vol. I). Princeton, NJ: Princeton University Press. (Original work published in 1947.)

Kearney, R. (1988) *The Wake of Imagination: Toward a Postmodern Culture*. Minneapolis, MN: University of Minnesota Press.

—— (1995) *Poetics of Modernity: Toward a Hermeneutic Imagination*. Atlantic Highlands, NJ: Humanities Press.

Kessler, R. (2000) *The Soul of Education: Helping Students find Connections, Compassion, and Character at School*. Alexandria, VA: Association for Supervision and Curriculum Development.

Kohn, A. (2004) *What Does it Mean to be Well Educated? And More Essays on Standards, Grading, and Other Follies*. Boston: Beacon Press.

Langer, S. (1942) *Philosophy in a New Key*. Cambridge, MA: Harvard University Press.

Mayes, C. (2005) *Jung and Education: Elements of an Archetypal Pedagogy*. Lanham, MD: Rowman and Littlefield.

Meier, C. A. (1984) *The Unconscious in its Empirical Manifestations*, trans. E. Rolfe. Boston: Sigo Press.

Miller, J. P. (1996) *The Holistic Curriculum* (revised and expanded edition). Toronto: OISE Press.

Modell, A. H. (2003) *Imagination and the Mindful Brain*. Cambridge, MA: MIT Press.

Nemeroff, C. and Rozin, P. (2000) The makings of the magical mind: The nature and function of sympathetic magical thinking. In K. S. Rosengren, C. N. Johnson and P. L. Harris (eds) *Imagining the Impossible: Magical, Scientific, and Religious Thinking in Children*. Cambridge: Cambridge University Press.

Neville, B. (2005) *Educating Psyche: Emotion, Imagination and the Unconscious in Learning* (2nd edition). Greensborough, Victoria: Flat Chat Press.

Piaget, J. (1962) *Play, Dreams and Imitation in Childhood*. New York: Norton.

Reed, H. (1996a) Close encounters in the liminal zone: Experiments in imaginal communication, Part I. *Journal of Analytical Psychology* 41: 81–116.

—— (1996b) Close encounters in the liminal zone: Experiments in imaginal communication, Part II. *Journal of Analytical Psychology* 41: 203–226.

Schwartz, J. M. and Begley, S. (2002) *The Mind and the Brain: Neuroplasticity and the Power of Mental Force*. New York: Regan.

Schwartz-Salant, N. (1989) *The Borderline Personality: Vision and Healing*. Wilmette, IL: Chiron.

Von Franz, M.-L. (1983) On active imagination. In M. F. Keyes (ed.) *Inward Journey: Art as Therapy*. LaSalle, IL: Open Court.

Wallas, G. (1926) *The Art of Thought*. London: Jonathan Cape.

Weisberg, R. W. (1993) *Creativity: Beyond the Myth of Genius*. New York: W. H. Freeman.

Woodman, R. (2005) *Sanity, Madness, Transformation: The Psyche in Romanticism*. Toronto: University of Toronto Press.

Chapter 9

The symbol as teacher

Reflective practices and methodology in transformative education

Darrell Dobson

Central to the kind of education I want to discuss is an acceptance of the symbol as a teacher. Such a basis for facilitating educative experience remains a radical position in the context of western schooling practices, which have been founded upon industrial and positivistic values and practices, creating school systems based explicitly on the paradigms of industry and factories (Bobbitt 1918, 1924; Tyler 1949). Overvaluing these aspects of the human experience does not contribute to the healthful development of the whole human being or of human societies, and these values persist in public schooling systems today. Industry, commerce and an entrepreneurial culture continue to increase the pressure for education to justify itself through relevance to their values, such as standardization, competition, meritocracy and the protection of self-interest (O'Sullivan 2002). Students are considered more in terms of human capital or human resources than as persons; market demands dictate how to shape these 'raw materials' (Greene 1995). Education has become a process of training employees and consumers and preparing to compete in a global economy is now seen as the primary purpose of schooling our children (Miller 2000).

An impoverished understanding of science is also implemented in mainstream educational contexts, not as a subject matter but as guiding principles for all pedagogical endeavours (Eisner 2004). Our culture and educational systems are subjugated by an outdated scientific materialism and objectivism that suggest that the scientific method is the only acceptable way to control and understand reality, and that the only reality is physical, observable, testable – positions now brought into question even in the realm of science itself (Palmer 1998). But there remains a general sense in schools and society that reality is controllable through rapid technological advancement, which is prized, while meaningful personal development is ignored.

Within this dominant context there are a growing number of teachers and educational researchers who argue instead that the purpose of education is the student's intellectual, emotional, physical, social, creative, intuitive, aesthetic, moral and spiritual development (see, for instance, Miller 2001). Within the field of education, Jungian studies are only beginning to make an impact on research and practice. Education has integrated numerous psychological perspectives, especially behaviourist, cognitive, developmental and constructivist. Psychological researchers and theorists such as Piaget, Vygotsky and Maslow are well known to educators and educational researchers. Educational psychology tends to study how children learn through a focus on intelligence, motivation, achievement, development, self-concept and self-esteem. Egan (1986: 1) points out several characteristics of psychological knowledge common to teachers: 'children's learning proceeds from the concrete to the abstract, from the known to the unknown, from the simple to the complex, and from active manipulation to symbolic conceptualization.' Egan also argues that such principles lead to an inappropriately mechanistic way of thinking about teaching and learning and ignore the educational uses of children's imagination. The dominant psychological approaches to learning remained rooted in Enlightenment presuppositions and retain the limitations that inhere to such perspectives. The main limitation is that they focus primarily on the intellect and overlook or undervalue the influence of extra-rational aspects of human experience on the processes of human learning and development. Goleman's (1995) work on emotional intelligence and Gardner's (1983) research on multiple intelligence theory has begun to push against these boundaries. However, none of these perspectives considers the role of the unconscious mind, which exerts a profound influence on the intellect, emotions, imagination, intuitions, body and spirit – and thus on learning. Given over a hundred years of research, inquiry and theory relating the profound influence of the unconscious mind on human learning and development, it is folly for an education system that purports to pursue the goal of maximizing human potential, whether academic, economic, social, ethical, personal or spiritual, to so neglect the implications and beneficial potential of depth psychology.

This chapter is a summary of the findings of my PhD dissertation (Dobson, 2007), a qualitative inquiry I conducted into the professional knowledge and reflective practices of four teachers who promote transformative learning based on their long-standing personal and/or professional practice in analytical psychology and the arts. I focus on their approach to teachers' reflective practises and teaching methodologies. The first participant in the study is Ann Yeoman, a practising Jungian analyst who teaches Jungian studies and literature classes at undergraduate level at the University of Toronto. The second participant is Austin Clarkson, a musicologist who has created classes and workshops based on his experience and knowledge of analytical psychology (Clarkson 2002, 2005a, 2005b, 2006, in preparation; Clarkson and Worts 2005; see Clarkson's Chapter 8 in this book). These classes use artistic activities in order to facilitate the creative imagination and the individuation process and have been offered to fine arts majors and to students in both Bachelors and Masters of Education programmes. The third participant is Lily, a high school English teacher near the beginning of her career, and fourth is myself. I was a high school drama and English teacher for over ten years before and during graduate school. Lily is a pseudonym. Ann and Austin declined the option of anonymity.

Methodology

Narrative inquiry is a methodology of arts-informed qualitative research pioneered and developed by Connelly and Clandinin (e.g., Clandinin and Connelly 2000). In this methodology, narrative is both that which is studied and the means of conveying the findings; narrative is 'phenomena under study and method of study' (ibid.: 4). My research uses the stories and self-reflections of its participants as data. Human beings lead fundamentally storied lives; we do not just tell stories but rather we 'lead storied lives on storied landscapes' (ibid.: 8). Narrative and story are foundational means of knowing; they are a paradigm of meaning creation, a powerful and basic means of making sense of experience (Polkinghorne 1988). Human beings experience the world narratively, and education is understood to be the construction and reconstruction of personal and social stories. Since experience is understood narratively, narrative inquiry is the most appropriate way to research experience. Further, according to Clandinin and Connelly (2000), the telling and retelling, construction and reconstruction, of stories, facilitates change and can be understood as one example of Dewey's (1938) emphasis on the reconstruction of experience as educative. In narrative inquiry researchers and participants acknowledge the temporal quality of the research and its findings, and recognize that the experiences represented therein are subject to reinterpretation and reconstruction and that the research begins and ends in the midst of an ongoing process of professional and personal development.

The primary method of data collection in this study is interviewing the participants, a long-established method of collecting qualitative data and a recognized and appropriate method of arts-based, qualitative research, including narrative inquiry (Connelly and Clandinin 1986; Dobson 2005). This study uses the method of unstructured interview, a process by which each researcher uses somewhat unique elements and often does so in distinctive combinations, and in which creative interviewers adapt to the particularity of each participant and situation in an interview process that might take place over many days in multiple sessions. Three three-hour open-ended interviews were conducted with each participant over a period of six to twelve months. Interviews were taped and transcribed.

I also collected data by observing each participant in teaching situations for at least five hours and read any related books, articles or unpublished manuscripts written by the participants. In addition, I recorded my observations, thoughts, reflections and ideas in a professional journal. The results of such an inquiry provide insight and knowledge without pretending to be a representation of an 'objective reality'. According to Eisner (1991):

No narrative that seeks to portray life experience can be identical to the experience itself; editing, emphasizing and neglecting through selection are all ineluctably at play. Hence we seek not a mirror but a tale, a revelation, or a portrayal of what we think is important to say about what we have come to know. This narrative should be supported by evidence, structurally corroborated and coherent, but ... [t]here is no telling it like it is, for in the telling, there is making. The task is to do justice to the situation and yet recognize that all stories, including those in the natural sciences are fabrications – things made.

(Eisner 1991: 191)

Narrative inquiry is a collaborative and relational research process. Consultation with the participants takes place over written materials through a sharing of interim texts. Participants received and commented on the Interim Narrative, a 30–40 page document created after the second interview, and the Final Narrative, a 30–50 page document created after the third interview. This process allowed the participants to collaborate in a dialogical fashion on the construction of the findings of the study. The emphasis here is less on the accurate reporting of 'what happened' but rather more on the portrayal of the participants' identity and knowledge (Ellis and Bochner 2000).

Archetypal reflectivity

Teacher reflectivity has become significant to practice and research in teacher education and development. Influenced by Dewey (1933), Schon (1983) and others, a body of literature has developed that centres around teacher reflectivity as a response to competency-based methods of training teachers in skills and knowledge. In contemporary research and practice, teacher reflectivity has come to refer to the numerous processes by which teachers respond to the dilemmas or opportunities of their teaching contexts. Reflectivity involves a meta-cognitive process by which educators increase their awareness of the implicit attitudes, beliefs and knowledge that inform their practice – in order to transform their practice. In this reflective approach to teacher education and development, in-service and pre-service teachers consider influences that contribute to their professional knowledge and practice. These usually tacit filters serve to accept or reject the experiences and understandings encountered both in teacher education programmes and in practice. Reflective practices help teachers to analyse their values and beliefs in order to more effectively identify and seek to address the problems they encounter in their work. Strategies used tend to include journal-keeping, autobiographical writing, seminar dialogues, action research projects, and debriefing after practice (Knowles 1993; Valli 1993).

That description of teacher reflectivity is similar to Mezirow's (1991) definition of transformative learning as a process by which previously uncritically assimilated assumptions, beliefs, values and perspectives are questioned and thereby become more open, permeable and better validated. Viewing teacher reflectivity as a form of transformative learning provides a new perspective on emerging developments in the field. Just as Dirkx critiques Mezirow's exclusionary emphasis on intellectual analysis (Dirkx et al. 2006), so have researchers in teacher reflectivity begun to consider the role of the extra-rational. Teacher reflectivity tends to focus on the pedagogical, biographical and political dimensions of teacher knowledge and practice (Mayes 1999). However, Tremmel (1993) argues that much of what passes as reflective practice remains limited by its ongoing reliance on the scientific analysis and 'technical rationality' critiqued by Schon (1983), who emphasizes the role of intuition and artistry in reflective practice. Valli (1993) also finds that the programmes of teacher reflectivity tend to value 'an analytical method that stresses objectivity and emotional detachment' (ibid.: 19), and she argues that emotion, intuition and contemplation must serve a role in reflective practice. LaBosky (1991) suggests that an emotional reaction or sudden intuition can serve as the impetus to reflection, and can serve as Dewey's 'felt difficulty', a state of hesitation, perplexity or doubt that instigates reflection. LaBosky (1991: 34) writes, 'I suggest that . . . flashes of inspiration and creative insights or intuitions function within the framework as a potential impetus for reflection. They may operate similarly to 'felt difficulties' but in a more positive sense'. Below, I return to these arguments in a discussion of 'archetypal reflectivity'.

The findings of the current inquiry concur with Mayes' extension of teacher reflectivity into the transpersonal and psychospiritual domains through the concept and practices of 'archetypal reflectivity' (Mayes 1999 2002, 2003, 2005a, 2005b). Mayes introduces 'archetypal reflectivity' because

> In addition to reflecting biographically and politically . . . it is at least equally important that teachers be able to refresh themselves emotionally and spiritually by reflecting on their work in timeless, transpersonal terms. Seeing their teaching as integral to their transpersonal quest helps teachers satisfy their hunger for the mana of 'psychic rewards' which is arguably their primary motivation for teaching.
>
> (Mayes 1999: 13)

Mayes argues that the omission of the transpersonal dimension from teacher reflectivity limits its effectiveness, and he describes practices in which the archetypes of hero, sage, ogre, clown, Icarus, shaman, spirit and shadow can contribute to new ways both to understand teacher practice and to enact oneself more authentically and effectively as a teacher. In these ways, teacher education and educational research has begun to catch up with Jung, who in the early 1950s argued that the primary focus of teacher education and development should be the personal or psychological development of the teacher (Jung 1954).

My inquiry further illustrates how the use of archetypes can provide a more powerful experience of reflectivity and transformation, and it contributes to the developing field of archetypal reflectivity in its expansion of the archetypes used as stimuli and frame for reflective practices (such as teacher-student, facilitator, judge, artist, shaman, Royal, Warrior, Magician, Lover, as well as individual mythic figures such as Gulnara, Ash and Perceval). For the participants in my inquiry, archetypal images make available practical alternatives as the participants plan and carry out their work as teachers. These images allow them to recognize their conduct and outlook in the past and present, and the images serve as a source of possibility and promise as they look ahead. They find that reflecting on archetypal images can contribute to new ways to understand their practice as teachers and to new means to enact themselves more genuinely and effectively as teachers. The participants are aware of the dangers of over-identifying with an archetype, which they describe as ego-inflation and a restricted ability to notice the shadows in the image.

I want to differentiate several possible methods of archetypal reflectivity. In the first, the instructor suggests using a particular archetype for investigating the nature of professional knowledge and practice – as Mayes (2005b) does with the shaman, I do with the Royal, Warrior, Magician, Lover (Dobson 2006; cf. Moore and Gillette 1990), and Neville (2005) does with the Greek gods. Similarly, Rosenstein (2002) uses Disney's *The Sorcerer's Apprentice* to illustrate Schon's (1983) concepts of knowing-in-action, reflection-in-action and reflection-on-action. Here, the speaker, instructor or author informs the group, class or reader about the obvious and subtle ways in which interacting with this archetype exemplifies the author's reflective practice and hopefully illuminates aspects of teachers' professional knowledge and practice in general.

In the second approach to archetypal teacher reflectivity, teachers could be asked to consider the ways in which an archetype – say the mature archetypes and immature bipolar shadows of the Royal, Warrior, Magician and Lover – manifest in their teaching. Or based on Mayes' (2005a) work, teachers could be asked to reflect on how the archetype of the hero and the hero's journey illustrates their experience as learners and teachers. Neapolitan (2004) provides a fruitful example of just this kind of analysis and synthesis in an article entitled 'Doing professional development school work: A tale of heroes, allies and dragons at the door'. This means of teacher reflectivity is similar to the uses made of metaphor and image in teacher education, development, and research (Munby 1986; Bullough 1991; Hunt 2001; Perry and Cooper 2001). Connelly and Clandinin's (1988) description of an 'image' bears significant resemblances to Jungian perspectives on symbols and archetypes:

> By image we mean something within our experience, embodied in us as persons and expressed and enacted in our practices and actions.

Situations call forth our images from our narratives of experience, and these images are available to us as guides to future action. An image reaches into the past, gathering up experiential threads meaningfully connected to the present. And it reaches intentionally into the future and creates new meaningfully connected threads as situations are experienced and new situations anticipated from the perspective of the image. Thus, images are part of our past, called forth by situations in which we act in the present, and are guides to our future. Images as they are embodied in us entail emotion, morality, and aesthetics.

(Connelly and Clandinin 1988: 60)

Clandinin (1985), for instance, helps her research participant make explicit the tacit images that inform her teaching. Bullough (1991) describes practices of asking his teacher education students to identify a metaphor that conveys the essence of their teaching identity and attitudes. Perry and Cooper (2001) illustrate how women educators have used metaphor to explain change in their work lives. This is a helpful and informative approach to teacher reflectivity that tends to either draw on or concur with Lakoff and Johnson's (1980) work on 'metaphors we live by'. There is a similarity between Jung and Lakoff and Johnson in their shared assertion of the wide symbolic or meta-phorical underpinnings of most and perhaps all thought, belief, and action. This argument is also made by Northrop Frye (1983). However, there is a vital distinction to be drawn here between the work of Lakoff and Johnson (and Frye) and that of Jung. For Lakoff and Johnson (1980) and Frye (1983), interaction with metaphors occurs on a fairly conscious, rational level – by this I mean there is no deliberate acknowledgement of the role of the unconscious mind in the process. Generally, the meaning of the metaphors is understood to be fairly clear. Metaphors used in this way are more like what Jung would call signs (Jung 1956 [1952]: para. 180). A related but even more significant difference is that for Jung, symbols reveal meaning and purpose that guide the increasingly conscious development of personal and professional identity. They are transformative in intent. This element is missing in Lakoff and Johnson (1980) and in Frye (1983).

The third approach to archetypal reflectivity therefore involves methods of accessing the unconscious, the innermost Self, in practices of teacher reflectivity in a manner that augments, without replacing, rational analysis. In this way, it seems to me that archetypal teacher reflectivity can most effectively be a practice of transformative learning. To access the full trans-formative potential of archetypal reflectivity, experiences must be undergone that allow the teacher or teacher candidate to encounter and interact with spontaneously generated images. Here, I return to the assertions of Schon (1983), LaBosky (1991) and Valli (1993) that intuition, emotion, contempla-tion, inspiration and creative insight ought to play more of a role in teachers' reflective practices.

The symbolic communications of the Self do not manifest only in images; they also present through the emotions, intuitions and physical symptoms. In this view, there is an extra-rational logic at work in the emotions and intuitions that can be valued as an impetus to reflective practice. The idea that inspiration and creative insight can and ought to play more of a role in reflective practice concurs with Austin Clarkson's use of exercises in active imagination, meditative visualizations and creative activities such as drawing, painting, writing, drama and mask-making to facilitate archetypal teacher reflectivity as a kind of transformative learning. Analysis of the meaning of aesthetic experiences, by which I mean considering one's responses to arts-centred experiences, suggests another extra-rational means of initiating archetypal reflectivity (Dobson 2004, forthcoming). In Austin's examples, the symbol is created by the individual; in my own example, the symbol is apprehended as the participant becomes aware of projections and inquiries into their nature. The images thus encountered are transformative in nature and purpose – they arise in order to direct personal and professional development. Drawing on the perspective of the unconscious mind allows the current or prospective teacher to discover and work with a symbol that inherently seeks to guide the personal and professional development of the individual at a unique, deep and authentic level. This inquiry suggests an approach to archetypal teacher reflectivity that includes an extra-rational and highly individualized dimension in the choosing of an archetype. It would be more apt to say that educative experiences need to be created that allow the archetype that chooses the individual to be encountered and engaged consciously.

Either of the first two methods of archetypal reflectivity described above could further facilitate transformative learning if more opportunity were made for participants to choose and interact with the images. For instance, after an introduction, the participants then work with one of the twelve images of the mature and immature Royal, Warrior, Magician or Lover. A participant chooses the one for which she feels the strongest affinity or revulsion (by confronting her revulsion she would thereby work on shadow issues). Or she could choose and work on the element of the hero's journey she feels is most relevant to her as a learner and teacher. As long as the participants are provided with an opportunity for choice and encouraged to follow their intuition or feelings rather than merely their intellect – as long as projection is allowed to function in the matter of making the choice – the image may then function as a symbol.

Methods of transformative learning

According to the participants in this inquiry, there is no one correct method of transformative learning. In their experience, both traditional and progressive teaching methods can be used to create conditions conducive to transformative education. However, for the participants, transformative learning tends to involve the four steps:

1   *Creation:* the formation of, apprehension of, or interaction with symbols felt to be personally relevant to the student.
2   *Reflection:* intellectual rumination upon the personal and archetypal meanings of the symbols and conscious analysis of previously incorporated attitudes.
3   *Integration:* the emergence of a more expansive, integrated, and differentiated conscious attitude.
4   *Action:* the taking of action in the midst of daily life that enacts this renewed perspective.

In the methods they use, participants seek to provide opportunities and support for each of these steps. The first two elements, creation and reflection, are relatively easy to facilitate in the classroom. The second two elements, integration and action or application, require substantial self-directed learning and action on the part of students. The process is rarely linear and often is characterized by multiple movements between and betwixt phases and is marked by pauses, returns and repetitions. The practice spirals forward as the completion of one round leads into the beginning of the next.

Traditional methods

In general, Ann's classroom is similar to other university English classrooms and Lily's is similar to other high school English classes. Students read pieces of literature and discuss them with each other and with the teacher. Students take turns presenting seminars or presentations on the work being studied. Students write large and small essays. The teaching methodology is mainly Socratic questioning interspersed with mini-lectures on relevant aspects of the course content. In using traditional teaching methods, these teachers promote the first step of transformative learning, the creation or apprehension of symbols, when they choose works to study that are symbolically rich, like myth, fairytale or literature. In studying such pieces, these teachers provide as much opportunity for individual choice as possible, either in the works studied or in the process of analysis, such as study questions, assignments, essay topics, seminar interests, group work and class discussion. These teachers promote as much freedom as possible – within the practical boundaries of systemic education – in order to encourage students to encounter the experience as meaningful. Student aesthetic response is itself understood symbolically as projection or transference – as an indicator of latent potential seeking to emerge.

These teachers address the second phase of transformative learning, reflection upon the symbolic content, when they use analytical psychology as an interpretive lens for exploring the literature. For instance, Ann follows von Franz when she suggests approaching literature with the hypothesis that every piece 'is a relatively closed system compounding one essential psychological meaning, which is expressed in a series of symbolic pictures and events and is discoverable in these' (von Franz 1970: 2). This means that, for Ann, a piece of literature addresses a transformation or attempted transformation of consciousness that is communicated using symbols, the language and grammar of the unconscious mind. Ann therefore understands that the beginning of a literary work tends to present a problem that provides the purpose for the story. Like von Franz, her approach is to describe the problem from a psychological point of view rather than from a literary perspective. The introduction will set up a problem, an imbalance or one-sidedness, that needs to be rectified, and the story will be a symbolic attempt to work through the problem. She understands that not all stories successfully resolve the problem presented, even when the tale states that the ending is happy. Ann's process of literary analysis involves investigating the symbols and amplifying the material, which entails considering comparative material from other sources, such as mythology, fairytales and other works of literature or art. Amplification means 'enlarging through collecting a quantity of parallels' (von Franz 1970: 43). Then Ann translates the amplified story into psychological language.

In Ann's approach, a story can be interpreted on many levels, including the 'intra-psychic', where the entire contents of the narrative are considered as symbolic manifestations of a single person's psyche. The story then symbolizes an attempt at personal transformation. The whole tale could also portray the psychic situation of the society or collective from whence it springs. The story then symbolizes an attempt at social transformation. The tale could also be considered as a symbolic manifestation of a family's psychic situation, or as if the protagonist were an actual person. The tale works on all of these levels, and possibly more, at once.

While Ann engages in such literary analysis, she is careful to remember that the symbolic nature of the narrative prevents any interpretation from being comprehensive or exclusively correct. There is always more to be discovered in the story. Ann cautions against considering any interpretation to be definitive or complete, and understands that her interpretations are relative. Ann asserts that any interpretation is partial and situated, affected by the psychic location and sociocultural context of the teacher and students.

In their use of traditional teaching methods, these teachers hope to facilitate the third phase of transformative learning, integration resulting in a new attitude, through the course activities: the discussions, activities, assignments and projects. They also hope that, as the course continues, these same avenues may serve the fourth phase of transformative learning, through taking action based on a renewed perspective. For instance, a stance taken in a class discussion is a kind of action, as is the topic chosen for an essay or class presentation.

Experiential methods

Each of these teachers also uses progressive methods of teaching and learning. Lily and Ann both use dramatic enactments of course material, and Lily and Austin use group projects and cooperative learning activities. I use drama activities and improvisation while teaching both secondary drama and English classes. Austin's extensive use of experiential teaching methodologies includes a variety of creative, arts-based approaches, including mask-making, puppet-making, storytelling, drawing, painting, collage, sculpture, movement, dance and song. Austin also uses the creative and experiential methods of active imagination and visualization. These experiential activities are used effectively in the first phase of transformative learning: creation. Active imagination and the arts-based activities, such as mask-making, drawing and puppet-making, encourage the formation of spontaneously generated symbols and provide further opportunity to interact with and explore the symbols.

The experiential first phase is then followed by reflection, the second phase of transformative learning, involving analysis of the personal and archetypal meanings of the symbols created by the students and conscious analysis of previously incorporated attitudes. Here, Austin again relies on more traditional teaching methods, such as class discussion, mini-lectures, research, reading and journal writing.

All of these educators use experiential activities in the hope that any of the traditional or experiential methods will promote integration, the third phase of transformative learning, the emergence of a new conscious attitude. According to Austin, almost all of the participants in his creativity classes report the discovery of a new insight in their final performances. This new perspective might emerge slowly and only after great struggle and moral effort, or it may burst forth in full flower. It may develop during a reflective period or during an experiential exercise. It may not ripen for days, weeks, years after the course finishes, or it may never emerge at all. The new attitude is more comprehensive – it allows the student to see more and more clearly. It is more integrated, in that aspects of the personality that have been left out or left behind are brought in. It is more differentiated, so that which was murky is clearer, that which was unformed is further shaped. This is not merely a change in an intellectual stance, though it likely includes such an adjustment. It is holistic in nature, and so also involves the emotions, intuition, body, ethics, aesthetics and spirit.

The experiential activities and traditional assignments also provide an opportunity for the fourth phase of transformative learning, the taking of action based on a new perspective. This is true throughout the course and particularly true of summative or final projects and assignments. Here, the students have an opportunity to enact their new perspectives experientially in a performance or through writing in a more traditional assignment or evaluation. Once again the four phases of transformative learning are rarely experienced in a linear fashion. As well, a student may feel that she is enacting her new perspective in her final project only to discover – in the very midst of the project or performance – a further nuance to her understanding or a new symbol arising – and so the cycle may begin again.

These educators use experiential methods as much as possible in order to provide educative experiences for their students. They assert that transformative learning can not be merely intellectual in nature and that experiential activities are used to appeal to, and draw out, more of each student's active and latent potential. Such activities allow students to draw on the strengths of their psychological type preferences, and they also provide a safe structure for exploring the students' less developed functions. Activities are planned so as to provide a flow of experience through each of the functions and attitudes, asking students to draw on intuition, sensation, feeling, thinking, extraversion and introversion. The holistic and experiential nature of such encounters regularly possesses what students describe as spiritual or numinous qualities and the shared quality of the classroom experience can contribute to an experience of communitas (Turner 1995 [1969]), a sense of cohesion within the group that transcends – without erasing – particularity.

The symbol as teacher

Austin uses the metaphor of the 'image as teacher' to convey his knowledge of the role symbols play in the process of transformative learning:

> The core learning is to gain a trust in the image, to accept the image as your teacher, which requires breaking through the ego-controlled attitude that insists there is nothing beyond the ego's horizon. To trust that the unconscious has messages for the conscious mind that it had better wake up and learn about. Trust that the Self has a more comprehensive view of what is going on than the ego does. Trust that it is for the best. You can only come into contact with the Self through images, and it involves activating the ego-Self axis, Edinger's (1972) model, which is easy to explain but difficult to experience. The Self is seeking to reconnect with the ego through images, even though the ego may not know it. The ego has to step aside and let happen that which should happen – as indicated by the Self through the images. If you do establish that confidence, you don't see such a partial view; you can see more of the whole picture. You can then trust the things that are happening even though you don't control them. This is a big learning: to trust the images and not the concepts. A symbolic attitude is something that can be learned if it hasn't come naturally somehow, and it is the symbolic attitude – an acceptance of images as sources of symbolic guidance – which makes it possible to find the correspondences between the inner and outer life.
>
> (Interview 2, 22 August 2006)

The participants in this study have faith in the symbol as a teacher because they follow Jung in experiencing and understanding the Self as the centre and the circumference of the total personality, which includes both the conscious and unconscious dimensions (Jung 1953: para. 41). For the participants, the Self is the fundamental generative force of the entire psyche, the ultimate psychic authority. The language and grammar of communication from the Self are symbolic, and these images are directed toward the actualization of the innate, latent potential of the individual. The images are teachers because they arise from the comprehensive perspective of the Self in order to compensate the inevitable one-sideness of the conscious ego. The participants concur with Jung's position that developing such a symbolic attitude involves understanding a symbol as 'an expression of an intuitive idea that cannot yet be formulated in any other or better way' (Jung 1966[1931]: para. 105). The symbol can become a teacher through the process of linking personal associations with archetypal amplifications of an image.

Here is an example from the larger study in which I reflect on my interest in the Grail story of Parzival (de Troyes 1987 [ca. 1170–1190]; Wolfram 2004 [1200]) and learn to consider that image as a teacher. My awareness of my transference or projection onto the literary figure stimulated a time of reflection on the nature and role of masculinity in my ongoing personal and professional development. Learning from the symbol involves a process of linking personal associations and archetypal amplifications of the image. As part of the process of amplifying the image I drew on Moore's description of the archetypes of the Royal, Warrior, Magician and Lover (Moore and Gillette 1990; Moore 2006). At various times throughout the myth Parzival exemplifies the mature and immature forms of each of these archetypes. I considered my personal associations and these archetypal amplifications in the context of my teaching and investigated the ways in which my professional knowledge and practice also exemplified the mature and immature forms of these archetypes.

For instance, I found Parzival to be a relevant role model of the Warrior archetype, in that he not only protects the innocent, but also diverts the rebel Kingrun into the service of King Arthur and the company of the Knights of the Round Table. I understood this scene as a symbolic representation of the high school teacher's task with the 'disruptive' student. Here is an excerpt from my professional journal kept in the larger study:

> In my grade 11 drama class, during a lesson based around theatrical movement, Kent refused to concentrate on the activity, and his comments, laughter, and attitude were interfering with the ability of the other students to engage in it. Having taught high school for ten years, I can easily imagine how this incident might have worked itself out earlier in my career. I might have asked Kent to stop his behaviour, and he might have done so for a few minutes and then continued to be disruptive as

soon as my attention focused on someone or something else. This cycle might have continued until I grew frustrated and felt that Kent's behaviour was a personal insult. I might have soon believed I had no choice but to send Kent to the office.

Instead, I called Kent aside, out of the activity, while the others continued. Kent and I stood by the side of the theatre, while the rest of the class continued a small group movement exercise: four students stood in a diamond shape and mirrored the movements of the leader through space, using a variety of levels and seeking to have the movement look choreographed, with all of the members in sync, rather than the improvisation that it was. It was now going well, and the class resembled a park full of T'ai Chi practitioners. Kent leaned his shoulder against the theatre door, body language and face defensive.

I quietly said, 'Look Kent, I like you. I think you are smart and talented. I don't have any problem with your need to be rebellious. There are lots of things in our lives against which we need to rebel, but I also can't have you interfering with the learning of the others. Instead of using your need to rebel to subvert whatever we are doing, use what we are doing as an instrument of that rebellion. Make it the content of any and every activity, if you need to do so.'

Kent looked relieved – and surprised. He raised his eyebrows, looked at me as if I was a bit peculiar, and said, 'Ookaaay.' He returned to his group, and when it was his turn to lead, he created movements that were angular, grotesque, and angry. There were no more 'classroom management' issues that day, and Kent was able to express and explore a vital aspect of his burgeoning identity – within the safe container and appropriate boundaries of the drama activity.

I consciously kept the image of Parzival as mature Warrior in my mind during this 'classroom management' incident with Kent. Like Parzival, I was focused on protecting the others but also on diverting Kent's energy into the service of the grail quest. It was clear to me that Kent himself was potentially a knight of the round table and that I should treat him as such. I believe that Kent and I both found the encounter and its outcome to be satisfactory – perhaps even satisfying. In this way I trusted the image of Parzival as a teacher that could guide my professional and personal development.

Conclusion

The teachers in this study are all seeking to promote transformative learning. They are each attempting to create educative conditions that encourage increased consciousness, that facilitate altered and expanded attitudes. They hope to draw out a renewed perspective that is more genuine, relational, vigorous and spiritual in nature, one that aligns the inner and the outer lives, as well as the personal and the social lives. For these educators, transformative education involves the development of a symbolic attitude, one that promotes the perspective that each person has a particular and individual nature, and that this nature has an agenda of its own, separate from conscious intention. Transformative learning leads to the development of perspectives that are more comprehensive, integrated and differentiated.

According to the participants, transformative learning promotes individuation. Individuation is an inherently holistic process, as it leads to a further integration of thought, feeling, intuition and sensation. It is the process of incorporating and transcending the apparent dichotomies of body and spirit, matter and mind, secular and sacred. In a seeming paradox, the participants argue that each of these elements retains and enhances its own particularity as it is incorporated into a more complex and integrated perspective. This kind of learning leads to relationships that are more authentic, respectful, caring and just. It promotes deepening relations with family, community and nature – not to isolation. It leads to humility, not self-absorption. The participants assert that transformative learning as a process of individuation leads students and teachers towards a state of increasing wholeness, a condition that is advanced but never reached. In this view, individuation is a process, not an end state. There are notable advances but no completion.

In order to promote transformative learning, the participants teach for understanding, for depth, not for breadth, facts, or accepted ideas. For these teachers, skills and knowledge are not gained in isolation, or for merely utilitarian purposes; they are acquired in service to individuation, in a context made meaningful through understanding. Skills and knowledge are obtained in a context that considers and values the extent to which they make individual and social life more meaningful and authentic. The focus is on a depth of engagement with the content that leads to a renewed understanding of human nature and so of one's own nature.

The professional knowledge of these teachers centres around their understanding of the symbol as teacher. The synthesis of their personal and professional expertise in analytical psychology and the arts results in understandings and practices that are unique within the research literature in fields of teacher education and development. Based on this qualitative inquiry with these four teachers, this study has suggested original approaches to archetypal reflectivity and teaching methodology in the pursuit of transformative learning at the elementary, secondary, undergraduate and graduate levels. Situated firmly in the midst of the challenges and joys of their daily teaching practices, these maverick educators attempt to transcend the one-sidedness of the dominant collective approaches to public education by enacting stories contrary to the prevailing institutional narratives. Ann reminds us why they do so:

We may turn to art to learn better how to create and continually recreate ourselves, and to remember that the fully and consciously lived life is a life of deeply committed symbolic action.

(Yeoman 1998: 119)

References

Bobbitt, J. F. (1918) *The Curriculum*. Boston, MA: Houghton Mifflin.

—— (1924) *How to Make a Curriculum*. Boston, MA: Houghton Mifflin.

Bullough, R. V. (1991) Exploring personal teaching metaphors in preservice teacher education. *Journal of Teacher Education* 42: 43–51.

Clandinin, D. J. (1985) Personal, practical knowledge: A study of teachers' classroom images. *Curriculum Inquiry* 15: 361–385.

Clandinin, D. J. and Connelly, F. M. (2000) *Narrative Inquiry: Experience and Story in Qualitative Research*. San Francisco, CA: Jossey-Bass.

Clarkson, A. (2002) A curriculum for the creative imagination. In T. Sullivan and L. Willingham (eds) *Creativity and Music Education*. Edmonton. Alberta: Canadian Music Educators' Association.

—— (2005a) Educating the creative imagination: A course design and its consequences. *Jung: The e-Journal of the Jungian Society for Scholarly Studies* 1(2) www.thejungiansociety.org (accessed 18 December 2007).

—— (2005b) Structures of fantasy and fantasies of structures: Engaging the aesthetic self. *Current Musicology* 79–80: 7–34.

—— (2006) Exploring creativity in depth: Assessment of an elementary school program for activating the creative imagination. Paper presented at the Conference of the Jungian Society for Scholarly Studies, June 2006, Toronto, Ontario.

—— (in preparation) The intelligence of the imagination: Personal stories of the creative process.

Clarkson, A. and Worts, D. (2005) The animated muse: An interpretive program for creative viewing. *Curator: The Museum Journal* 48: 257–280.

Connelly, F. M. and Clandinin, D. J. (1986) On narrative method, personal philosophy, and narrative unities in the story of teaching. *Journal of Research in Science Teaching* 23: 292–310.

—— (1988) *Teachers as Curriculum Planners: Narratives of Experience*. New York: Teachers College Press.

De Troyes, C. (1987) *Arthurian Romances*. London: Everyman's Library.

Dewey, J. (1933) *How We Think: A Restatement of the Relation of Reflective Thinking to the Educative Process*. Boston: D. C. Heath.

—— (1938) *Experience and Education*. New York: Collier Macmillan.

Dirkx, J., Mezirow, J. and Cranton, P. (2006) Musings and reflections on the meaning, context, and process of transformative learning: A dialogue between John M. Dirkx and Jack Mezirow. *Journal of Transformative Education* 4: 123–139.

Dobson, D. (2004) Aesthetic experience and the transformation of self: The mature masculine. Paper presented at the Conference of the Jungian Society for Scholarly Studies, August 2004, Newport, Rhode Island.

—— (2005) From spotlight to fluorescent bulb: aesthetic dimensions of personal, practical knowledge in an actor training to be a high school teacher. *Research in Drama Education* 10: 327–340.

—— (2006) Royal, Warrior, Magician, Lover: Images of teachers' professional knowledge. Paper presented at the Conference of the Jungian Society for Scholarly Studies, June 2006, Toronto, Ontario.

—— (2007) Transformative learning: Constructing professional knowledge through interacting narratives. PhD thesis. Toronto: Ontario Institute for Studies in Education, University of Toronto.

—— (forthcoming) Seeking the mature masculine in pop culture and high art. In J. Baumlin, K. Polette and S. Porterfield (eds) *Perpetual Adolescence: Jung and Contemporary American Culture*. Albany, NY: State University of New York Press.

Edinger, E. (1972) *Ego and Archetype: Individuation and the Religious Function of the Psyche*. London: Shambhala.

Egan, K. (1986) *Teaching as Storytelling: An Alternative Approach to Teaching and Curriculum in the Elementary School*. London, Ontario: Althouse Press.

Eisner, E. (1991) *The Enlightened Eye: Qualitative Inquiry and the Enhancement of Educational Practice*. New York: Macmillan.

—— (2004) What can education learn from the arts about the practice of education? *International Journal of Education and the Arts* 5(4) http://ijea.asu.edu.v5n4/ (accessed 20 October 2004).

Ellis, C. and Bochner, A. (2000) Autoethnography, personal narrative, reflexivity. In N. Denzin and S. Yvonna (eds) *Handbook of Qualitative Research* (2nd edition). Thousand Oaks, CA: Sage.

Frye, N. (1983) Literature as a critique of pure reason. *Descant* 14(2): 7–21.

Gardner, H. (1983) *Frames of Mind: The Theory of Multiple Intelligences* (10th anniversary edition). New York: Basic Books.

Goleman, D. (1995) *Emotional Intelligence: Why it Can Matter More than IQ*. New York: Bantam.

Greene, M. (1995) *Releasing the Imagination: Essays on Education, the Arts, and Social Change*. San Francisco, CA: Jossey-Boss.

Hunt, C. (2001) Shifting shadows: Metaphors and maps for facilitating reflective practice. *Reflective Practice* 2: 275–287.

Jung, C. G. (1953) Psychology and alchemy. *The Collected Works of C. G. Jung* (Vol. 12). Princeton, NJ: Princeton University Press.

—— (1954) The development of personality. *The Collected Works of C. G. Jung* (Vol. 17). Princeton, NJ: Princeton University Press.

—— (1956) Symbols of transformation. *The Collected Works of C. G. Jung* (Vol. 5). Princeton, NJ: Princeton University Press. (Original work published in 1952.)

—— (1966) On the relation of analytical psychology to poetry. *The Collected Works of C. G. Jung* (Vol. 15). Princeton, NJ: Princeton University Press. (Original work published in 1931.)

Knowles, J. G. (1993) Life-history accounts as mirrors: A practical avenue for the conceptualization of reflection in teacher education. In J. Calderhead and P. Gates (eds) *Conceptualizing Reflection in Teacher Development*. London: Falmer.

LaBosky, V. (1991) A conceptual framework for reflection in preservice teacher education. In J. Calderhead and P. Gates (eds) *Conceptualizing Reflection in Teacher Development*. London: Falmer.

Lakoff, G. and Johnson, M. (1980) *Metaphors We Live By*. Chicago, IL: University of Chicago Press.

Mayes, C. (1999) Reflecting on the archetypes of teaching. *Teaching Education* 10: 3–16.

—— (2002) The teacher as an archetype of spirit. *Journal of Curriculum Studies* 34: 699–718.

—— (2003) Alchemy and the teacher. *Teacher Education Quarterly* 30(3): 81–98.

—— (2005a) *Jung and Education: Elements of an Archetypal Pedagogy*. Toronto: Rowman and Littlefield Education.

—— (2005b) The teacher as shaman. *Journal of Curriculum Studies* 37: 329–348.

Mezirow, J. (1991) *Transformative Dimensions of Adult Learning*. San Francisco, CA: Jossey-Bass.

Miller, J. (2000) *Education and the Soul: Toward a Spiritual Curriculum*. Albany, NY: State University of New York Press.

—— (2001) *The Holistic Curriculum* (revised and expanded edition). Toronto: OISE Press.

Moore, R. (2006) A way forward for Jungian psychoanalysis and research: Elements for a neo-Jungian structural psychoanalysis. Paper presented at the Conference of the Jungian Society for Scholarly Studies, June 2006, Toronto, Ontario.

Moore, R. and Gillette, D. (1990) *King, Warrior, Magician, Lover: Rediscovering the Archetypes of the Mature Masculine*. New York: HarperCollins.

Munby, H. (1986) Metaphor in the thinking of teachers: An exploratory study. *Journal of Curriculum Studies* 18: 197–209.

Neapolitan, J. E. (2004) Doing professional development school work: A tale of heroes, allies and dragons at the door. *Reflective Practice* 5: 79–90.

Neville, B. (2005) *Educating Psyche: Emotion, Imagination and the Unconscious in Learning* (2nd edition). Greensborough, Victoria: Flat Chat Press.

O'Sullivan, E. (ed.) (2002) *Expanding the Boundaries of Transformative Learning: Essays on Theory and Praxis*. New York: Palgrave.

Palmer, P. J. (1998) *The Courage to Teach*. San Francisco, CA: Jossey-Bass.

Perry, C. and Cooper, M. (2001) Metaphors are good mirrors: Reflecting on change for teacher educators. *Reflective Practice* 2: 41–45.

Polkinghorne, D. E. (1988) *Narrative Knowing and the Human Sciences*. Albany, NY: State University of New York Press.

Rosenstein, B. (2002) The Sorcerer's Apprentice and the reflective practitioner. *Reflective Practice* 3: 255–261.

Schon, D. (1983) *The Reflective Practitioner: How Professionals Think in Action*. New York: Basic Books.

Tremmel, R. (1993) Zen and the art of reflective practice in teacher education. *Harvard Educational Review* 63: 434–458.

Turner, V. (1995) *The Ritual Process: Structure and Anti-structure*. Hawthorne, NY: Aldine de Gruyter. (Original work published in 1969.)

Tyler, R. W. (1949) *Basic Principles of Curriculum and Instruction*. Chicago: University of Chicago Press.

Valli, L. (1993) Reflective teacher education programs: An analysis of case studies. In J. Calderhead and P. Gates (eds) *Conceptualizing Reflection in Teacher Development*. London: Falmer.

Von Franz, M.-L. (1970) *The Interpretation of Fairy Tales*. London: Shambala.

Wolfram, V. E. (2004) *Parzival*. London: Penguin. (Original work published in 1200.)

Yeoman, A. (1998) *Now or Neverland: Peter Pan and the Myth of Eternal Youth*. Toronto: Inner City Books.

Chapter 10

Arts-informed learning in manager-leader development

Sue Congram

> When we create artistically to learn more about ourselves, we open to laughter, tears, anger, fear, excitement, and wonderment. Rarely are we left empty handed or untouched.
>
> (Barry 1996: 411)

Conventional management and leadership learning has paid little attention to the self or encouraged reflective practice in the management-leader role. Instead greater emphasis has, until now, been given to the role incumbents' capabilities in meeting practical and measurable imperatives. In the workplace the potential contribution of imagination has been greatly subordinated by know-how. That is until now; it appears that the arts are confronting the borders that created this split. Adler (2006) describes how the arts are inspiring creative and improvisational skills with corporate leaders and that leading business schools worldwide are beginning to add arts-based courses to their curriculum. The corporate world is beginning to take interest in the human capacity for imagination and the value of imaginative learning methods (Nissley 2002; Darsø 2004), but what is arts-based or arts-informed learning and what added benefits can it bring to management education?

In this chapter I use the term arts-informed learning to broadly refer to ways that the arts can be used in management and leadership learning. Similar terms are also used in the literature such as arts-based learning, arts-centred learning and arts-informed inquiry (McNiff 1998; Nissley and Jusela 2001; Nissley 2002; Adler 2006). All of these terms imply that there is a process of bringing together the arts and a discipline outside of the arts, such as management development, where the arts inform and assist learning in that discipline. The arts can be organized to facilitate and inspire learning in a number of ways:

- Art as an inspiration for leadership; visiting galleries, reading, listening to music and being involved with stage performance, painting and creative photography.

- Art as metaphor for leadership; such as through theatre work and Shakespeare (e.g., Olivier 2001; Olivier Mythodrama, www.oliviermythodrama.com; The Praxis Centre www.thepraxiscentre.com; Arts and Business, www.aandb.org), storytelling (Gabriel 2000), the orchestra conductor as a metaphor for organizational leadership (Koivunen 2003) and jazz improvisation (Barrett 1998).
- Using the arts such as poetry (Whyte 2004) for learning interventions to illustrate points, and for knowledge creation (Nissley and Jusela 2001).
- Engaging in art as a process of inquiry and as representation of unconscious, unknown and unspoken material in context of the role in the workplace (Edwards 1995).

The last two approaches were used in the professional development programme discussed here. Examples of how they were used are described throughout the chapter. This programme was for manager-leader development; that is, people in management roles with leadership responsibility. My colleague, Josie Gould, and I designed a programme based on arts-informed learning. As a photographer, artist and personal development coach, Josie brought a wealth of experience to the programme, combined with my many years' experience of management and leader development, using a Gestalt-centred approach. Additionally, we had both studied Jung through a long-term programme with Jungian analyst, Marion Woodman (www.mwoodmanfoundation.org), experiencing the practice of deep personal work using active imagination and the arts.

This chapter describes how the rich combination of arts-informed learning, active imagination and Gestalt-centred learning informed the design and facilitation of the manager-leader programme outlined here, ending with some reflections on the potential benefits to management and leadership education through arts-informed learning.

The programme outline

The programme sought to balance the development of conventional practices of management education, *doing*, with development of the self and reflective practice, *being*, through arts-informed learning. *Doing* and *being* were two strong interweaving threads that formed the basis of the six-module programme.

The programme was aimed at developing women in management, in a region of the UK where the number of women in management positions was statistically low. In view of this the programme was funded through European Social Funds, which meant providing a qualification on completion of the programme. We established this through the Institute of Leadership and Management (ILM). In order to enter the programme, women had to be either already in a management role, working towards this in their career, or managing their own business. Eighty-five women in total participated in the programme. Each programme ran for six modules over a period of nine to twelve weeks. We ran several programmes over a period of twelve months. All the women had available to them group and one-to-one tutoring for a management project, which they had to undertake and write up as part of the qualification requirements. The qualification meant that those entering the programme were expected to meet learning objectives, which were assessed against measures set by the ILM. It also meant that we, as leaders of the programme, had to meet required standards in the way that we managed and facilitated the programme. A written report of a work-based project needed to demonstrate a capability of putting together a clear, well-presented document (as a manager would need to do in practice) as part of the qualification requirements.

The function of the arts

The function of art was central to learning within every aspect of the programme design. Body movement, mask work, visual art, poetry and storytelling were used so as to facilitate active imagination towards the development of the self. Towards developing management knowledge and skills, we designed arts-based activities in visioning, problem solving, planning change, Force Field Analysis, decision-making and leadership. So, every aspect of teaching included some form of art, exercising both logic and creative modes of learning. We built on the idea of *being* and *doing* in the manager-leader role, maintaining a focus on these two interweaving threads throughout the programme and developing an appreciation of how one impacts the other. Women entering the programme knew that it was arts-based but did not know how learning would be achieved.

The arts methods we used were all linked to learning objectives, as follows.

Pencil drawing, pastels and painting

Drawing and painting provided methods for learning core management skills such as visioning, problem solving, decision-making and planning change. For example, we taught students how to represent feelings and emotions through free expression, using pencil, pastel and paints (Edwards 1995). They learned how to be curious, to ask open questions, and to observe and 'read' their work without analysis, such as to notice how lines changed, differed in their appearance and moved in different ways across the paper, to discover the relationship between different aspects of the picture, and with the whole image. This leads to perceiving issues in a different way, changing perspectives and adding new meaning. I illustrate this in a problem solving exercise later in the chapter.

Poetry

We used poetry as a facilitative tool to accentuate learning, or as novelty to enliven learning. In talking about the way that literary arts can support learning, Nissley (2002: 39) states that 'the novel provides a vehicle for bringing the subject matter to life in a way that can make it easier for students to explore the experience of managing and organizing'.

David Whyte (2004), a poet, believes that people connect with poetry at a profound level when a poet reflects deeply on issues that concern him or her personally. In that deep place within, a connection is made with collective concerns that are reflected in the poetry (ibid.). In my experience, students feel significantly seen when a few lines of a poem are appropriately used to reflect their personal struggles and insights.

Storytelling

A particularly insightful moment for me was watching Nicola Shindler (2002) giving the Huw Wheldon Memorial Lecture on television in 2002. In that lecture she illustrated the difference between *plot* and *story*, modifying a distinction which was originally given by Forster (1974 [1927]). According to Forster, a story (an archaic term for history) is a chronicle of events arranged in a time-sequence, whereas a plot (*mythos*) tells us why it happened. His famous example: 'The king died, then the queen died' is a story; 'The king died, and then the queen died of grief' is a plot (ibid.: 60). Shindler paraphrased Forster's example but reversed the terminology, defining *plot* as what happens, and *story* as why it happens and what it means to the people involved. I adopt Shindler's usage below. The distinction is perhaps self-evident to writers and filmmakers, but hearing Shindler make it with fluency and inspiration has set me thinking about what this means in the workplace. There is a question here about whether the responsibility of the manager-leader is to add 'story' to the 'corporate plot' (the strategy, vision and stated values); for example, to create a great place to work. Although we did not set out to teach this as such on the programme, we invited a 'story' to be told early in the programme, and to experience how much more engaging that is than reporting facts.

Journaling

Journaling is a private exercise, which we encouraged. Written as a *text* it bridges imagery with language, recording reflections, insights and internal thoughts. Journaling in *images*, such as through drawing, painting and photography, can free thought and rational thinking, representing feelings and personal learning imaginatively and aesthetically. Journaling is not simply keeping a diary; it is a private record of learning, questioning and personal insight. The process of journaling encourages reflective practice, can educate imagination and often brings new meaning.

Mask work

There were two reasons for designing mask work into the programme – for development of self, and linking this with the manager-leader role in an imaginative way. Creating the mask was the main process used for active imagination. The purpose of the mask work and active imagination was to bring into consciousness the 'unlived life': the side of a woman that she has not, or cannot let free. In my coaching work with women in management and leadership roles, a large number of women have described feeling like their 'wings are clipped', 'being locked in a cage', or wanting to release a 'free spiritedness and freedom to be themselves' in their work. When addressing this issue in groups, mask work offers an imaginative way for women to take steps to change this and to discover what that means in life and work.

We used a gum-strip method for making the mask (Foreman 1999) so the basic shape of every mask was unique. The colourful features of the mask developed out of earlier artwork. As I explain later, in active imagination the image 'comes up' from the unconscious, which gives form to the mask. An alternative would have been to develop the mask through imaginative expression of known aspects of the self, such as the 'persona' mask (ibid.). There are many ways of working with mask; the direction is determined by the objective of the exercise.

Movement and dance

The body has held no place in the history of management and leadership education, but psychology and personal development professions know that the body and body awareness play a significant role in learning, in imagination and in life (Berry 1982; Woodman and Dickinson 1996; Parlett 2002).

On the programme, we worked with the body from the beginning to bring body awareness in as a meaningful source of learning. Movement, supported by music, facilitated the first stage of active imagination, and *authentic movement*, a process where the mover is witnessed (Wyman-McGinty 1998; Stromsted 2001), aided a clearer focus to the authentic inner experience of the emerging mask qualities. Finally, working with gesture sharpened and imprinted meaning from the mask, as a form of integration.

Jung's concept of active imagination

The concept of active imagination was one of Jung's major contributions to analytic practice. It is a process of bringing to consciousness deeply authentic aspects of the self and integrating these into life, a process of individuation.

Individuation is a term that Jung used to describe personality development: 'A person's becoming himself, whole, indivisible and distinct from other people' (Samuels et al. 1986: 76).

Jung differentiated between two forms of imaginative practice. He related *imaginative activity* to the personal and conscious expectations, linking fantasy and invention, to 'the surface of personal things and conscious expectations' (Jung 1976b [1935]: para. 397). He related *active imagination* to the deeper unconscious where 'images have a life of their own and . . . symbolic events develop according to their own logic' (ibid.: para. 397). A distinction between surface activity and depth leads to a differentiation between sign and symbol (Schaverien 2005). This differentiation is particularly significant for arts-informed learning. *Motifs*, such as a heart, tree or house, which are signs, are closer to life experiences and involve personal memory, whereas *symbols*, which are more abstract and indefinable, touch depth, do not require explanation, are not dependent on personal memory, and are understood to be deeply held in the body. In our learning methods, our interest was to engage the unknown and to represent that through art, working with abstract forms and discouraging the use of known motifs.

There is another distinction to be made in active imagination that is between analytic *method* and analysis as a *process*. My reason for wanting to emphasize this distinction is that transforming unconscious material to conscious meaning is not methodological in a way that human consciousness can determine or control. Jung seems to have been in many minds on this point, referring to the concept of active imagination as a 'method', 'technique' and a 'natural process' over the years that he developed this analytic practice (Chodorow 1997).

On the other hand, a wide range of different *methods* can be used to facilitate the process of active imagination, such as art, dance, poetry and, in our programme, mask work. Jung encouraged his patients to engage in dance, movement, painting, poetry and drawing or mandala. Chodorow (1997) provides a useful resource of key readings on active imagination from Jung's *Collected Works*, where examples could be found, such as a reference to women dancing mandalas (Chodorow 1997: 78): 'Among my patients I have come across cases of women who did not draw mandalas but danced them instead. In India there is a special name for this: *mandala nrythia*, the mandala dance' (Jung 1976a [1929]: para. 32).

Jung structured active imagination into two stages.

Stage 1: a meditative process to let the image come up

In this process, suspension of the ego takes place and the body is able to connect to its own rhythms. As Jung describes it, ' when we concentrate on an inner picture, and when we are careful not to interrupt the natural flow of events, our unconscious will produce a series of images which make a complete picture' (1976b [1935]: para. 398). Furthermore, 'when we concentrate on an inner picture, and when we are careful not to interrupt the natural flow of events, our unconscious will produce a series of images which make a complete picture' (ibid.: para. 398). Woodman (1993: 35) writes about the image in terms of energy located in the body, such as an impulse: 'I look at a work (drawing, painting, a poem, whatever the analysand presents) to try to locate the energy and to discover where the energy wants to go. Where is the energy blocked if it is blocked?' Bringing the image and the felt experience into form, into an outer picture, enables the experience to become meaningful.

Stage 2: living it in life

This stage is a process of making meaning of the experience and integrating emerging insights into life. When new insights arrive they tend to carry high energy and vibrancy in their owner. Other issues pushing for attention become an aside for a while until a new balance is established in the life of the student. In this second stage the unconscious image meets the ego as it comes into consciousness. In Jungian terms, that positions the ego in a vital role, initially *identifying* with the archetypal image. Schaverien (1999: 23) describes a process similar to this in analytical art psychotherapy where 'the picture becomes an embodiment of the processes which operate within the individual'. The student then moves into a *relationship* with the picture and, in doing so differentiates from it. This is demonstrated through the difference between a student saying 'I am this image' and 'I can relate to qualities of this image in me'. Becoming fixated in or paralysed by the identification, 'I am this image', can become pathological. Jung established that 'the characteristic feature of a pathological reaction is, above all, *identification with the archetype*. This produces a sort of inflation' (Jung 1968 [1950]: para. 621, italics in the original). So, although identification is a necessary part of the process it can also be problematic. As a way of avoiding this problem, Schaverien (1999) recommends five stages through which this process of differentiation needs to go through – identification, familiarization, acknowledgement, assimilation and disposal – arguing that this is far from a linear process and may take place over a few hours through to months or years.

Facilitating mask work in active imagination

There is a deep, cultural and anthropological background associated with masks, with connections to the spiritual world and the divine. Nowadays, masks continue to be regarded as sacred objects in parts of Africa, Central and South America and Asia, where they are worn in tribal rituals and healing ceremonies. In the west, the major significance of the mask tends to be theatrical where the mask both reveals and conceals, and in festivals or carnivals as dynamic art forms. A comprehensive study of the origins of mask is beyond the scope of this chapter, but as a facilitator of this work, history tells me that the mythological and the spiritual is deeply rooted in the symbolism of mask, whether I choose to explicitly work with it with students, or not. So the learning potential for mask work in education is wide-ranging and linked to learning objectives. Students can enjoy the gifts of their own imaginative activity and personality in mask work, just as they can explore the depths of their individuality.

The starting point of active imagination is in the body, where 'energy' is located in a mood, a feeling, a sense, an emotional state, an impulse. On the programme we started the mask work through a meditative process followed by dance and movement. In this process the women (unknowingly at the time) were 'letting an image come up'. The feelings and emotions generated through movement were taken into free-expression painting and eventually into a mask. To put this in context of the programme, body movement and art form were facilitated on the first module, and the mask developed in relation to the original art form, on the second module a week or two later.

When completed, we worked with the original painting and the mask as an inter-connecting whole to inform learning in the management role. An example of a mask and connecting artwork is shown in Figure 10.1. This is the work of a student on the programme, who has since successfully established a life coaching business.

Students naturally identify with their artwork as it emerges, where the mask image and student are very connected. I catch myself in awe as I observe this process; it is beautiful to watch and to see the emerging form of each mask. This is the process of *identification* with the emerging mask image – the 'I am this mask' described earlier. Facilitating a process of inquiry at this point opens up an interrelational space between the mask and the student and the potential for separation. I see my work here as guiding the student to observe and experience, in the body, the fully formed image in front of them. So, students would explore a single line, a colour, shape or artefact from the mask and ask 'What is this in me? What are the gestures and feelings that I experience?' and 'How might the quality I experience with this line appear in my work and life?' The focus of learning at this stage is in developing a relational practice with the mask.

Our task on the programme was to facilitate a process where the women could begin to understand and integrate the new meaning represented in the mask. Our goal wasn't to force understanding, but to teach a process of experimenting and testing out the essential qualities of the mask in the context of working life. We achieved this by imagining how the represented qualities in the mask/self might react to real life management issues.

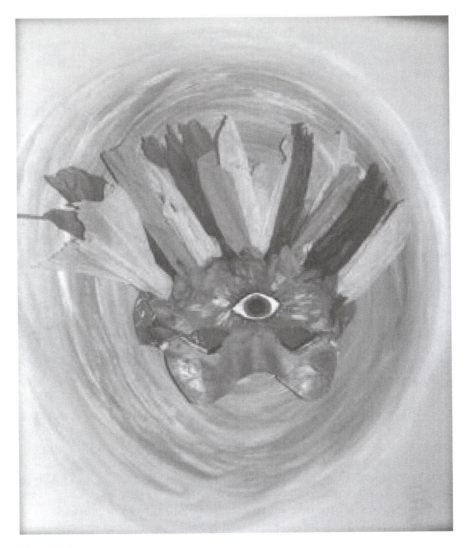

Figure 10.1

Gestalt: the facilitator as artist and educator

Gestalt-centred learning has informed my consultancy work for many years. I was attracted to Gestalt in the mid-1980s, for its imaginative interventions, diversity, use of artistic materials and drawing methods from the arts (Zinker 1978; Spagnuolo Lobb and Amendt-Lyon 2003). At the heart of Gestalt theory and practice is creative licence, which means not only permission to be creative in the therapeutic or educational context, but also greater *freedom* to be creative. Gestalt-centred learning works from the heart of the practitioner's creative capacity and draws on the imagination of the student.

Like Jungian psychology, Gestalt-centred learning is interested in bringing unconscious material into *consciousness*, but in Gestalt the term *awareness* is more widely used. Definitions of these two different terms are variable and problematic (Stern 2004). Stern describes *consciousness* as 'the process of being aware that you are aware', which requires self-reflection, and *awareness* as concerned with 'a mental focusing on an object of experience' (ibid.: 123). The term *awareness* as it is commonly used in Gestalt is a process of being aware of an experience in the here-and-now *and* becoming aware of that awareness.

Having evolved out of Gestalt therapy (Perls et al. 1951; Clarkson and Mackewn 1993; Spagnuolo Lobb and Amendt-Lyon 2003), Gestalt-centred learning offers a holistic approach to education. There is no scope here to provide full details of the Gestalt framework; instead, I will describe five distinct elements of Gestalt-centred learning in this context: response-ability, relating, self-reflecting, imagining and experimenting, and embodying. These five elements are informed by a progressive approach of Gestalt-centred learning originally conceived by Parlett (2002, 2003) as 'five abilities'.

Response-ability

A particular skill of the manager-leader is the ability to respond to whatever situation he or she is faced with. That means making the best of opportunities, taking risks and being creative towards problems, decisions and obstacles that get in the way. It also means recognizing that nothing occurs in isolation, and that there is a wider phenomenological field which impacts on imagination, attitudes, choices and decisions (Parlett 2003). We all respond differently to the challenges that life throws at us; our ability to refine this process and to adapt requires us to become more aware of how we respond in the moment when we most fully experience a situation, without prejudice. The ability to respond is deeply connected to 'empowerment, to taking authority and response-ability for one's own life' (ibid.: 55). In our programme, it was also about taking empowerment, authority and responsibility in the manager-leader role.

Paying attention to the here-and-now is a valuable strength of gestalt-centred learning. Educational interventions guide the student towards focused awareness and self-reflection in a way that is close to the flow of experience. Reflecting observations, or attending to 'what is', facilitates learning using an approach in Gestalt described as the *paradoxical theory of change*. Gestalt tends not to be diagnostic or prescriptive in its approach to learning, instead trusting the ability of the individual to adapt and change through awareness of 'what is' and through self-reflection.

Throughout the programme, we would heighten 'responding' awareness in the group by inviting the women 'to notice what happens as you . . .' or we would reflect an observation, 'what I notice is . . .'. We would work with the whole group and individuals in this way, a method that the group also used in coaching each other on the programme. In a more focused way, attention to response-ability was brought out in the mask work described earlier, when the women imagined how the qualities in the mask might react to work situations.

Relating

In the workplace relationships are important, and the skill to relate to others at all levels in the manager-leader role is essential. Learning to discuss, debate, share concerns, really listen, articulate well, give feedback, collaborate, lead teams, deal with conflict, inclusion and communicating ideas, all involve relating, whether it is face-to-face, on the phone, through written reports or by email. Particularly today, it is well known that managing all these forms of communication is necessary, and that email is no substitute for the benefits gained from face-to-face contact.

The notion of 'contact' is important here, the Gestalt view is to establish and build good quality contact in the process of relating. Contact in this sense means the level at which a person engages with others and with life. At a surface level contact is objective, clichéd, practical, intellectual, there-and-then rather than here-and-now. At a deeper level contact becomes subjective, personal, emotional, intimate, profound, centred in the here-and-now, and at the deepest level, spiritual. There is no judgement about right or wrong levels of contact; the learning is in developing a wide range of contact capabilities, choice-fullness and discernment, within any given situation. Most of us have a preferred way of relating to the world that we tend to stick to until it no longer works for us, or we decide to expand our range of capabilities. Work cultures tend to invite formal, clichéd and intellectualised conversation. The rich fabric of more personal, imaginative, humorous and intimate contact disappears into the drapes and folds of cultural norms. The Gestalt challenge is to bring personal preferences and social norms into the awareness of students and question them, perhaps experiment and test out different possibilities.

On the programme many of the arts-based activities carried relational learning potential in a variety of ways. For example, one of the first exercises that the women engaged in was in small groups where they each told a story about themselves to their group. They were asked to tell a story about what inspired them to come on the programme and what they wanted to learn from it, while another member of the group noted down the main story lines and key words as it was being told, as a reflective record for the storyteller. By bringing in the arts and personalizing exercises in this way, greater meaning is attached to learning and to relating; the range of contact, and therefore the range of learning, becomes expansive.

Self-reflecting

In the wider field of learning there are a range of terms that are linked to self-reflecting such as self-awareness, self-understanding and self-recognizing. These are outcomes from self-reflection, and have in common the ability to be aware of one's self as an active agent in relation to the social and physical world, also, to know what is happening internally, such as imaginings, thoughts, feelings, physical sensations, as the ongoing connection with the outer world is made. This idea is not unique to Gestalt, what Gestalt brings to learning is to observe, and reflect on the fine, subtle, telltale signs which indicate when the potential for quality 'contact' is interrupted and when it is at its best.

Imagination plays a key role in self-reflection and in making meaning of the inner world. Imagination can also lead to an either inflated or diminished view of one's self. For example a number of women on our programme reported feeling 'not good enough' in their job, with a fear of being 'found out'. This overactive self-critical thinking is made worse by an inflated view of others, such as believing the other to be more skilled, knowledgeable and experienced than reality. The ability to know the difference between fiction and fact, to be able to shift from imaginings to observing 'what is', is necessary for healthy self-reflection. Pencil drawing, mentioned earlier and described in the next section, teaches students how to make detailed observations of a piece of artwork and develops skills for seeing 'what is'. Facilitating this process means keeping students aware of their observations and how shapes, images and interpretations occur in the imagination which are not in the drawing. The learning for students is in developing awareness of the ongoing flow of experience, not in a right or wrong way of doing the exercise.

However, it was in the mask work that we were able to build and grow a positive self-view. In this sense a little inflation goes a long way as long as the process is facilitated towards a 'relational' outcome.

My experience as a facilitator has shown me many times that some of the most powerful learning can be achieved through imaginative, contactful, interventions, in response to a momentary flicker of an interruption to healthy self-reflection in the student. The work of the facilitator is itself art-full.

Imagining and experimenting

Improvising, as in jazz or improv theatre, is pure experimenting. In other fields of activity it is 'to fly by the seat of one's pants' or 'to make it up as you go along'.

(Parlett 2003: 61)

Gestalt-centred learning is achieved through experiential and experimental practice, so facilitation is often highly improvisational. This requires imagination by the facilitators at many levels: in designing learning activities, in creating the right environment for learning, in their relationship with students, building trust and support to enable learning, and in responding to emerging group needs. The idea of experiment refers to testing something out in a new way; breaking old patterns through trying new possibilities. This process requires imagination between the facilitator and the student; it is co-created, not prescriptive, and cannot be planned in advance. Although unformed, working in this way is not wildly chaotic, but calls for focused attention (ibid.). An experiment develops out of the relationship between the student/s and facilitator/s and is intended to take a further or deeper step in learning.

The following example from our programme illustrates how a well-developed exercise becomes an experiment, where improvisation takes a student's exploration to a deeper level.

The exercise is an arts-based technique developed by Edwards (1995), which she calls 'Upside-Down Problem Solving'. A problem or issue is reflected on, and then represented on white paper using a pencil or charcoal within a frame, as shown in Figure 10.2. This is achieved through the simplest of movements (not known images or motifs).

Building on a process of observation and inquiry, the image is explored

Figure 10.2

and understood for what it is in terms of space, shapes, relationship, texture, movement and connectedness. This is written down. The observational commentary for the picture above started like this:

> I see ribbon-like shapes of different sizes they look like they are moving and connected to a central filled black sphere. The picture looks three dimensional, there is shadow and light which gives it depth and movement, there are also very strong spiky lines connecting to the centre, except for three that appear to have broken away and are flying off. The ribbons also seem to be breaking away and flying off.
>
> I wonder what the black centre is, it looks strong and revolving, with ribbon circling around it, opening in places against the movement of the ribbons and spikes. The whole image appears to be moving. The spikes and ribbons are not connected; they look like they are flying out of the picture at me – fast. That's how this problem feels, I don't feel in control of the situation.

These observations continue into the finer detail, keeping close to the observed image rather than the problem at hand. When complete the students are asked to turn the paper upside down, and to repeat the observation exercise, but this time noticing differences compared to the first perspective (see Figure 10.3).

Figure 10.3

One of the observations noted down from this upside-down perspective was:

> I see ribbons and spikes, but this time they appear to be moving towards the centre rather than away from the centre, like a magnetic pull. There is a ribbon coming in from the bottom left. I wonder if it is moving into that empty space, as though it is the missing piece of a puzzle. The movement is considered and flowing. This is significant. I had not realised this before.

This exercise can yield transformative insights towards the original problem. The particular point that Edwards (1995) brings attention to is in seeing 'life' problems from an abstract upside-down perspective.

We improvised with our students by inviting them to imagine what might happen next in their picture. We asked: 'Where are the impulses?', 'What direction are lines and shapes going?' Staying with the picture rather than intellectualizing the problem, they took bigger sheets of paper and extended the upside-down image beyond the boundary of the original frame and paper. Finally each student added a simple colour or artefact somewhere to the picture in a way that symbolised a resonance. Some women danced the image forward.

The real value of experiment is that the new insight is always there to be known, the artwork and the experiment do not produce the new perspective but aid a process of reflection, imagination and seeing the problem in a different way.

Embodying

Embodying means taking in and living what we learn and believe. It also means listening to the messages in the body – the gut feel, intuition, a deep sense – and being informed by those messages. Gestalt-centred learning means more than drawing on purely mental skills, it involves the body and engages learning through experience. The difference between being embodied or not in Gestalt terms lies in the extent to which rational living has taken over from embodied living. Arts-informed learning is well placed to assist this process. Parlett (2003) is concise in his assertions when saying that the arts involve the whole body. I don't think that any artist would disagree with him on this. But this is not just about students learning through arts-based experiential methods. It is also about students not only discovering how to be interested in the physical reactions of others, their emotional and physiological processes, without judgement or interpretation, but also learning how to listen to their own emotional and physiological inner world in response to the outer world. 'To know from the inside what embodying is' (ibid.: 59) means to respond to the messages that are available only through the body, such as intuition.

The use of the arts accentuates learning through experience, through the body. On the programme, our facilitation reinforced this. We reflected back our sense of the group process, we encouraged movement and engagement with the body, and we developed exercises that invited self-awareness. Significantly, in the mask work we avoided intellectual meaning making, working with the body throughout and only engaging rational thinking at the point of integrating the mask qualities with life and workplace issues.

So . . .

What added benefits can management education gain from the arts? Art therapists, Jungian analysts and Gestalt-centred practitioners have long known that the arts can offer compelling ways to frame current understandings, much more than straight reasoning can achieve. On the programme described in this chapter, arts-informed learning facilitated a wide range of learning that conventional methods do not seek to cover; such as educating the imagination, development of the self/Self, self reflection, raising into consciousness the unspoken and the unknown, widening perceptions and linking together *being* and *doing*. The full value of arts-informed learning leans towards the human contribution rather than the practical, operational, skill-based, knowledge-driven, aspects of management learning. So the arts offer access to new meaning making, a different vantage point with wider perspectives for management and leadership learning, just as Jungian psychology and Gestalt offer different ways to understand human experience. For me this is like walking around a mountain; I can see changing contours and wider landscapes from many different vantage points, but I can't possibly see the whole mountain by standing in one place. In that sense, the value added by arts-informed learning is unquestionable.

There is a growing wave of research and increasing recognition of arts-informed learning in management education; much of this is usefully documented by Adler (2006) and Nissley (2002). As Nissley points out, this wave of interest also increases the need for adequately trained arts-based practitioners, which raises questions as to what is meant by 'adequate training', what does a facilitator need to learn in order to effectively use the arts to facilitate learning? This is an area that could greatly benefit from wider research, but my personal reflections on co-facilitating these programmes have reinforced the value of working with my artist colleague, and the potential advantages of bringing together artists and people in professional roles in a learning capacity. What is more, when viewing the art process from an archetypal or Gestalt perspective, art-making activities take on a new importance as an agent of learning and exploring the unknown, requiring additional knowledge, skills and experience. Significantly when considering facilitation training, both Jungian and Gestalt practices are non-directive, process oriented and engage a mode of inquiry. Whether the facilitator is

Jungian-centred, Gestalt-centred or other-centred is a professional choice and will influence the direction of learning. It seems to me that the fundamental skills of a facilitator are process-centred, non-directive and imaginative, with the ability to position facilitation in *context*. There is a necessity to ground learning in context; of life, of the workplace and in the role, otherwise arts-informed learning can become meaningless, mystical and without substance. The important thing here is for facilitators to develop in themselves what Chodorow (1997: 12) describes as a 'self-reflective, psychological attitude that draws from both the aesthetic passion for beauty and the scientific passion to understand'; facilitating both meaning (mythos) and understanding (logos) in the educational process.

Many of the women arrived on our programme lacking confidence and self belief, with their full potential for a manager-leader role obliterated by this. The opening storytelling exercise confronted this issue, initiating a process of sharing, listening, reflection, imagination and discovery, which continued through the art and mask work. The fact that learning occurred over several weeks, rather than a single event, was useful in positioning learning in a work context. We have been in contact with a number of women since the end of the programme who have told us of the significance of their learning in this way and the deep impact that it had, and continues to have on their professional work and personal lives. This was echoed in an email to us from a student some months later: 'Your approach to learning using arts and discussion was so much more powerful, and indeed accessible than the usual text based information-giving. . . . [this way of learning] is truly exceptional!'

References

Adler, N. J. (2006) The arts and leadership: Now that we can do anything, what will we do? *Academy of Management Learning and Education* 5: 486–499.

Barrett, F. J. (1998) Creativity and improvisation in jazz and organizations: Implications for organizational learning. *Organization Science* 9(5): 605–622.

Barry, D. (1996) Artful inquiry: A symbolic constructivist approach to social science research. *Qualitative Inquiry* 2: 411–438.

Berry, P. (1982) *Echo's Subtle Body*. Dallas, TX: Spring.

Chodorow, J. (1997) *Jung on Active Imagination*. London: Routledge.

Clarkson, P. and Mackewn, J. (1993) *Fritz Perls*. London: Sage.

Darsø, L. (2004) *Artful Creation: Learning-Tales of Arts-in-Business*. Gylling, Denmark: Narayana Press.

Edwards, B. (1995) *Drawing on the Artist Within: How to Release your Hidden Creativity*. London: HarperCollins.

Foreman, J. (1999) *Maskwork*. Portsmouth, NH: Heinemann.

Forster, E. M. (1974) *Aspects of the Novel*. London: Edward Arnold. (Original work published in 1927.)

Gabriel, Y. (2000) *Storytelling in Organizations: Facts, Fictions, and Fantasies*. Oxford: Oxford University Press.

Jung, C. G. (1968) A study in the process of individuation. *The Collected Works of C. G. Jung* (Vol. 9.i). London: Routledge and Kegan Paul. (Original work published in 1950.)

—— (1976a) Commentary on the secret of the golden flower. *The Collected Works of C. G. Jung* (Vol. 13). Princeton, NJ: Princeton University Press. (Original work published in 1929.)

—— (1976b) The Tavistock Lectures: On the theory and practice of analytical psychology. *The Collected Works of C. G. Jung* (Vol. 18). Princeton, NJ: Princeton University Press. (Original work published in 1935.)

Koivunen, N. (2003) *Leadership in Symphony Orchestras: Discursive and Aesthetic Practices.* Tampere, Finland: Tampere University Press.

McNiff, S. (1998) *Art-based Research.* London: Jessica Kingsley.

Nissley, N. (2002) Arts-based learning in management education. In C. Wankel and B. DeFillippi (eds) *Rethinking Management Education for the 21ˢᵗ Century.* Greenwich, CT: Information Age Publishing.

Nissley, N. and Jusela, G. (2001) Using arts-based learning to facilitate knowledge creation. In J. Phillips (ed.) *Measuring and Monitoring Intellectual Capital.* Alexandria, VA: American Society for Training and Development.

Olivier, R. (2001) *Inspirational Leadership: Henry V and the Muse of Fire.* London: The Industrial Society.

Parlett, M. (2002) *Human Strengths: Five Abilities in an Interconnected World.* Knighton, UK: Raft.

—— (2003) Creative abilities and the art of living. In M. Spagnuolo Lobb and N. Amendt-Lyon (eds) *Creative Licence: The Art of Gestalt Therapy.* New York: SpringerWien.

Perls, F., Hefferline, R. F. and Goodman, P. (1951) *Gestalt Therapy.* London: Souvenir Press.

Samuels, A., Shorter, B. and Plaut, F. (1986) *A Critical Dictionary of Jungian Analysis.* Hove, UK: Brunner-Routledge.

Schaverien, J. (1999) *The Healing Image: Analytical Art Psychotherapy in Theory and Practice.* London: Jessica Kingsley.

—— (2005) Art, dreams and active imagination: A post-Jungian approach to transference and the image. *Journal of Analytical Psychology* 50: 127–153.

Shindler, N. (2002) Once upon a time. Huw Wheldon Memorial Lecture, 12 November 2002, www.rts.org.uk (accessed 26 April 2007).

Spagnuolo Lobb, M. and Amendt-Lyon, N. (eds) (2003) *Creative Licence: The Art of Gestalt Therapy.* New York: SpringerWien.

Stern, D. N. (2004) *The Present Moment.* London: Norton.

Stromsted, T. (2001) Re-inhabiting the female body: Authentic movement as a gateway to transformation. *The Arts in Psychotherapy* 28: 39–55.

Whyte, D. (2004) *The Power and Place of Poetry: An Irish Radio Interview.* Langley, WA: David Whyte and Many Rivers Company (CD recording 1989).

Woodman, M. (1993) *Conscious Femininity: Interviews with Marion Woodman.* Toronto: Inner City Books.

—— (1996) *Dancing in the Flames.* Dublin: Gill and Macmillan.

Wyman-McGinty, W. (1998) The body in analysis: Authentic movement and witnessing in analytic practice. *Journal of Analytical Psychology* 43: 239–260.

Zinker, J. C. (1978) *Creative Process in Gestalt Therapy.* New York: Vintage.

Chapter 11

Learning assistants for adults

Nick Stratton

This is an informal account of an ongoing quest. It all began when I had a dream some thirty years ago. I lived above an antiquarian bookshop in Cambridge at the time. I was in my mid-thirties and in a period of transition from my career in industrial chemistry to one in psychology. The bookshop had an accessible roof with a number of small gables. In my dream I was on the roof at night when I was accosted by an invisible stranger. A struggle ensued until he had me pinned against a low parapet, with the street four storeys below. I suddenly had the idea that I could get rid of my adversary by throwing him over my head into the void. Which I did. Maybe this was not a propitious outcome, but it did convince me of the reality of archetypal figures, no matter how induced. I was reading 'The Structure and Dynamics of the Psyche' (Vol. 8 of Jung's *Collected Works*) at around this time, in which he states,

> Significant dreams . . . are often remembered for a lifetime, and not infrequently prove to be the richest jewel in the treasury house of psychic experience. How many people have I encountered who at the first meeting could not refrain from saying 'I once had a dream!'
>
> (Jung 1969 [1948]: para. 554)

The persistence of such memories points to the powerful 'engagement' qualities of archetypal figures that presumably arise from the characteristic combination of theme, imagery and emotion. In later years it occurred to me that such engagement might be borrowed for supporting learning.

The second notable event was the success of a project at the Open University, where I was a research fellow a few years later. I worked in a small group specializing in the general design of student assessments. It had always seemed strange to me that assessments occurred at the end of a course (for credit purposes) when they could have much greater value before and during the course for guiding and strengthening learning, that is for diagnostic purposes. (There might be a personal reason for this. I have never performed well under time pressure, beginning with the 11 + IQ test, which I failed initially.)

The university operated a computer-marked assignment (CMA) system, where the results for units were reported as grades. With the help of the technology faculty and a mainframe programmer, I designed a new CMA for a Systems Technology Unit that, rather appropriately, provided diagnostic feedback in the form of individual letters to students. The evaluation showed that students were delighted with this supplement to the standard system (Stratton 1979). And I was pleased with the success, which led to a continuing interest in supporting learners with feedback.

From 1980 to 1996 I worked for the City and Guilds Institute, eventually becoming their research manager. In this capacity I participated in the government-inspired radical changes to the system of vocational qualifications, resulting in NVQs, GNVQs and Key Skills. My role was to assist in the design of the assessment systems for such awards. This field was particularly congenial to me as I had started out my working life with a five-year apprenticeship and felt very much in tune with the vocational world. But I pick up the thread of this story subsequent to 1996 when I became a freelance consultant. One of my first clients was the Qualifications and Curriculum Authority (QCA) which was planning a revision to the Key Skills awards. My job was to lead the redevelopment of the Problem Solving Key Skill (Stratton 1998). I culled the relevant literature for ideas and good practices, and eventually arrived at a general model for problem solving that consisted of a problem solving cycle, supported at each phase by strategies and techniques. In effect this was a universal problem solving toolkit, intended to apply to all vocational contexts and activities from fault-finding to strategic planning. It included a very wide range of techniques, some analytic, some creative and others social. It is also notable that problem solving cycles closely resemble learning cycles (e.g., Kolb 1983) and thereby provide a stepping stone towards intervening personal factors such as learning styles.

At this point, the occasion arose to develop a student support system by combining ideas about motivation (preservation), assessment for feedback and the problem solving toolkit. On a visit to a university in south-west England in 2000, I met with an engineering lecturer whose students were experiencing difficulties during their extended project work, when they were less well supported by staff. This problem, considered to be more widespread, could result in poor performance by students, or even in them dropping out altogether. We had the idea of designing a virtual (software-based) learning assistant that would be available to support students in their project work. We wrote a proposal ('Investigating Motivating Factors in Problem Solving'), planning to review the motivational literature in order to design and evaluate such a system, and seeking funding from the Economic and Social Research Council. Unfortunately we were turned down. The reviewer was intrigued by our ideas but felt that our approach to evaluation fell short of certain requirements. However, the ideas had started to jell, and, being fired up, I decided to go at it alone. My consultancy work allowed me time to develop, or at least to prototype, learning assistant software. I was already acquainted with suitable authoring software (Mediator) and in a position to commence.

Conceptualizing motivation

My first problem was that, if I were to design a general purpose learning assistant for adults (18+), as opposed to the context-specific Plymouth project, I would need to take into account an even wider range of motivational factors. When is learning support needed? Typically, when the learner is indecisive about direction or when obstacles arise, or when distraction sets in. Clearly I would need to take into account the motivation-to-learn literature so as to arrive at the key motivating and demotivating factors – focusing on those intrinsic to learning. These turned out to include effort, capability, confidence, aspirations, self-management, learning style and role fitness in organizations. In a sense, the perceived effort needed for learning incorporates the other factors.

This is illustrated by research findings by the psychologists Sternberg (1988) and Cziksentmihalyi (1992). Sternberg (1988: 296) provides a substantial list of *failures of self-management*, which he describes as motivational and emotional blocks that get in the way of our proper use of intelligence:

- lack of motivation
- lack of impulse control
- lack of perseverance and preservation
- using the wrong abilities
- inability to translate thoughts into actions
- lack of product orientation
- inability to complete tasks and follow through
- failure to initiate
- fear of failure
- procrastination
- misattribution of blame.

Csikszentmihalyi (1992: 49) describes *flow* experiences, where effort is minimized and enjoyment maximized. Eight conditions are singled out, all necessary for *flow*, where the person

- has a good chance of completing the task
- can concentrate on the task
- has clear goals
- is given immediate feedback
- acts with deep but effortless involvement
- exercises a sense of control over her actions

- loses her concern for the self
- experiences an altered sense of time (contracted or expanded).

He adds that, if flow is to be experienced, the task should be neither overly challenging, which might induce anxiety, nor require merely well-rehearsed skills, which might result in boredom (ibid.: 74).

It is clear that both authors are concerned with self-management and that the two lists complement one another. For example, 'losing concern for self' would prevent fear of failure and blame, and 'can concentrate' would facilitate completion of a task.

Thus made aware of such complexities, I opted for a simplifying model, grouping motivational factors by:

- *The past* – when I walk through the door, what do I bring with me? (my work and learning habits and capabilities)
- *The present* – how do I see myself and how do others see me and I them? (social roles and projections)
- *The future* – what does the future hold for me and is what I am doing relevant? (aspirations, goals).

Learning is about effecting changes in oneself of (e.g.) attitudes, competences and understanding. Hence it would be helpful to implement a further group that addresses and promotes such change:

- *Effecting change* – how can I alter my self-perceptions and expand my 'learning to learn' repertoire of strategies? (self-management).

Bear in mind that my attitude was pragmatic; that is, intended to develop a useful product, rather than to conduct research on learning.

Jungian studies

At this time (2000), a crucial event occurred. I noticed that the only MA in Jungian and Post-Jungian Studies in the UK was available on my doorstep at the University of Essex. This was serendipity – if I were to be accepted (as I proved to be), I could both follow up my long-standing interest in Jung and, by gaining greater insight into Jungian concepts and procedures, aid and abet my project. For now my focus remained on archetypal figures, but at later points, amplification procedures and individuation have come into the picture. My attitude continued to be pragmatic. I wished to learn more about analytical psychology in order to apply it with confidence. Transferring ideas across contexts – from the therapeutic to educational worlds – might prove tricky.

Learning assistant roles

Having settled on the four-part *past/present/future/change* structure for motivation, I needed to subdivide the learning assistant into corresponding sections, and to provide labels that would convey the part each played. An analogy could be with computer-based adventure games, where the game player is typically the hero or heroine, who grapples with a villain with the help of a sidekick and is supplied with an amorous interest, all of whom are involved in a quest. In fact, the designers of such adventure games sometimes explicitly use Jung's archetypal figures as models for characters in their games (Dare 2004). Inspiration struck: could I not do likewise by associating archetypal figures with each role in the learning assistant 'game'? This would necessitate 'fitting' each role that relates to past, present and future aspects of motivation to its nearest archetypal figure. In this way, it might be possible to borrow some of the 'engaging' qualities of such figures.

Jung (1967[1952]) used various mythologems, including the hero/heroine quest myth to represent his individuation process, where the goal is to enhance self-development and psychic wholeness by increased self-awareness and accommodation to unconscious aspects of the psyche. This process is aided and/or obstructed by several figures which might appear in dreams or be represented in artwork. Such figures include persona, shadow, anima, animus, trickster, wise old man/magician, great mother, divine child. These figures are regarded as collective – they retain their identity for all individuals. Their nature does not depend on personal history. However, an exception is the shadow, which comes in both collective and personal forms.

The following sections each take one of the roles representing an individual's motivational past, present, future or change. This role is assigned a name (label) that is descriptive of the role. It is then associated with the nearest archetypal figure and this figure used to amplify the role.

The personal past

How can my past get in the way of learning? I have a repertoire of 'can do' attitudes and competences, some of which may facilitate learning. However, equally I have a number of 'can't do' attitudes – possibly stemming from bad experiences. Perhaps I can't do algebra, dance or paint, nor collaborate with others. Some such attitudes and competences may be to do with poor self-management, such as little appreciation of my capacity to learn. These exclusions are both protective and preventive – they confine me to a safe zone, where I am competent and not blamed. If one of our learning assistant roles is to address such matters, an apt name for it would be the Guard.

The Guard thus presented would possess some of the features of the personal shadow.

This [shadow] is made up of all the personal tendencies, motives and characteristics that we have barred from consciousness, whether deliberately or not. It is, of course, typically projected onto other people; but if we look and listen honestly, we will also learn about it, and thus about ourselves, from our dreams, from self-reflection, and (last but not least), from the responses of others. The admission of the shadow is the *sine qua non* of individuation.

(Hart 1997: 92)

The personal present

As I type this, I am aware in the background of a variety of feelings to do with my collaborators and potential readers. Am I meeting the expectations of colleagues? Perhaps I am letting them down. Will my readers understand and appreciate what I have written? What impression have I given of myself and my involvement with this project? In the general case of learning, I have expectations of others and they of me.

If these expectations are inappropriate or false, my learning may suffer. I have called the learning assistant role that focuses on such issues the Mirror. The Mirror thus presented would share some of the features of the persona.

Reinforcing a purely external image of oneself is the 'mask' known as the persona – the personality which, wittingly or unwittingly, one presents to the world. This external picture can be, and often is, vastly different from the inner reality of the person, with his or her hidden emotions, attitudes and conflicts. . . . if the image it represents is too far removed from the person within, there will be a fundamental instability.

(Hart 1997: 94)

The personal future

Do I have a sense of direction regarding my life? I often have short-term goals, but may be largely unaware of where I am heading in the long run. If I could clarify some of these long-term goals of fulfilment, perhaps I can derive some relevance to my current learning activities. This might help both to motivate me and to inform my activities such that they serve current purpose and long term ends, making the fulfilment of life more likely. The Guide seems an appropriate name for this learning assistant role.

The Guide, so presented, could borrow some of the features of the anima.

The figure of the anima differs from other female figures in dreams in a number of ways: the characteristics of the figure can be categorised as evincing fascination, strangeness, radical fervour, wisdom, bring about the initiation of transformation, and helping us in a dangerous situation. . . . The anima as the mysterious stranger could be subdivided into the anima as guide, anima as guide to transformation, and anima as stranger.

(Kast 2006: 124)

The various archetypal figures manifest as either male or female, regardless of the gender of the beholder. As Kast (2006: 122) points out, according to Hillman, 'these archetypes are equally important for males and females. He rejects the idea that an archetype can be gender specific. He also points out that in clinical work we find images of the anima in women.'

Facilitating change

The above roles of the learning assistant focus on various obstacles to learning, but not specifically on second order learning, that is learning to learn. We all tend to prefer particular styles of thinking and learning (e.g. abstract or concrete, serial or parallel, visual or verbal, active or reflective). We tend to be stuck in our ways, but these are not immutable There are strategies and techniques for shifting or expanding these preferences that involve seeing problems from different perspectives.

I have labelled this last learning assistant role the Joker. It's a job is to find unconventional ways of making progress. The Joker as delineated has much in common with the trickster archetype:

> As one of the few truly universal figures in world mythology, the trickster deserves a theory that can adequately explain his omnipresence and significance. . . . [The] trickster represents an archaic level of consciousness, an 'animal' or primitive self given to intense expressions of libido, gluttony and physical abuse. . . . Although in essence mischief-makers these trickster gods are at the same time great benefactors, and in Native American mythology the trickster is often the main culture-hero.
>
> (Russo, 1997: 242)

Status of roles and archetypal figures

When speaking of the learning assistant roles (especially once implemented as software), there is a danger of anthropomorphizing them – assigning person-like agency. However, they are mere devices, designed to fulfil the function of learning aids. Similar remarks apply to archetypal figures, which are regarded here as merely manifestations of psychological processes. The relation between learning assistant roles and archetypal figures is loosely thematic.

Towards designing 'learning assistant' software

By combining the above elements, there is a potentially manageable basis for connecting motivational feedback with a follow through using problem solving strategies. Put crudely, if a motivational blockage is encountered, diagnose it and dissolve it by adopting a new strategy for the problem in hand.

The four motivational roles described above were operationalised as software. Each of the four roles (Guide, Mirror, Guard and Joker) functions interactively by asking the user questions about the perceived relevance of a set of motivational factors, then by preparing a user profile suggesting priorities and strategies for development. This amounts to straightforward diagnostic assessment that serves to raise the user's awareness of their motivational factors. Each role includes fifteen questions, which represent three factors for feedback. Hence the assessment is merely indicative, and not statistically reliable. This is not problematic, provided the assessment does not bear consequences beyond the control of the user. Note that the software is not prescriptive – the user can override it.

The software also incorporates the wide-ranging problem-solving toolbox, which is used to help users to explore learning strategies and techniques that go beyond their present repertoire. Finally, the software includes a progress-tracking and review system. In short, the four roles (referred to as 'agents' in the software) help to identify developmental goals, and the problem solving section suggests the means for making progress towards these goals.

The application was developed for PCs using Mediator authoring software and made available on CD-ROM. It is self-contained, complete with advice on how to use it. Details of the learning assistant system are provided below.

Exposures

The first audience was my circle of friends, who, having tried out the software system, found it intriguing and expressed encouragement (as friends tend to do). They focused on the first part of the system (the four roles), responding to the sets of questions and noting their resulting profiles and prioritized targets for personal development. At this stage, the graphic style and the 'personalities' of the roles were informal. I had assumed it would help to engage with the roles if each had its own character (challenging, confiding, cautious, cheeky) and if they sometimes challenged each other. And, indeed, my friends did appreciate this aspect.

The next exposure was a demonstration to a group of staff at my local further education college, Colchester Institute. They too liked the informal style and suggested making it even more so, to engage students. However, this was followed by a demonstration to executives of a business-oriented software company, who were interested in the ideas but found the graphics style, format and formality to be inappropriate for staff. They felt that the software should conform to the style and format of Windows business applications.

A third port of call was Guildford Educational Services (GES) – a consultancy that conducted much evaluation for government agencies. In particular, they were familiar with a variety of educational software. They felt the software was unique in its approach and had considerable potential. They also suggested that the four roles should be more challenging towards the user, preventing the latter from remaining in a comfort zone. About this time I also presented a short paper on motivation at a Further Education Research Association conference (Stratton 2003); however, the response was muted.

Finally, the system (complete with a theory and practice manual) was demonstrated to a human resources development manager at a college of higher education in London, who was interested in supporting their administrative staff. The software was tried out by one consultant and the manual read by another. The first found the software interesting to use and that the problem-solving toolbox was valuable, but commented that the four roles should be more consistent and demanding. The second consultant reported that the software had a sound theoretical basis. It was agreed to set up a small pilot study, provided that the software emphasized professional development, rather than personal development. It would also be helpful if delivery were to be via the Internet rather than CD-ROM. Unfortunately, the mooted trial was postponed indefinitely, since following an organizational review it was decided to overhaul their entire approach to staff development.

Re-evaluation and technical matters

There was now an interlude to consider the issues arising from those demonstrations and trials. Could the tensions between those who wanted a formal, professional version and those seeking a more personal version be resolved? Is it a matter of presentational style, or is it more fundamental, say to do with differences in long-term goals for the individual? The latter issue is explored below (developmental pathways), where it may be that a common underlying approach can be preserved. For now, the focus would be on the development of the professional version (e.g. for office staff), as it was felt that this would demand a certain rigour of design, which could subsequently form the basis for a more personal version (for students and individuals). A description of Professional Agent is found at my website (Stratton 2005).

A second issue was whether and how to switch to delivery of the software by downloading it from the Internet. This turned out to be problematic initially. I had the means to produce a modular system based on the Internet that would run on both PCs and Macs (using a Java authoring programme, Jamba). I devised a set of modules, based on the original materials, but formal in tone, to meet the professional market. However, I ran into technical problems: downloading to PCs encountered security problems; holding a data file for the user at a website also gave rise to downloading problems (caches) and Microsoft stopped installing Java with Windows. There were also potential Data Act problems with holding user information on a website. The alternative was to create a set of modules using Mediator (Windows only) that could be downloaded as required and kept and run on the user's PC, which would also hold the data file. This last approach appeared to be by far the best technical solution, and I began work to demonstrate this.

After this technical hiatus, Jungian inspiration returned on two fronts – personification and individuation – as described below.

Personification

Although the four roles within the learning assistant had defined functions and characters, they remained neutral regarding their identity. So why not ask each user of the software to create a personification for each agent in order to maximize their personal engagement? A trial module was created for the Joker, where the user is invited to select a figure (real or fictional) who is regarded as charismatic, has popular appeal (ensuring a degree of collectivity) and who potentially fits the Joker's role and style. This figure is then amplified in Jungian fashion to flesh it out with personal memories, images, feelings, and imagined interactions, in effect creating a mini-complex. This process would then be repeated for the remaining agents. The result is a new, personalised front end for the learning assistant software that may have greater potential to sustain interest.

In my own case, I would choose to identify the Joker with Lewis Carroll's Cheshire Cat. The Cat has a number of tricksterish qualities that qualify it for the role of Joker. It first appears to Alice when she is lost in the forest. It is friendly when approached in the right way but otherwise contrary; it is disrespectful of authority; it has an ironical sense of humour; it can transform itself, appearing and disappearing at will, either instantly, slowly or partially; it can see into the future; it proves that it is mad (through some very dubious logic). As a possibly over-rational individual, I find the Cat fascinating, and would be happy to consult it when facing a challenging situation. I have a number of visual memories of it, each accompanied by feelings: Tenniel's pictures, cartoons, films (including animation), television productions.

Individuation and developmental pathways

The second initiative is to pay more attention to paths to individuation. Defined as 'the lifelong development of personality', individuation refers to 'the process of becoming the personality that one is *potentially* from the beginning of life. . . . it so often fails to reach its proper destination due to genetic, circumstantial, social and cultural obstacles' (Stein 2006: 198). Jung's model of individuation – to harmonize the ego with the unconscious Self – is essentially introverted. But there may be extraverted parallels such as personal development through action or learning. Steps in individuation (so conceived) might include learning about one's current preferences and limitations, then setting goals and finally adopting a strategy for self-development. If the result tends towards greater autonomy and harmony, then that could be considered as a step towards individuation.

Several authors have recently discussed such developmental paths. Zohar and Marshall (2000) collated and matched a number of approaches, including first, Holland (1997 [1958]) personality types based on vocational preferences; second, Jung (1971 [1921]) psychological types; and three, Cattell (1957) motivational categories. The result is six paths, each with a characteristic style and motivation as shown in Table 11.1, where the columns are based on Holland, Jung and Cattell respectively after Zohar and Marshall (2000: 298). Zohar and Marshall's suggestion is that a person is likely to have a strong, though not exclusive, preference for one of these paths. Taken together, the scope of these paths is very broad and encompasses most of the population.

Table 11.1 complements the model underlying the learning assistants, which so far has focused on the motivation to learn with attention to factors which promote learning effectiveness. The paths could provide life contexts in which to anchor self-development or individuation. They are compatible with occupational perspectives, not surprisingly as Holland's research is based on analyses of occupational preferences, interests and abilities, which underpin his six personality types.

Further conceptual development

While the six paths point to orientations and potentials, they lack indications of the extent of development, that is of how far someone might have progressed along a chosen path. Like Jung, Wilber (2000) collated and attempted to integrate a large number of philosophical and psychological theoretical systems, both East and West (the 'perennial philosophy') which he shaped in diagrammatic form. He aimed at devising a general theory of spiritual

Table 11.1 Six developmental pathways

Path	Occupation	Type	Motivation
Duty	Conventional	Extraverted/perception	Gregariousness
Nurturing	Social	Extraverted/social	Parental
Understanding	Investigative	Introverted/thinking	Exploration
Transformation	Artistic	Introverted/perception	Creativity, Eros
Brotherhood	Realistic	Introverted/feeling	Construction
Leadership	Enterprising	Extraverted/thinking	Self-assertion

development. One such diagram is an 'integral psychograph' which provides a powerful developmental model by combining a set of developmental lines (paths) which pass through a common sequence of stages or levels. In Wilber's case, the paths are labelled as *physical, relationships, institutions, emotional, mental, spiritual* and the stages are four 'centres of awareness' – *body, mind, soul, spirit* (Wilber 2000: 31).

It is possible to create a parallel model to suit the educational context by substituting Wilber's model with the six paths described by Zohar and Marshall (2000). To reflect Wilber's spiritual approach, the focus could be on the 'width' of awareness when engaged with learning or with a challenging task. The four equivalent stages would then be: *passive (responsive), anticipatory (pro-active), reflective (self-aware)* and *strategic (wider perspectives)*. This model would encourage increased autonomy, effectiveness, self-awareness and awareness of others. It would also enrich the design of learning assistant roles by elaborating and strengthening the role of the Guide, itself related to anima figures. In fact, the initial design of the Guide was based in part on such a model. But there is considerable scope to refine it. No doubt similar considerations apply to the remaining agents.

I can at this point note an increasingly Jungian turn in the design basis of the learning assistant. This started with the concept of guidance roles based on archetypal figures. Next, I considered personalizing these roles by means of personification and amplification, with the intention of maximizing engagement. Lastly I found a strengthened basis for assigning individuation-like processes to the Guide. It remains to elaborate the other three roles in similar terms. In effect the original, diverse motivational factors are gradually subsumed by a more encompassing and satisfying psychological developmental perspective.

Description of the learning assistant system

The following description of the learning assistant software is based on the User Guide for Professional Agent prepared in 2005. Sentences in italics are added to indicate future development. The system is available either complete on CD-ROM or by downloading modules from the Internet. Both systems are organized as nine modules. The system has prototype status.

Module 1 – Introduction

This describes the intended benefits of Professional Agent, how it is structured, and how to use it. The user's data file is explained – it accumulates information as the user works through the modules, and uses this information to offer priorities and advice (feedback). A remote adviser is available via email to assist the user in the use of the software, if need be. If the user's data file is made available, the adviser can see exactly what progress the user has made.

Module 2 – Guide

This is the first of four professional agents. It is designed to help the user to reflect on certain self-development themes. It asks the user twelve questions. The responses are used to offer indicative priorities (high, medium or low) for attending to each of three themes:

1   What is your attitude to challenges at work?
2   To what extent do you consider others at work?
3   How would you like to develop at work?

'Work' includes any learning opportunity, whether an occupational task or a project. (Note: these themes are expected to be related more closely to the longer term development lines as described above.)

Modules 3–5 – Mirror, Guard, Joker

These modules follow the same pattern as that for the Guide.
   The respective development themes are:

Mirror

4   Do you feel self-sufficient at work?
5   Do you appreciate colleagues at work?
6   How much do you enjoy risk-taking at work?

Guard

7   How systematic are you at work?
8   Do you need to avoid blame at work?
9   Do you need to take more risks at work?

Joker

10   How effective are you at learning?
11   Do you tend to learn through action?
12   Do you tend to learn through reflection?

Each Professional Agent can be personalized to a limited extent by choosing and inserting the name of someone the user finds charismatic and appropriate. (Note that it is planned to devise preliminary modules where the user personalizes each agent in depth by amplifying all their associations to the selected representatives.)

Module 6 – Selecting a project and targets

Here, the user is invited to pick a project (possibly in conjunction with a supervisor). The user is then asked to select up to four of the twelve development themes to pursue during the course of the project. Clearly the project should provide appropriate learning experiences. There is advice on choosing projects and targets. In particular the user is urged to select one of two development strategies – either to build on strengths or to plug gaps in competence.

Modules 7 and 8 – Project problem-solving stages

These modules guide the user through the four stages of the problem solving process (which might involve hopping back and forth between them – life is rarely tidy).

Module 7	stage 1	exploring and clarifying the problem
	stage 2	identifying and selecting solutions
Module 8	stage 3	carrying out the chosen solution
	stage 4	evaluating methods and outcomes.

These stages are supported by a range of strategies and techniques.

Strategies

- Reframe the problem, make comparisons, simplify the problem, check problem clarity.
- Reframe possible solutions, compare with other solutions, simplify solutions, choose the best solution, analyse risk, consider resources.
- Plan your actions, allow for contingencies, check resources, maintain momentum, adapt your plan, monitor progress.
- Inspect outcome product, evaluate outcome process, check quality of methods used, review alternative methods.

Techniques

Over forty techniques are organized into fourteen tool groups:

- First thoughts (analytical)
- Open questions (creative)
- Similar solutions (creative)
- A helping hand (creative)
- Taking risks (analytical)
- Scheduling (planning)
- Impact on people (analytical)
- Situations and reasons (analytical)
- Time to change? (analytical)
- Coming up with ideas (creative)
- Being systematic (analytical)
- Gaining support (planning)
- Facilitating (monitoring)
- Measurements (analytical)

(Note: this toolbox is gradually accumulating an increasing number of self-awareness techniques.)

Module 9 – Reviewing progress

This module allows the user to track the impacts of the techniques they have used at the various stages of their project. One form of impact refers to its effectiveness for the project. The other refers to progress made towards the selected development targets. This progress is entered incrementally, then summarized. (Note: in principle, this developmental progress could be fed back to modify the priorities indicated by the four agents in Modules 2–5, thus closing the cycle.)

References

Cattell, R. B. (1957) *Personality and Motivation Structure and Measurement*. New York: World Book.

Cziksentmihalyi, M. (1992) *Flow: The Psychology of Happiness*. New York: Harper and Row.

Dare, R. (2004) Games and the imagination, www.gamedev.net/reference/design/features/gati3/ (accessed 18 December 2007).

Hart, D. L. (1997) The classical Jungian School. In P. Young-Eisendrath and T. Dawson (eds) *The Cambridge Companion to Jung*. Cambridge: Cambridge University Press.

Holland, J. L. (1997) *Making Vocational Choices* (3rd edition). Odessa, FL: Psychological Assessment Resources. (Original work published in 1958.)

Jung, C. G. (1967) Symbols of transformation. *The Collected Works of C. G. Jung* (Vol. 5). London: Routledge and Kegan Paul. (Original work published in 1952.)

—— (1969) On the nature of dreams. *The Collected Works of C. G. Jung* (Vol. 8). London: Routledge and Kegan Paul. (Original work published in 1948.)

—— (1971) Psychological types. *The Collected Works of C. G. Jung* (Vol. 6). London: Routledge and Kegan Paul. (Original work published in 1921.)

Kast, V. (2006) Anima/animus. In R. K. Papadopoulos (ed.) *The Handbook of Jungian Psychology*. Hove, UK: Routledge.

Kolb, D. (1983) *Experiential Learning: Experience as the Source of Learning and Development*. New York: Prentice Hall.

Russo, J. (1997) A Jungian analysis of Homer's Odysseus. In P. Young-Eisendrath and T. Dawson (eds) *The Cambridge Companion to Jung*. Cambridge: Cambridge University Press.

Stein, M. (2006) *Individuation*. In R. K. Papadopoulos (ed.) *The Handbook of Jungian Psychology*. Hove, UK: Routledge.

Sternberg, R. (1988) *The Triarchic Mind*. London: Penguin.

Stratton, N. (1979) Some procedures for generating and evaluating computer-marked assignments and associated diagnostic feedback materials. Unpublished report for the Open University, UK.

—— (1998) Redevelopment of the Problem Solving Key Skill: Report on Phase II. Unpublished report for the Qualifications and Curriculum Authority, UK.

—— (2003) Personal motivation at work. Paper presented at the Further Education Research Association Conference: Motivating Learners at College and Work, January 2003, London, www.fera.uk.net (accessed 18 December 2007).

—— (2005) Professional Agent website, www.p-agent.com (accessed 18 December 2007).

Wilber, K. (2000) *Integral Psychology*. Boston: Shambala.

Zohar, D. and Marshall, I. (2000) *SQ Spiritual Intelligence: The Ultimate Intelligence*. London: Bloomsbury.

Chapter 12

Chasing the shadow

Carolyn Mamchur
with Vandy Britton, Linda Apps and Michelle Robert

How do we do our best work? With an informed mind and a generous heart. How can we, as educators, create the conditions that lead our students to a place where they develop both? This chapter is about one path of that journey experienced with a group of graduate students at Simon Fraser University. Interestingly, we sought the light of our wisdom by 'chasing the shadow'.

The opportunity

It was January, a new year, a new class, a new course: 'Educ 819: Interactions in the Classroom'. This course outline advertised Educ 819:

> Northrop Frye suggests that two of the responsibilities of the educated imagination are to understand and be understood.
> This course embraces that belief. It will focus on the use of psychological type to both understand the self and other; and to develop skill in being understood.
> There will be four areas of focus:
> First on the self. On being the most developed and generous self that one can be. On being an autonomous decision maker.
> Second on the other. On being able to listen to the other from a vantage point of deep understanding and caring.
> Third on the art of communication. On being able to speak in ways that take into account individual differences.
> Fourth on the ability to be a creative and critical thinker and writer. On being able to express oneself with pathos, ethos and logos and teach others to do the same. On being able to use writing as a way to tell one's personal story and make meaning of life.
> Jungian psychological type theory will be examined as a means of understanding individual teaching and administrative styles, as a way to develop personally and as a way to develop one's creative processing.
> The quality of interaction that one has with others depends upon many factors. One is the quality of the individual's own personal development

and maturity. Another is one's ability to listen to and understand the other.

The first night, the small group of sixteen graduate students and I revisited the several options for the focus of the course. 'I'd like to make this course as personally meaningful as possible for you,' I told them. 'I am limited by the expectations of the university and by what I know.' But given those parameters, we could concentrate on any one of these options – self, the other, the art of communication, the ability to be a creative and critical thinker and writer and divide our time equally among them. Or we could focus most of our energy on one of the four areas.

At first, the class wanted all of them. But by week three, a preference had clearly emerged. They wanted to focus on personal development.

I could guess that this focus might have been prompted by the fact that the class had largely adult learners beginning to feel a need to individuate. Most of my students agreed with Jacobi (1965) in her view of individuation, which suggests that it is a mistake to unremittingly search for 'happiness':

> The true goal is a task that continues right up to life's evening, namely, the most complete and comprehensive development of the personality. It is this which gives life an incomparable value that can never be lost; inner peace, and therewith the highest form of 'happiness'.
>
> (Jacobi 1965: 17)

The development of personality involves looking at the dark side of our being, which unconsciously affects us. Putting the unconscious into the light is a fascinating and informative process that this class was eager to experience:

> Life may be compared to a piece of embroidery, of which, during the first half of his time, a man gets a sight of the right side, and during the second half, of the wrong. The wrong side is not so pretty as the right, but it is more instructive; it shows the way in which the threads have been worked together.
>
> (Schopenhauer 2004: 67)

Why such a cry for personal development?

It is both fascinating and troubling that at a time when schools are moving toward a dangerous bureaucracy of accountability, businesses are turning to the work of such gurus as Hermon (1994), who revisits the work of educators such as Carl Rogers, Abraham Maslow and Fritz Perls promoting every individual's need and responsibility to build personal power.

'We are witnessing a radical redefinition of the task of public education, driven by the widespread belief that by focusing our attention on externally imposed constraints', such as government standardized testing, 'we can both produce higher achievement and restore public trust in our schools' (Meier 2002: 95). It was the belief of this class and of many educators that there is a growing phenomenon of fear and mistrust and reduction of professionalism that educators must rise up against.

The question, of course, is how?

> In the face of the daily onslaught of media persuasion, business-speak, falsification of feeling, the stealing of our right to perceive, experience, . . . taxonomies, theories, appeals to science, and measurement of results (accountability) whatever the situation, the resulting insensitivity to individuality and difference, the looting of the earth, constant engine noise, not to mention the many conflicts and injustices in the world, I am constantly asking myself how best to do my job (as an art educator), how best to live in today's world.
>
> (Richmond 2005: 76)

Bruno Bettelheim (1960), in the inspiring book he wrote as a result of his surviving a concentration camp in Nazi Germany, insists that it is essential for all of us to become autonomous decision-makers. This autonomy has to do with human beings' inner ability to govern themselves based not as a revolt against authority, but rather as an acting out of inner conviction, leading to an increasing consciousness which forms the basis for the human deepening sense of identity, self-respect and inner freedom. This internal autonomy is necessary if the members of any organization and any country are to function as responsible citizens who 'live the good life in that society and create anew in each generation the good society for himself and others' (Bettelheim 1960: 75).

As the class work emerged we recognized we were creating an opportunity for ourselves to represent a group of educators who fiercely promoted a different kind of accountability. A personal accountability. 'The alternative to standardization is real standards. Standards in their genuine sense have always depended upon the exercise of that suspicious quality of mind – our fallible judgment – and training ourselves, to the better exercise of such judgment' (Meier 2002: 132). Bettelheim says that to make choices we must first understand ourselves, who we are, what we value, what we are prepared or not prepared to give up. 'I know of no more encouraging fact than the unquestionable ability of man to elevate his life by conscious endeavor' (Thoreau 1964 [1854]: 343).

The tools

Given our chosen mandate, what tools did we use to do the job of conscious endeavour, of personal development, of being strong enough amidst the terrible surge of externally enforced accountability, to offer the gift that counted most, ourselves?

Jungian psychological type theory

Jung (1971 [1921]) has given us a model with which to elevate our lives by conscious endeavour. His system, called psychological type theory, is a practical psychology, which moves the unconscious into the conscious so that we can make choices. He believed the difference between the conscious and the unconscious to be very significant, primarily because every conscious choice is at the same time, an ethical choice. One of the jobs of the individual is to move through the stages of life leading to the final stage, individuation, when we become the most whole we can be.

As Corlett and Millner (1993: 49) point out, 'Jung saw individuation, not as a self-centered path, but as a search for balance in which both self-understanding and connections with others interact and enhance one another.' Psychological type theory is not a trait theory, as many wrongly assume, but is rather a developmental model designed to move us through the various stages of life from perfection (using the dominant function) to balance (using the auxiliary function) and finally to individuation (consciously using the inferior function) and 'using the task of individuation as a time to incorporate all our psychological preferences to be available as needed – not developed equally, but used appropriately' (ibid.: 48).

In order to understand this progression, Jung had to label aspects of mental behaviour. He classified all of human behaviour into two choices that could not be simultaneously experienced. The first choice was a preference for perception. That is, a preference to be open, adaptive, a preference for discovery, for finding out, for being aware of. 'Perception includes the many ways of becoming aware of things, people, events, or ideas. It includes information gathering, the seeking of sensation or of inspiration and the selection of the stimulus to be attended to' (Myers and McCauley 1985: 12). The second choice is a preference for judgement. That is, a preference to be closed, decided, a preference for having a plan, making a decision, taking action. 'Judgment includes all the ways of coming to conclusions about what has been perceived. It includes decision making, evaluation, choice, and the selection of the response after perceiving the stimulus' (ibid.: 12).

Because it is so difficult for us to make sense of things, which are presented in a chaotic and complex manner, it is an especially important breakthrough when someone can simplify information or ideas by categorizing them.

Jung had that unique and precious ability to simplify and categorize (see Figure 12.1).

Jung decided that this judging/perceiving categorization was not complete enough. He added what have come to be known as the four functions. There are two perceiving functions, sensing and intuition, and two judging functions, thinking and feeling. One of those four is dominant (or superior), one is auxiliary (aids the dominant), one is inferior (or undeveloped and childish) and one is tertiary (aids the inferior or the auxiliary, depending upon the state of the person). (See Figure 12.2.)

Each function has its own job (Myers and McCauley 1985: 13):

- Sensing (S) seeks the fullest possible experience of what is immediate and real.
- Intuition (N) seeks the broadest view of what is possible and insightful.
- Thinking (T) seeks rational order and plan according to impersonal logic.
- Feeling (F) seeks rational order according to harmony among subjective values.

Jung then added the final component of Extravert and Introvert to his matrix (see Figure 12.3). Extraverts extravert their favourite or dominant function, using it in their outer world, the extraverted world where actions and interactions dominate attention and energy. Introverts introvert their favourite or dominant function, using it in their inner world, the introverted world where

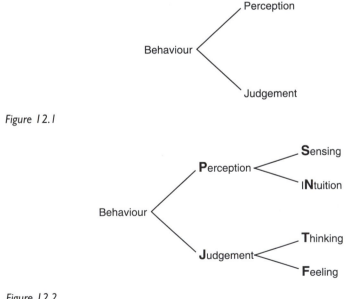

Figure 12.1

Figure 12.2

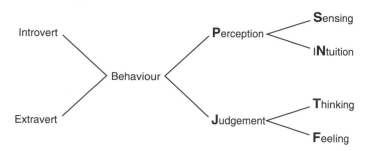

Figure 12.3

reflection and consideration take priority on a private level inside the introvert's head.

The functions

What is the dominant function? It is the core of the method used by the personality to function, the conscious leader of our psychic energy. It is that function to which we naturally turn to get us through the day. The auxiliary is that function which we need to balance our dominant function. It serves to round out our psyches, giving us both perception and judgement. If we lock ourselves into our dominant functions we run the risk of one-sided behaviour and decision-making. Perceiving types can get locked into the dreaming, full of great ideas that never get actualized. Judging types can get locked into the taking action part, determined to see a thing to its bitter end, even if the 'thing' isn't worth doing in the first place.

The inferior function, sometimes referred to as the shadow function, is the least developed, most unconscious, most tyrannical function. If you know your dominant function you know your inferior function: it is always opposite your dominant. That is, if your dominant function is sensing, your inferior is intuition, and vice versa. If your dominant function is thinking, your inferior function will be feeling and vice versa. Both your dominant and inferior functions are in the same family of perception or judgement. Consequently, if you are dominantly a perceiving type, both your best and worst experiences, your most and least satisfying experiences will occur in the perceiving mode. The same is true, of course, for the person who prefers judgement. It can be very disconcerting to experience such a negative reaction to events when the inferior function affects the way we perceive or make judgements.

This is especially true if you have a well-developed dominant function that serves you well. The inferior function is there to tap you on the shoulder when you least expect it, to remind you that you still have a lot of growing to do. The inferior function, being the least developed, most child-like function, usually forces its entry into our lives when we are under stress. It pops up just when we least welcome or think that we need it. Jungians, however, feel that the inferior function is very useful, offering opportunity for growth and insight and giving a burst of new energy in mid life. The inferior has some common features. At first, a tendency to ignore that function, then a tendency to get troubled or irritated by it, and finally, falling into the grip of it and becoming fixated.

As an intuitive type, you may, at first, simply ignore the inferior function of sensing and make mistakes with details. However, if you get in the 'grip' of your inferior function you become obsessed with the very details you might otherwise ignore or not pay much attention to. You might notice a mole and you will be sure that you have cancer. Even though tests and doctors assure you that the mole is just a mole, you will not believe it. You will be able to convince yourself that the doctor doesn't want to tell you, the test was wrong, the cancer has moved somewhere else.

If sensing is your dominant and intuition your inferior function, the very things that the intuitive is good at haunt you. You may, at first, simply be quite uncomfortable with being asked to project into the future or to 'guess' at how to do something when you don't have the necessary data or expertise. However, if you are in the 'grip' of your inferior function you become obsessed with the future and its unpredictable nature. The sensing in the grip will feel a terrible sense of loss of control over what he values – the facts. Instead, he feels impulsive and at the worst stage catastrophizes. Your 18-year-old daughter is late coming home from a trip. You project all sorts of horrors, the plane has crashed, she has been kidnapped, she has married a bank robber. Your husband, an intuitive, tries to assure you that nothing is wrong. She simply missed the plane or changed her plans and will be calling you soon. You wonder why you married him? Doesn't he care?

If thinking is your dominant function, feeling will be the inferior. The first level of experiencing feeling is to avoid it, not to pay attention to it, even when someone else may wish you would. You might respond to someone's need for understanding by trying to solve the problem for them, rather than getting up close and actually seeing it from their point of view, with empathy. However, in the grip of your feeling function, you will not ignore your feelings, ignore the values-laden issues that affect harmony and get people feeling comfortable and safe. Instead, you will be overwhelmed by feeling, over-responding with anger, or joy, or sadness. You will become an explosion or a puddle of emotion embarrassing yourself and surprising others.

When feeling is the dominant, thinking is the inferior function. The first level of experiencing thinking is to reject the notion of objective thought. Feeling types do not actually believe that there is such a thing as objectivity and would argue that in a most rational way. They can overlook results and focus on intentions. Feeling types can overlook such things as cause and effect when it comes to making choices about purchases, even as big as houses. With a dominant function of feeling, you may be moved to purchase a home because the porch reminds you of your grandmother's porch. You may ignore location. I know I have done exactly that, bought a home and didn't notice it was on one of the busiest streets in Regina, Saskatchewan, next to a football stadium. But in the grip of thinking, the feelers become cold, aloof, with a biting sarcasm and seeming indifference which terrifies those accustomed to their more cooperative, caring orientation. 'Why should I?' asks the feeler in the grip and believes she is acting in a way that is totally appropriate for the situation. At least, that's how the feeler experiences the situation and her response while in the grip. Once she gets out of the grip, deep remorse can be crippling.

All of the students in the class had experienced the crippling effect of being trapped in the grip of the inferior function. Some were in the grip when we met. They hungered for individuation.

> The possibility that everyone can have his own direction, his special purpose and it can attach a sense of value to the lives of those who suffer from the feeling that they are unable to measure up to collective norms and collective ideals.
>
> (Singer 1973: 158)

People sometimes confuse the inferior function and the shadow. The two are closely related. Quenk (1993) offers a useful analogy regarding the inferior and the shadow. She says: 'Metaphorically, the inferior function is the skeletal form and the shadow is the flesh that gives it substance and life' (ibid.: 52).

Imagery

Another of the tools we embraced was active imagery. 'The images of the unconscious place a great responsibility upon a man. Failure to understand them, or a shirking of ethical responsibility, deprives him of his wholeness and imposes a painful fragmentariness on his life' (Jung 1961: 193). Our use of imagery was based on a belief that we already know those things in life which are important for us to know. We have but to listen. Or look.

> To address the unconscious in logical terms is not particularly effective. In order to reach the unconscious . . . we have to speak in its own terms. One should attempt to use the mode in which the unconscious normally operates, which is by way of symbols.
>
> (Assagioli 1970: 180)

We began with images in the present. A field. A meadow. What was the present telling us? I played classical music, turned down the lights, invited folks to go for a walk in a field, a meadow and just pay attention to what they saw. The idea was not to intellectualize, not to force, just to be open and receptive.

I was surprised to find a chair appear in the middle of my meadow.

I invited the class to let the item that appeared say something to them.

My chair told me to sit down.

Exactly. Sit down. I was doing too much. I was over extended. I was about to burn out. I needed to sit down.

We all received messages. The class was amazed at what was for most, their first experiences with metaphorically inviting the conscious into their lives.

Narrative

We learned to recognize our stories by sharing narratives. Often our narratives were written. Sometimes they appeared as song; or dance; or painting. We told the stories of our lives and our city and our culture.

We need to inhabit stories that encourage us to pay close attention, we need stories that will encourage us toward acts of the imagination that in turn will drive us to the arts of empathy, for each other and the world.

(Kittredge 1996: 164)

Our stories began to reveal some ancient and some current edge of our vulnerability. It was not a matter of confession. It was a matter of discovery with real discipline and focus.

The conditions that permit such learning to occur

Acceptance

'The process of making peace with our stories requires us to identify, under-stand, accept, and embrace everything in our past that has caused us pain' (Ford 2002: 103). When you have a mix of students of different ages, sexes, experiences, it is only normal that folks will have different developmental paths. It is essential that there are no predetermined expectations, but rather attentiveness and an open acceptance and celebration of whatever comes.

Some Jungians have finely tuned the paths to individuation, moving away from accommodation (when our ego is developed and as its name implies, we accommodate society, make a 'name' for ourselves, get security and meet the demands of life) to travel through three stages identified by Stein (1977) as 'the rite of separation' (breaking down the masks we have hid behind), the 'rite of liminality' (feeling chaotic, feeling we should go back to the familiar rather than forge ahead to challenging new directions) and the 'rite of reintegration' (a subtle movement out of the steep curve of liminality to a more gentle acceptance of and belief in the possibility of rebirth).

Because these rites involve change, they feel a bit overwhelming, and can take time as we tell and listen to our own stories. The rite of separation may feel like giving up a dream. New roles for ourselves emerge and replace them. But in that process, we go through liminality where we feel lost, perhaps chaotic, searching, closer to our unconscious self. At this stage it is important to pay attention to what our stories are telling us.

Things calm down a bit for us in reintegration, we become more comfortable in our changing skins and we can trust the renewed energy and understanding that is ahead. Reiteration brings a more comforting sense of harmony to the individual. We can appreciate others more; we are more connected to our spiritual self and more aware of the world around us. This is often described as mindfulness. To nurture mindfulness, that meaning making that is significant to one's sense of self, we need to open up spaces for play, contemplation and intuition. This is not always easy or welcome in an overly rational world.

This leads me to the second condition needed for this kind of learning to occur: irrationality.

Irrationality

Although I offer my students a particular curriculum that is composed of specific bits of knowledge, such as Jung's psychology, and writing process, it is never the thing upon which we rely. Instead, those specific bits of knowledge create space between the ideas and the students. And in the magic of those spaces, the real work happens. This is a notion of curriculum as Jacques Daignault might explain it, as 'a participation' in 'continuing creation'. We see the space between is a multilayered complex interplay of dimensions which spans breadth, depth, height and time (Irwin and Sameshima 2006: 4).

It is as if we were walking between these things and discovering something new, something deep and sincere that is difficult to learn in a strictly rational analytical manner. We trust our intuition in the process of making connections. In the words of one of the students (reproduced with her permission):

Power of the Unsaid

I always wondered why black and white photos fascinate me. They're just black and white; yet I see so much in the shades in between.

I like to sketch the shadows. The image lies in the spaces between my pencil lead. It is in these gaps where important things hide. I love it when my mind fills in the spaces my eyes cannot see.

Our body sees what our eyes do not.

On a trip to the lake one April day when I was eight, I felt the coldness of the water underneath the sunshine when my mother laid her hand on my left shoulder to prevent me from jumping into the lake with my brothers.

When I was in grade seven, Math became a perplexity for me when Mr. Ellis chose John Porter's 'A' over mine to represent our school in the district Math Quiz.

At sixteen, my limbs were paralyzed when my brother Ben got to drive the family car though I aced the driving test and he barely did. When I finally got behind the wheel, my courage faltered when my father said: 'This traffic jam must have been caused by a female driver in front of us.'

Every year, I could feel my throat constrict when no one heard my suggestions as my brothers decide where to go for our family vacation.

Is it voodoo? Is it magic? Why do I feel disempowered? No, it is the power of things left unsaid.

Perhaps that's why I love to fill the spaces. The gaps. Once I fill them, they lose their power over me.

(Karen de Jesus, student)

Building a community of learners

Personal Connection, modelling explicit instruction, dialogue, assessment for learning with a focus on community sharing and learning from one another were essential ingredients to this course. We all presented at a conference on Innovative Teaching. Students reported on what made our course a community. These were the phrases they used: 'Began the first class by making personal connections with us.' 'A feast of hot home made spaghetti and buns waited for us when we walked in the room. What was this?' 'We all brought food. We ate and laughed and cried.' 'She shared some of her personal stories and invited us to share ours. But she took the first risk.' 'We got to choose what we wanted to learn.' 'She honored us by only starting class when we were all present.' 'She expected and required that we attend all classes because we had much to learn and we all needed to be there. We were a community.' 'She believed in us.' 'She taught using explicit instruction that allowed us to practice what we were learning in a safe environment and then she slowly relinquished more of the responsibility to us so that we would experience success independent of her.' 'The class became ours.' 'I'll never forget these people. We are family.' 'When I had to go to court over a custody battle, they all showed up to support me.' 'When my sister's baby died, they sent flowers.' 'When I told them my gay boyfriend called me fat in the shower, no one laughed. They understood. I had never told anyone I was gay before.'

'I wrote to my sister. I shared my story. We hadn't talked in seven years. She's coming to Vancouver for Xmas.'

What happened to us was the creation of communion – the sharing or exchanging of intimate thoughts and feelings. The key that allows communion to develop is dialogue, which has several capacities. One of these capacities is a spirit of openness or inquiry. It is also a willingness to be vulnerable. Somehow it happened. We were open, full of inquiry, willing to be vulnerable. Why? We trusted one another. We trusted ourselves. We trusted the process.

The garden

> Experiences in nature might be for emerging writers or artists a sort of lived physics: attentiveness in nature that enables them not only to articulate attunement with wilderness or develop mindful respect for nature, but also to have a 'hand in the creation' of themselves (Thoreau 1999: 192).
>
> (Haggarty 2005: 25)

When I first purchased the three acres overlooking the ocean, I had visions of secluded beauty and hours of writing solitude. I did not know that the frail ferns whispering into the bark of an eighty foot maple would speak to me and I would find myself creating a botanical garden. I did not know that the garden would become a haven for my students semester after semester, a sacred crucible for our most important learning.

We walk in the garden, we talk in the garden, we work in the garden, we feast on halibut and blue berries which abound in the area, we swim in the ocean less than a mile away, we soak in the hot tub. In the evening, we read our poems and play our instruments. We tell stories and paint and sculpt and photograph. And on this occasion, with these students, we chose to face our demons, and to chase them away. On this occasion we decided we would heal in the garden.

We built a fire and ritualistically burned messages of pain; we gathered stones, heavy, dirty and hauled them to a place down a steep bank where we wanted to form a dry creek bed. It was a hard job, a dirty job. We dumped the rocks. And then we shaped. We created a path of stone to a lovely statue, a small pool with gold fish. Beauty emerged. Creativity flourished. I decided to turn the dry creek bed into a waterfall. I purchased a pump. Water flowed. Birds gather there now. And frogs. Maples flank the sides of the waterfall. It is a spot alive with memory and renewed life.

Three personal stories

Michelle's journey

Michelle was new to Vancouver. She was new to Canada. She had been selected by her government to come to Canada to earn a degree and return to Mexico with a Master's degree and new found knowledge. When I met Michelle I would not have known that she had been a principal of a school, strong and wise and able to make decisions which affect hundreds of people. Michelle was full of three things that were drowning her spirit. She was full of sadness and anger and defeat. One of her professors was giving her so much negative feedback on her English and on her 'style' that she felt demoralized and afraid she would return to her home country a failure. For a woman in a patriarchal society that would bring shame and ridicule.

'I took this course because someone told me you were a good teacher and you would teach me how to write. But I don't think you can. I am a terrible writer. My English is so bad.' It was one of the first things Michelle told me.

'We'll see,' I told her.

The first assignment I gave the class was an invitation to write about an embarrassing moment. Michelle described a time when she had given her daughter permission to go to a chaperoned party, and the daughter had become sick and had to be taken to hospital. This is an excerpt from what Michelle, the non-writer, the person who could not make herself understood, wrote:

> A doctor went out and then another, some nurses walked by me, people here and there while I was standing frozen in the middle of nowhere.
>
> My husband, himself a physician, was outside of the ER surrounded by friends and colleagues. He was not by my side where he should be, letting me know what was happening. He wasn't with me; and I wasn't with him.
>
> I wanted to embrace him, to comfort him, to tell him that I didn't understand what was happening to our beautiful teenage daughter. His icy glaze stopped me. My feet were paralyzed. His cold eyes told me he didn't wanted to talk about anything, so I returned to my place in the middle of the hallway, standing by myself stuck to the ER door . . . then I began to pray.
>
> Many hours later the three of us drove home in complete silence. I put my child to bed and went to my room alone; there, in the still of the night trying not to be heard, I cried . . .

Michelle read her story to the class. Her voice quavered, but she did not cry. There was a silence and then – applause. And then a circle of people surrounded her and she began to weep.

Three months later, at our mythological day of ridding ourselves of our shadows, Michelle used the expression that had turned the class to laughter many a day. 'Kill, kill, kill!' she said as she threw sheet after sheet into a huge bonfire we had built together. The sheets contained descriptions of the many ways she had been mortified as a woman, as a wife, and an immigrant.

And then she produced her work of art. A crucifix of silver, upon which she had engraved a scene of the church in her home town of Chihuahua, using a repousse technique. It was a gift to me. It hangs on the hugest tree in my garden. It blesses all who enter.

As Michelle worked on the silver, her hands deftly punching each perfect indentation, she confessed to the class that she had been ready to die rather than return a failure to Mexico; rather than return to a husband who didn't love her.

Today she is making changes in how schools are being run in her country. She is a leader. She is a voice to be heard. She has a story to tell and people listen. Her shadow had lifted. She had become a woman of power.

Linda's journey

I'd known Linda for a long time, since she was just a girl. Actually we were both girls, just a few years apart; I, a young high school teacher, she my student. And here she was again, doing her PhD with me. It was a special treat. I knew Linda to be carefree, open, loving, with a bright curious mind and hunger to release a creative talent. The woman who came to me was still bright and curious and had become an artist. But there was something about her face that would, without warning, some times flash a hint of pain and disappointment. There was something about her manner that suggested reservation and careful self protection.

What had happened in the years between the easy laughter and the laughter that could easily turn to tears? But didn't. Not in front of you. Didn't. Not at all. What had happened probably had its birth in her home with a mother never quite prepared for motherhood. But the young girl had only experienced surprise in her youth, perhaps a bit of anger. She was still full of rebellion and youth and self discovery. The young girl became a woman, a wife and mother. The woman had gone through a divorce and a separation from her children. The woman had been torn in her desire to be free, to do her art, to be a single mother, responsible for two children.

And now, twenty-five years later, she entered my classroom in a manner that was more reserved then I had expected. As we progressed with our studies in the class, examining the shadow, the dark side of our beings that haunted us, Linda was quite silent. She spoke a bit about her sons; one a super responsible fairly cautious mechanic; the other a wildey beast, full of worry and discontent, full of addiction and a vulnerable desire to belong and a killing belief that he was not worthy.

Part of the work we were doing was to recognize the shadows that haunted us, and to ritually shed them and to find a creative way to heal. We used my cabin setting as a place to do our ritual shedding. Around a fire, Linda told us she was haunted by feelings of guilt and failure around her son. He broke her heart. He just couldn't create a life for himself, he drifted in and out of jobs, in and out of debt, in and out of depression. And then she began the work which became her arts-based dissertation. She began to explore the topic of touch.

What did it mean to be touched? There is the touch of a loving hand, an angry hand, a healing hand. When you are touched, what do you experience? When you touch others, what is left behind?

She explored her topic as an artist. She took photographs of herself touching herself. She produced these photos (see Plate 7).

And she realized her story was all about boundaries. She had discovered the great tension of her life. To love or not to love. To let some in or not to let them in. To care, but not too much. To commit, but not too far. To lose oneself in another? Where was the balance?

Boundaries. What an interesting life's work. She presented at conferences on the topic. Her dissertation was a success, a beautiful piece of work. She 'moved the shadow into light'.

In the second half of life our shadow, our inferior function, gives us a new source of energy. She will explore this subject for many years. She will examine and re-examine. She might even forgive herself for giving her son to her husband to take care of in a crucial time of his leave. And it will feed her creative passions, her teaching, her work.

Will it heal? I don't know. But it will serve her. Of that I am sure.

Our demons often become our angels. Consciously using our demons is a very empowering process. I have a suspicion the angels of many a great teacher, artist, person have a birth in their demons.

Vandy's journey

If you met Vandy you would see a drama teacher, a PhD student, a woman of extreme beauty and grace and joy. You would not imagine Vandy to have a dark side haunting her dreams. Yet her shadow was the darkest of all.

I knew her early story. She had written of it in a Creative Writing course she had taken with me two years previously. I knew that as a child, Vandy had experienced the unimaginable. She had witnessed her father shoot her stepmother, aim the gun at the girl and then lift the gun to his own head and kill himself in front of his 8-year-old daughter's eyes, leaving her alone in a deserted forest campsite. Miraculously, Vandy had been rescued and returned to her mother.

Miraculously, Vandy survived and became a woman of more love and open acceptance than one can hope for. It was as if all the horror had been lifted from her young life and she was free to enjoy the sunshine days forever.

It took time for Vandy to address her shadow. It started in small moments of description of the challenges associated with raising a son with Asperger's Syndrome:

> I hit my son today. Hard. I didn't mean to do it. I certainly didn't want to do it. But I did it. I hit him.

But it wasn't until the day at the cabin when we shared our darkest thoughts and threw them into the fire that we all realized the depths of her anxiety and guilt. She read a letter to her son, huge gulping sobs forcing the words to be distorted, tortured. The words spoke of not wanting a child, of being afraid of motherhood, of contemplating abortion. Did he know? Had he sensed it in her womb? Was this the reason he struggled so? Was she the cause of all his disconnect with the world?

No one tried to tell her it couldn't be so. We knew there were no words. We knew she had heard them all before. We knew she would have to find her own words.

And she did. The next week. In our classroom. She looked pale. Her hands shook. She told us she wanted to share something she had written. She had written the music and the lyrics.

She sat at the piano and played. She sang in a beautiful voice, a song entitled; 'I work the night'. Vandy sang her sorrow for us. She sang of her own childhood, of a young girl who was forced to see the darker side of humanity too soon.

> I gave it all to you.
> I had to throw my hope away.
> I gave it all to you.
> So I could live from day to day.

Through her song, Vandy gave that child a voice.

> I had to survive somehow.
> I didn't put up a fight.
> But what did you make me do?
> I work the night.

We gathered around Vandy. We felt so close. All of us standing there, surrounding her as she sang. It was our last night together.

Vandy has now finished her PhD. She is writing about the moral responsibility attached to being a drama teacher. She is teaching two classes at the university. Her students love her. She is the kind of teacher whom students describe as 'wonderful' and 'inspiring', 'the best instructor I've had in my entire university career'.

She brings her child out to my cabin. Her husband accompanies her. They visit the pond, they visit the stream, we roast hot dogs and marshmallows over an open fire.

The parents are alert, sensitive to the child. They do not over-stimulate. They never let him out of their sight. When he tires they sit calmly, offer food and drink. He takes a nap in the cabin. We share a bottle of wine and we all know life is good. And I know how fortunate this child is to have these parents, this mother. I know the child knows, too. And hopefully, so does this beautiful woman, this Vandy.

*

The light outside has changed through the enormous windows and the cedars have gained their evening sober elegance. Their tops wave, dark and lovely, their live green scent mingles with the smoky breath of just-lit evening fires.

(Claire Murray, student)

References

Assagioli, R. (1970) *Psychosynthesis: A Manual of Principles and Techniques.* New York: Viking.

Bettelheim, B. (1960) *The Informed Heart.* New York: Avon.

Corlett, E. and Millner, B. (1993) *Navigating Midlife: Using Typology as a Guide.* Palo Alto, CA: CPP Books.

Ford, D. (2002) *The Secrets of the Shadow: The Power of Owning your Whole Story.* New York: HarperCollins.

Haggarty, R. M. (2005) Photo/synthesis: photography, pedagogy and place in a northern landscape. Unpublished PhD dissertation. Simon Fraser University, British Columbia.

Hermon, S. (1994) *A Force of Ones.* San Francisco, CA: Jossey-Bass.

Irwin, R. and Sameshima, P. (2006) Rendering dimensions of a liminal currere. In C. Snowber (discussant) *Interweaving Boundaries: Art, Education, and Spirituality.* Symposium conducted at the meeting of the American Educational Research Association (AERA), San Francisco, CA, April.

Jacobi, J. (1965) *The Way of Individuation.* New York: Harcourt, Brace and World.

Jung, C. G. (1961) *Memories, Dreams, Reflections.* New York: Random House.

—— (1971) Psychological types. *The Collected Works of C. G. Jung* (Vol. 6). London: Routledge and Kegan Paul. (Original work published in 1921.)

Kittredge, W. (1996) *Who Owns the West?* San Francisco, CA: Mercury House.

Meier, D. (2002) *In Schools We Trust: Creating Communities of Learning in an Era of Testing and Standardization.* Boston, MA: Beacon Press.

Myers, I. and McCauley, M. (1985) *Manual: A Guide to the Development and Use of the Myers-Briggs Type Indicator.* Palo Alto, CA: Consulting Psychologists Press.

Quenk, N. (1993) *Beside Ourselves: Our Hidden Personality in Everyday Life.* Palo Alto, CA: CPP Books.

Richmond, S. (2005) On city sights and being an artist: Pondering life and education in a market economy. *Canadian Review of Art Education: Research and Issues* 32: 75–92.

Schopenhauer, A. (2004) *The Essays of Arthur Schopenhauer: Counsels and Maxims*, www.gutenberg.org/catalog (accessed 7 February 2007).

Singer, J. (1973) *Boundaries of the Soul: The Practice of Jung's Psychology*. Garden City, NY: Anchor.

Stein, M. (1977) *In Midlife: A Jungian Perspective*. Dallas, TX: Spring.

Thoreau, H. D. (1964) *Walden*. In C. Bode (ed.) *The Portable Thoreau*. New York: Viking. (Original work published in 1854.)

—— (1999) The Maine Woods. In R. Finch and J. Elder (eds) *The Norton Book of Nature Writing*. New York: Norton.

Index